The Fox and the Jewel

Location of Inari Worship Centers

Map of Japan showing major centers of Inari worship mentioned in text.

The Fox
and the
Jewel

Shared and
Private Meanings in
Contemporary
Japanese
Inari Worship

Karen A. Smyers

University of Hawai'i Press
HONOLULU

© 1999 University of Hawai'i Press

All rights reserved

Printed in the United States of America

04 03 02 01 00 99   5 4 3 2 1

Library of Congress Cataloging-in-Publication Data

Smyers, Karen Ann, 1954–
    The fox and the jewel : shared and private meanings in con-
temporary Japanese inari worship / Karen A. Smyers.
        p.   cm.
    Includes bibliographical references and index.
    ISBN 0-8248-2058-4 (hardcover : alk. paper).
    ISBN 0-8248-2102-5 (pbk. : alk. paper)
    1. Inari. 2. Foxes—Religious aspects. 3. Cults—Japan.
    I. Title.
    BL2211.I5S69 1999
    299'.561211—dc21   98-34604
                                                            CIP

University of Hawai'i Press books are printed on acid-free paper and
meet the guidelines for permanence and durability of the Council on
Library Resources.

Designed by Inari.

Contents

For my teachers
Hildred S. Geertz, Princeton University
Taitetsu Unno, Smith College
with deep gratitude

Acknowledgments

Many people and institutions have supported me during the research and writing of this book. Fieldwork was conducted under Fulbright-Hays and Japan Foundation dissertation fellowships. A sabbatical and leave from Wesleyan University provided the time for writing and revisions, which were completed at Nanzan University, Nagoya, Japan, with the support of a postdoctoral fellowship from the Japan Society for the Promotion of Science.

To my informants, for sharing their ideas and experiences, go my deepest thanks. The priests, staff, and communities of Fushimi Inari in Kyoto and Toyokawa Inari in Aichi gave me two very rich years of friendship and information. Priests and worshipers at numerous other Inari sites were also most helpful. Suzuki Kazuo, head priest of Tamatsukuri Inari, became almost as excited by my study as I was and assisted me in countless ways.

In Japan Hirai Naofusa, Naoe Hiroji, Miyake Hitoshi, Miyata Noboru, Ueda Masaaki, and Yoneyama Toshinao provided important advice and information at various stages of this study. David Plath, Harumi Befu, and William Kelly generously read research proposals early on and steered me in useful directions. For helpful readings of the manuscript, I would like to thank Robert J. Smith, Ian Reader, Jim Sanford (and fox), John Nelson, Scott Clark, Jackie Stone, Hilly Geertz, James Boon, Abdullah Hammoudi, Kelley Ross, and my anonymous readers. Colleagues at Wesleyan have provided friendship and advice—thanks particularly to Jan Willis, Susanne Fusso, and Spencer Berry. Listening to Alvin Lucier's musical composition, "The Sacred Fox," was one of the high points of 1995.

I thank the scholars and staff of the Nanzan Anthropological Institute and the Nanzan Institute for Japanese Religion and Culture for their many kindnesses. Peter Knecht, with his indefatigable energy and good cheer, has been a wonderful mentor and friend. Computer assistance from James Heisig averted disaster on several occasions. At the University of Hawai'i Press, Patricia Crosby has been most helpful, and I am grateful for her direction and warm encouragement. Don Yoder's masterful copyediting improved the manuscript in countless ways without even once upsetting the author.

Special thanks to Angela Davis-Gardner for her encouragement, to Richard Smyers for research assistance, and to David Macdonald for meeting with me at Oxford (and bringing along three fox cubs). Handa Shigeru designed the map and took the cover photograph. To him and his extended family (especially Kazue) I owe a special debt of gratitude for making this last stay in Japan the best yet.

Finally, I must thank my (furry) domestic partners, Tamayorihime and Himiko, for constant support even though they think my preoccupation with a member of the canine family is highly questionable.

Notes on Conventions

Japanese names in this text are given in Japanese order—surname followed by given name—unless it is a person who publishes primarily in English. The term "shrine" is used to translate *jinja (taisha, miya)*, and "temple" for *tera (ji, in)*, although religious sites may be complexly syncretic and may include both "Shinto" and "Buddhist" elements. The glossary lists characters for unusual terms, puns, and multiple ways of writing the same word.

My informants are all designated by pseudonyms, even though most gave permission for their names to be used in my study. I decided to conceal identities because the book sometimes deals with conflicts and tensions and I am reluctant to reveal names in this context when my informants themselves rarely spoke publicly about these matters.

All photographs, unless noted otherwise, were taken by the author.

The ratio at which I calculate the dollar value of the Japanese yen is ¥125 = $1, the exchange rate during 1989-1991 when I was in the field.

NKBT in citations refers to the *Nihon koten bungaku taikei*, 100 vols. (Tokyo: Iwanami shoten, 1958-).

The Fox and the Jewel

1
Introducing Inari

I think the most valuable thing I have learnt in my life is that there is so much to say on both sides of every question that there is little to choose between them. It has made me tolerant, so that I can listen with equal interest to you and to my cousin Algernon. After all, how can I tell whether Truth has one shape only, or many?

—W. Somerset Maugham, *The Merry-Go-Round*

The deity called Inari has been worshiped in Japan since at least the early eighth century, and today more than one-third of all Shinto shrines in Japan are dedicated to this *kami*.[1] Small Inari shrines without full-time resident priest, home and company shrines, tiny field and roadside shrines are everywhere. If these places were included, the registered number of Inari shrines would increase by ten to one hundred times the official figure (Gorai 1985:3). Inari worship is found throughout Japan in both rural and urban settings, and devotees include people from all social classes. Sacred Inari sites may be either Shinto or Buddhist, although the former are more numerous.[2]

Settings of Inari Worship

Sites of Inari worship can be found almost everywhere—in famous large shrines and temples, on factory rooftops, in lay religious establishments, in alleys of major cities, on sacred mountains, in rice fields. Here we consider three representative examples of Inari worship.

Morning Worship at a Tokyo Beauty Salon

The eight staff members of an upscale beauty salon in Roppongi arrive at work by 9:00 and are busily sweeping, dusting, and polishing every surface inside and outside the shop. The space is rather small, but well designed, decorated in elegant high-tech style. The workers are all young and very fashionably attired. When the owner arrives at 10:15, the cleaning stops, and the group lines up behind her under the Inari altar high on the wall just inside the entrance to the shop, complete with fox statues and a tiny offering box. She clasps her hands (glittering with tiny diamonds set into long red fingernails) in prayer, and all follow suit. One of her male assistants stands directly under the altar and formally leads the prayers. They all chant a Shinto *norito* prayer, the Buddhist *Heart Sutra*, then clap and bow twice, and turn and bow to the east, in gratitude to the sun. Private prayers are murmured, and the day begins.

Fall Festival at Toyokawa Inari

Hundreds of red and white paper lanterns decorate the stately precincts of a large Zen Buddhist temple. It is a beautiful fall afternoon, and people of all ages mill around the grounds, listening to the drumming performance of local schoolchildren and eating cotton candy, roasted corn with soy sauce, fried noodles, and other festival favorites. At 3:00, the climax of the festival begins: Inari (here called Dakiniten) is carried from the main sanctuary in a portable shrine *(mikoshi)* to a temporary resting place in front of the shrine of the deity who protects this Buddhist temple.

The procession begins with musicians dressed in ancient court style playing *gagaku* music on wooden flutes and a drum. Following them are eight priests in splendid brocade robes carrying silver and gold ritual implements, sutras, symbolic keys to the buildings, and a brocade-covered book containing a list of the faithful. As they walk, they purify the grounds and onlookers in three ways: one scatters drops of water from a goblet using a green leaf as a dipper; one carries incense in a receptacle fashioned as a dragon with a magic jewel in its claws; the last scatters flower petals (made of paper). People scramble to retrieve these petals, pushing and shoving anyone in their way. The lucky few who get one consider it to be an extremely efficacious charm and put it carefully into a purse or wallet.

Fall Festival, Toyokawa Inari. Devotees place small monetary offerings inside the mouths of the fox masks for good luck.

A line of fifty divine children *(chigo)* from age three to seven follows. Escorted by their mothers and wearing gold crowns and bright red, purple, and gold kimonos, they have powdered white faces and red lips like courtiers of old. Some cry in fear, others ham it up for the video cameras. The procession passes under a large stone torii gate and past the gazes of two pairs of large guardian fox statues. Finally comes the Inari deity, borne in a splendid gold palanquin by thirty young men and women in short pants and *happi* coats, sweating and groaning under the staggering weight. They weave drunkenly back and forth across the path, careening into the crowds, tipping and shaking the deity. Behind this, at a safe distance, walks the head priest of the temple, in a bright red robe, shaded by a large umbrella held over his head by an attendant. Two large white foxes prance along, oversize masks borne on the shoulders of two men, and worshipers place money into their open mouths as offerings for luck. The palanquin comes to a rest under a large tree, and the priests conduct a short Buddhist worship service. The head priest prostrates himself on the ground, offers incense, and chants a sutra. After the prayers, the priests slowly walk away, and the informal festival activities resume. In the evening, the paper lanterns are lit, shining a soft red into the black night.

Crossroads Divination at Hyōtan Yama Inari

The shrine known as Hyōtan Yama Inari is located in the outskirts of Osaka in the foothills. Its name derives from the shape of the hill on which it sits, which resembles a guitar-shaped gourd *(hyōtan)* lying on its side. This auspiciously shaped mountain was also used as a burial chamber *(kofun)* sometime between the third and sixth centuries. Now the shape of the hill is obscured by the tall buildings that cluster around it, but this shrine is still well known for crossroads divination. I visited it on March 4, 1990, with the head priest from another Inari shrine and his two young sons. The shrine grounds were impressive: although small, they contained a profusion of fox statues, *otsuka* worship stones, and various forms of popular devotion. Here the wish-fulfilling jewel usually found at Inari worship sites is not in evidence but has been replaced by the *hyōtan* gourd, which appears as decorative motif on most surfaces. Wanting to learn about the crossroads divination, we went first to the shrine office and got instructions about how to proceed. The priest there explained with a detailed map exactly what to do. First I made a small monetary offering at the main sanctuary and asked Inari for assistance in answering my question. Then I shook a cylindrical wooden box containing three long rods until one fell out the small hole at the bottom. It was Number 1, which indicated that I should pay attention to the first person who passed and note the manner of passing (walking, running, car, bicycle), dress, sex, items carried, and so on. Next I walked around to the left of the shrine and followed the path to the back gate, which looked out onto a paved road running perpendicular to the path. There was a stone to mark the spot, and there I waited. Soon the buzzing of a mini-motorbike could be heard, and I waited with interest for its arrival. In a moment, a man on a bright red motorbike passed from my left to right and disappeared over the hill and round a curve.

We went back to the shrine office and were seated in a tatami-mat room where we waited on cushions while the head priest concluded his previous audience. I was instructed to put on a white vest, a garment symbolizing my purity for the divination. Finally we were ushered into the priest's old-fashioned room, which held an Inari altar in the alcove consisting of a miniature antique shrine building of dark wood and two very old earthenware white fox statues. The priest asked me the particulars of who had passed, and he filled in the information on a printed worksheet. He then turned and sat facing the Inari altar and prayed. The question I had posed for this divination was whether my study of Inari would be published as a book. The priest said yes: because a *man* had passed from north to south, it meant this task was possible. Men work in the world, so this was a very good sign. Looking at the expression on my face, he hastened to point out that women work very hard too, but in Japan it is usually within the home. The motorbike indicated that the task would not take too long. The other priest thought that the bike's bright red color reinforced the meaning of Inari as subject of the book, because red is the distinctive color that identifies Inari shrine buildings. The head priest then told us in great detail of his fascination with the theory that the Japanese are actually one of the lost tribes of Israel. After discussing this question, we thanked the priest, took some photographs, and paid the 2,000-yen fee for the divination.[3]

In Search of Consensus

Inari worship may be conducted by Shinto or Buddhist priests, by nonclerical religious specialists, by lay worship group leaders, or by devotees themselves. Festivals involving the whole town or large numbers from an urban area celebrate Inari's blessings collectively, and priests conduct dozens of prayer services *(gokitō)* daily for individuals or small groups. Devotees ascertain the divine will in various "folk" methods of divination that do not require a priest or religious specialist and may even experience Inari personally through a possession or divine dream. I use the term "religious specialist" to differentiate the healers and shamans from the priests, both Shinto and Buddhist. In Japanese, these religious specialists are called *odaisan, ogamiyasan, reinōsha,* or *reikanshi.* They often head lay worship groups *(kō),* but to classify them with ordinary lay leaders slights the tremendous religious power they command. Followers often consider them to be far more religiously advanced than the priests, who they describe as "learning about religion from books, not by doing austerities." Chapter 2 examines the tension and cooperation between these two types of religious leaders. Additionally, I have tried to avoid using the term "believer" for worshipers of Inari because belief is not the most important characteristic of religiosity in Japan (Reader 1991a:1–22). Nelson discusses the complex anthropological conundrum concerning the relationship between behavior, motivation, and interpretation (1996:120–123) and presents fascinating data about what ostensible worshipers say they are actually doing at a shrine. Because my study focuses less on the sacred space and more on the ideas and behavior of people who define themselves as Inari's *shinja,* I use the terms "worshiper," "devotee," "practitioner," and "follower" to designate them. This does not mean these labels are appropriate for everyone who enters, or even prays at, an Inari shrine.

Many Japanese not involved personally with Inari told me they assumed that all Inari worshipers are elderly or interested only in financial gain. Older people and those praying for business prosperity *(shōbai hanjō)* are indeed numerous, but I also met worshipers from a fairly representative cross section of Japan: fashionable young hairdressers, an elite company president and his staff, housewives, families and children, a silk weaver, a truck driver, a medical doctor and his patients, musicians, gangsters, a photographer, spiritualists, a real estate agent, liquor store owners, an orange farmer, an alcoholic, students, very ill people, shopkeepers, a baker, flower arrangement and tea ceremony instructors, brewers, train workers, insurance workers, an oil company head, a doctor's wife, a chiropractor, geisha, sushi bar owners, and local politicians.

No matter where the worship of Inari takes places or who conducts it, one or more symbols most likely will be present: the fox, jewel, red torii, red worship hall, prayer flags, rock altar, cedar, fried tofu, and rice. Because of these symbols, Inari shrines are easy to distinguish—unlike so many other shrines where even the locals can only answer a generic *"kami sama"* (honorable deity) in answer to the question of what deity is enshrined there. Inari worship sites can almost always be identified by their red color and prominent pair of fox statues. But is Inari always the same deity? Are Shinto priests, Buddhist priests, and shamanic religious specialists worshiping the same Inari? Are there doctrinal differences between the different institutional centers?

Although settings of worship are diverse, they symbolize Inari in a fairly consistent way through the use of an easily recognizable set of symbols. But when people speak about Inari, this seeming unity quickly dissolves into a bewildering array of understandings—many of which are completely contradictory. It might be reasonably thought that this is probably the situation in most religions. Perhaps one should consult the experts, those who take as normative certain doctrinal or historical materials. To some extent, I attempted to do this. But I quickly learned there was little consensus among priests or scholars either.

Ideas about Inari

The most often heard ideas about Inari are that it is a Shinto *kami* that is (or is connected with) a fox. But when I asked Shinto priests about the identity of Inari, they had various ideas. Some identified Inari with Uganomitama no Ōkami, a *kami* from the classical mythologies; others linked Inari with Toyouke no Kami, the *kami* worshiped in the outer shrine at Ise; still others took Inari to be equivalent to any grain *kami*. The pamphlets distributed by Inari shrines throughout Japan include a bewildering array of *kami* enshrined as Inari. The one thing most priestly commentators agreed upon is that Inari has a deep connection to rice.

A bit more investigation, especially among scholars and priests, reveals that Inari is worshiped in Buddhist temples as well—often as the temple protector *(chinjugami)* but sometimes as the main object of worship. At Toyokawa Inari, the setting of the fall festival described earlier, the Buddhist form of Inari is called Dakiniten. At Saijō Inari in Okayama, a Nichiren sect temple, the main object of worship is the *Lotus Sutra,* but here it takes the form of a deity called Saijō-sama. Both Buddhist Inaris take the form of a bodhisattva carrying rice astride a flying white fox.

Worshipers at these various sacred sites had rather diverse ideas about Inari. Some were simply vague, such as the man whose family had worshiped for years what they assumed was Inari in their home shrine—only to open the doors and discover an entirely different *kami* enshrined there. Many were completely unaware of Inari's Buddhist form, and one man got very angry with me when I insisted that Toyokawa Inari was a Buddhist temple. Another was open-mindedly eclectic: "Inari is really a [Shinto] *kami* but is worshiped at Toyokawa as a Buddhist deity—but I really feel it is more of a *kami* than a Buddhist figure. I don't think Inari is different from other *kami*, and may even be the same as the Christian God. The point for me is that *kami* have a lot of power—the particular variety of that strength is not important." Others had more personalized views. One woman who worshiped both the *kami* of the new religion of Tenrikyō as well as Inari "discovered" Inari to be one of the ten deities of that religion. Another devotee, the fervent leader of an Inari lay worship group under the auspices of the Fushimi Inari Shrine, realized one day that Inari had been responsible for the economic recovery of the Volkswagen company. He had heard about the decline and recovery of the company, and when he saw that the logo of the company was a fox, realized that "Inari's powers work even in foreign countries."

When Inari is visualized by devotees or depicted in iconography, gender is variable (and so I use both masculine and feminine pronouns to refer to Inari). Unlike other well-known Japanese deities who have unambiguous gender in anthropomorphic form, Inari is thought to be either male or female; or both; or neither. Its most popular representations are as an old man carrying rice, a young female food goddess, or an androgynous bodhisattva on a white fox. Priests and devotees offer justifications for their understanding of the gender of this deity, but there is no theological orthodoxy on this question. The deity Inari was worshiped on the sacred mountain in Fushimi from at least the eighth century, and it was not until some centuries later that priests tried to identify this deity with others from the official mythology. Inari seems not to have been gendered at first: the female associations come from Inari's functions as a rice and fertility deity; the male associations derive from later Buddhist traditions (Yamaori 1986).

The one constant I did discover in priestly rhetoric about Inari, Shinto and Buddhist alike, was that it discourages the idea that Inari is a fox. Nevertheless, many people believe this to be the case. Some saw Inari to be a benevolent fox-*kami;* others were frightened of it. One said, "Dakiniten is a fox-*kami* who eats people and is terrifying." A souvenir shop near the grounds of the Fushimi Inari Shrine considered a statue of a fox to be the repository *(shintai)* of Inari and would not let me photograph it. The priests were appalled by the notion when I described it to them. Another idea I encountered almost as often as the fox identification was the notion that Inari is a snake (or dragon)—but this does not seem to upset the priests to the same extent that the fox does. From time to time I was told that Inari is incarnate in the body of a living devotee, usually a shamanic female who can speak for the *kami.*

Inari is both loved and feared. People involved with this deity tend to feel great intimacy with her; those less involved may be nervous about the stories of her retribution related with great relish even in modern-day Tokyo. In either case, people consider Inari to be a very powerful deity: the "rough" or "wild" side is not necessarily evil; it is simply the deity's inherent power to reward or punish. I was told by a very cosmopolitan Tokyo boutique owner about the recent removal of a tiny Inari shrine to build a skyscraper. An unusual number of accidents and injuries began to make the workers very nervous—but after they replaced the Inari shrine, the accidents stopped. Priests too respect the notion that Inari's anger is to be taken seriously. An Inari shrine in Kyushu was established in 829 on the basis of a divine dream to avert a plague. The traditional date to celebrate the festival to this Inari is September 20, but some years ago the priests moved the main part of the festival to the nearest Sunday so that more people could attend. In the late 1980s, one of the large floats fell over and killed three people during the festival. The head priest and two others made a pilgrimage of propitiation to the Fushimi Inari Shrine, fearing that Inari was angry because of the date change. Moreover, they tried to appease Inari by inviting priestesses *(miko)* from the Fushimi shrine to perform their sacred *kagura* dance at the Kyushu shrine as an offering.

For the majority of worshipers with whom I talked, however, Inari's other side was more important. People constantly told me of their personal connections to Inari, their profound intimacy with this *kami,* and their deep gratitude to Inari for countless blessings received. Still, even this special relationship gave them no license to slight Inari, and their intimacy did not include careless behavior toward this deity. It is important to note that people who may be very involved in Inari worship (as well as other religious practices) may not consider themselves particularly religious. This is partly a problem of semantics, for the term "religion" *(shūkyō)* implies adherence to specific religious groups and doctrines. But it also shows the contradictory positions a person may hold. A female lay worker at the Toyokawa Inari Temple provides a good example of this in her own "half belief/half doubt" along with great respect for the religious experiences of others:

Well, I sort of half believe and half don't *(hanshinhangi).* I suspect this is the attitude of most of the priests and lay workers at this temple: we are fairly practical about Inari because this is our job and livelihood. This is very different from the real devotees who come here, who are fervent about their faith. I imagine that this faith has a positive effect on their lives. One woman told me an experience she had when she returned to this temple to express her thanks. Her son was very sick, and she came here and prayed and got a talisman *(ofuda)* from this temple. Sitting by her son's sickbed, she dozed off and had a dream in which Dakiniten [Buddhist Inari] suddenly loomed up in the sky. When she awoke, her son's fever was gone, but her own chest hurt as if a weight were crushing down upon it. She did not see the talisman, and searched all over for it, finally locating it under a heavy book. When she removed it from under this heavy weight, her own chest stopped hurting.

People not personally involved with Inari tend to assume that all Inaris are the same deity, or at least "relatives." But those particularly caught up in Inari worship at a sacred center often distinguish their Inari from others: "We worship a Shinto *kami* and they a Buddhist one"; "Ours is a real Inari but theirs is not"; "Their foxes are black but ours are white." Few of the purported differences were based on actual research or experience; misunderstanding, stereotype, and hearsay predominated. Arguments based on the differences between the institutional affiliations of "different" Inari were usually emotional rather than rational. One of the male hairdressers who came monthly to Fushimi from Tokyo to conduct a pilgrimage of the sacred mountain explained in these terms:

> Toyokawa Inari worships a Buddhist form of Inari, and it is very dangerous to worship *kami* and buddhas at the same time. Buddhism is for dead spirits, and if you worship both at the same time, while you are religiously open, worshiping the *kami*, dead spirits may attach themselves to you and cause all sorts of trouble. Yes, it is true that the religious leader of our group says that one must worship one's ancestors or they may block prayers to the *kami*. But you must do the activities separately: first worship the ancestral spirits, then do pure Shinto worship. Yes, we do chant the Buddhist *Heart Sutra* when we pray to Inari, so I guess we are not totally consistent. But buddhas and *kami* were worshiped together for a long time in Japan, and even [the priest] Kōbō Daishi worshiped Inari, they say. But Toyokawa is definitely a different lineage of the deity. I do not know much about it, but I do know that it is not good to worship there.

In general, people who are actively involved in Inari worship believe that their object of worship is special if not unique, and even religiously superior to other forms of Inari, while those who worship more casually tend to think that Inari is Inari and are not aware of the distinctions.

If this brief compilation of ideas about Inari is confusing, it is a good approximation of the situation today in Japan. Contradictory notions are held, not just by believers at different sacred centers, but by priests at the same shrine or temple. No central authority has managed to standardize the mythology or traditions; no scriptures provide guidelines for orthodox beliefs and practices. Most people are not aware that their understanding of Inari is different (sometimes radically so) from that of other people. The complexities of contemporary Inari worship and its multilayered symbols are explored in more detail in the following chapters.

Implicit Theory

In the same way that certain communicative styles in Japan make their point without calling attention to themselves, I have attempted in this study to address certain theoretical issues without excessive use of methodological jargon. My primary orientation is Bakhtinian. That is, I wish to show that Inari practices and beliefs work as a "nonmonologic unity" (Morson and Emerson 1990:2): they do form some kind of unity, but they are not systematized or free of contradiction. I have tried to inscribe and describe the multiple voices and positions on Inari in their chaotic unity rather than impose my own organizing structures onto them. Although there are profound differences between the work of an anthropologist and a novelist, in at least one regard this study tries to emulate a Bakhtinian "novel." In Bakhtin's special sense, the novel is epitomized by the works of Dostoevsky, which contain autonomous voices and opinions of various sorts, not the single view of the author or narrator placed in the mouths of different characters. Bakhtin says that "Dostoevsky placed the idea on the borderline of dialogically intersecting consciousnesses. He brought together ideas and worldviews, which in real life were absolutely estranged and deaf to one another, and forced them to quarrel" (1984a:91). This is what I have tried to do for the multiple voices on Inari, which exist in a polysemic but not truly polyphonic condition in Japan: I have tried to render differences, in the words of Clark and Holquist, "into a tensile complex rather than into a static unity" (1984:10). Diversity exists, but it is not necessarily expressed: silent voices do not engage each other in true dialogue. Inari worship groups do not communicate much with each other; in fact, they often use verbal encounters to prevent substantive exchange of information. The very real differences that exist in the world of Inari beliefs are largely unarticulated in Japan but exist as potentials to be revealed in dialogue with an outsider (Morson and Emerson 1990:55). My dialogue with different people in Japan about Inari reveals the rich diversity not usually seen because of assumptions about cultural unity and homogeneity. And this is why my voice is present too: it is the necessary voice of the outsider who asks the kind of questions not usually asked within the culture.

By extension, one cannot explore the multiplicity within Inari worship with a single theoretical lens. A Bakhtinian perspective favors the multiple, the indirect, the inclusion of the culturally unarticulated other side; it rejects reification, single, narrow interpretations, and pompous universal claims. Rather than impose a single reading or theoretical position, or choose just one aspect of Inari to study, I allow the complexity to tell its own story. The text is open enough that scholars will be able to find other significances and raise additional theoretical questions from the material. The main focus of this study is the coexistence of astounding multiplicity and a strong cultural emphasis on unity. It also addresses the questions of power and resistance, the uses of rhetoric and silence in the maintenance of identities (both shared and private), and the means by which decentered cultural phenomena retain their identity in the face of other cultural change.

The study also takes inspiration from the radically different move Bakhtin makes in *Rabelais and His World* (1984b). In his explorations of carnival, grotesque realism, and folk laughter, Bakhtin celebrates "unfinalizability" and the enduring qualities of a people that enable them to resist tyrannical systems of "authoritarian" or "monologic" thought. For Bakhtin, Rabelais depicted the "rest of the story" that was left out of the official picture of the world: "Rabelais did not implicitly believe in what his time 'said and imagined about itself'; he strove to disclose its true meaning for the people, the people who grow and are immortal" (1984b:439). I find many aspects of the world of Inari worship to be "Rabelaisian" in Bakhtin's sense. In addition to quiet Zen rock gardens, cooperative agricultural festivals, and kimono-clad worshipers praying at the New Year, Japanese religion consists of worship of animal forms of the deity, prayers for money, associations with sexuality, and the extreme individualization of certain deities. Humor and terror often accompany popular images of Inari, particularly when depicted as a fox. Inari beliefs symbolize change in contrast to the continuity often stressed in descriptions of Japanese religious forms.

Bakhtin inverts our commonsense notion that systems of thought are universal and human lives transient. He shows that, in fact, "permanent" systems and institutions come and go; what remains constant is "the grotesque body," the material principle opposed to that which is abstract, never static but always becoming. In keeping with this insight, I have tried to present the world of Inari in a way that does not privilege the institutions but focuses on the popular energies—paradoxically the ever-changing constant in Inari worship. A study of Inari that considered the institutions to be normative and the actual practices of worshipers to be deviations would, I believe, misrepresent the actual situation: in fact, the centripetal and centrifugal energies within Inari are delicately balanced at the ritual centers, where they come together in a kind of unarticulated tension.

Organization of the Study

Although I argue that the centers of Inari are not truly central in shaping the practices and ideas of Inari worship, Chapter 2 considers two major centers of Inari worship, Fushimi Inari and Toyokawa Inari, where I did a year each of fieldwork. Even at these large centers, there is no single unquestioned tradition: tensions between factions, priestly and shamanic claims to authority, and institutional rivalries are expressed through contending attitudes, interpretive discourses, and organizational styles. Intense but uninformed and nonconfrontational factionalism characterize relations between many of the individuals and groups involved in Inari worship.

Chapters 3 and 4 present "thick descriptions" of the two principal symbols of Inari, the fox and the jewel. These two rich and multivocal symbols center Inari beliefs and practices in the absence of a centralizing institution and dogma and yet, by their very nature, allow a multiplicity of meanings. It is my contention here that the fox symbol is the key to Inari's long and continued popularity. Like the elusive, shape-shifting fox that refuses domestication, the symbol remains open and adapts to new situations. The fox symbol is not necessarily focused on by devotees, who may not have given it a great deal of thought, but it is iconographically ubiquitous at most Inari worship sites and is synonymous with "Inari" for many. By presenting a thick description of fox meanings in Japan I am not suggesting that all devotees are aware of these meanings. Rather, I am detailing the cultural background of the symbol. Priestly disapproval of the fox symbol is, in my reading, not because the fox is unimportant in Inari worship but precisely because it is so important. As evidence that the fox symbol is somehow "necessary" at Inari worship sites, one notes that disapproving priests do not remove the symbol but merely try to reeducate devotees concerning its meaning.

The most characteristic feature of Inari worship—the high degree of individualization and personalization of the deity—is the topic of Chapter 5. Inari provides a superb example of this feature of Japanese religiosity, an aspect that has been largely overlooked because it is not articulated in public modes of discourse. Not only do ideas about Inari vary regionally, but they vary individually, even to the degree that Inari is worshiped under thousands of different names chosen by individual devotees. The

Yearly ritual performed by Shinto priest at a company Inari shrine located next to the factory, Osaka. (Photo courtesy of Suzuki Kazuo.)

sacred centers of Inari worship, including the site of origin in Fushimi, have no single authoritative tradition or sacred narrative and thus are loci for multiple interpretive worlds. The fox symbol, I argue, is at one level a metaphor for individuality: its shape shifting is a cultural fantasy for people with restricted mobility and constraints on personal expression.

Chapter 6 asks why, in the face of this variation, diversity, and lack of clear center, Inari is taken to be a single phenomenon, on the one hand, and why on the other, the factionalism does not create the schisms so common in other forms of Japanese religion. The answer lies in certain communicative strategies—cultural and linguistic mechanisms that tend to present unity but preserve diversity. Finally, in Chapter 7, I argue that Inari's strength and adaptability lie in its power to embrace oppositions, contradictions, and seemingly negative elements. Inari remains continually relevant because its broadest meaning is growth and change, rather than cultural embodiment of this concept that might become obsolete.

A Brief History of Inari

A detailed consideration of Inari's history is beyond the scope of this study, but a short outline of major events in its development will provide some background against which to view the contemporary scene.[4] As the Meiji-period governmental separation of Shinto and Buddhism has thrown the pre-Meiji Buddhist forms of Inari into shadow, here I will discuss the reinvented Buddhist traditions after describing the history of the original Inari shrine, some of its offshoots, and related folk customs.[5] As we shall see, even the priests who valued Inari's history were not very well versed in it. Devotees knew little history and tended not to consider it important— more important than the historical origin of a symbol or practice was its meaning for them at the present. This brief survey traces the development of this *kami* and his worship as a backdrop to their present understandings.

Origins and Early Histories

The first occurrence of the word "Inari" in an extant document is in the eighth-century *Yamashiro fudoki* in a tradition that describes the origin of the Fushimi Inari Shrine in this way.[6] A distant rich ancestor of Hata no Nakatsuie named Irogu one day used a rice cake for target practice. When his arrow pierced the cake, it suddenly changed into a white bird and flew to the top of the mountain. He followed it and found that where it perched, rice was growing *(ine-nari)*.[7] (See the glossary for characters.) The story continues that descendants of Irogu uprooted small trees from this mountain and planted them in their gardens. If the tree took root, the family would prosper; but if it withered, this foretold bad times (*NKBT* 2:419-420). This story gives an account of the origin of the Inari shrine, although the characters used for Inari in the *Yamashiro fudoki* are phonetic and have no particular meaning. The first time the present-day characters "carrying rice" were used was in 827 in the *Ruijū kokushi* (Nishida 1983:248).

Scholars believe that worship at Inari Mountain was being conducted for some centuries before the official founding date of 711 (Higo 1983:10; Fushimi 1977:26-27) and use archaeological evidence to fill in the blanks in the earliest written sources.[8] Inari Mountain is the southernmost peak of the Higashiyama chain to the east of Kyoto. Rising only seven hundred feet or so above sea level, it has three gently rounded peaks covered with a dense cedar forest.[9] An excavation in 1966 uncovered a Yayoi-period (200 B.C.E.-250 C.E.) site at the southern foot of the mountain in the area subsequently called Fukakusa where the inhabitants most probably worshiped the deity who dwelled on the nearby mountain, the source of fertility and resting place of the ancestors (Higo 1983:5-6; Fushimi 1969:26;

1977:18-19). Two large tombs *(kofun)* have been discovered on Inari Mountain, probably from the latter half of the fourth century, which seem to be burial sites for the chieftains of these Yayoi-period clans (Ueda 1977:7). The arrival of the Hata clan around the second half of the fifth century precipitated major changes in this area. Although a tradition dating from the Heian period has it that the Hata were descended from the first Chinese emperor,[10] in fact they came directly from the Korean peninsula, probably from Shiragi. This group became the priests who conducted formal worship of Inari.

The name "Inari" appears nowhere in the classical mythologies describing the origins and exploits of the myriad Japanese *kami*. Higo, along with most other scholars, thinks that the association of the word "Inari" with *"ine,"* rice, points to an origin in the indigenous rice-growers' faith (1983:7); this view is plausible, as the association was made early. The characters "carrying rice" now used to write the word "Inari" developed from a Buddhist tradition, as we shall see, and throughout the centuries shrine records contained at least three other sets of characters for the name "Inari": "rice grows," "rice develops," and "food grows" (see the glossary) (Fushimi 1969:8). National Learning scholar Hirata Atsutane (1776-1843) surmises that Inari is a contraction of *inabari,* "granary" (Kirby 1910:46; Fushimi 1976:187), and numerous similar suggestions abound.[11] But there are endless associative possibilities between sounds and meanings in the Japanese language, which is rich in homophones, and although popular etymologies do create traditions of meanings, they are unreliable as historical proof. Another undocumented possibility was suggested to me by a priest at Fushimi Inari Shrine. The word "Inari" occurs for the first time in connection with the Hata clan, and the original characters used to write it had no meaning but simply represented the sounds "i-na-ri." This could point to a Korean origin for the word, perhaps corrupted into pronounceable Japanese sounds. None of the characters used is an exact fit to the sounds (most would be read *"ine-nari"* or *"ina-nari"*), and the great number of etymologies may result from the need to account for a word that was not originally Japanese.[12]

In this initial period a *kami* called Inari began to be worshiped on the three peaks of the mountain in southeast Kyoto in Fukakusa. Descendants of the Hata clan were conducting worship, and the *kami* at this time was most likely agricultural, protecting the rice in particular as well as other crops. But even at this early time, Inari seems to have taken on the wider functions of protecting the commerce and trade of the Hata clan and may have retained ancestral associations from the graves on the sacred mountain as well.

Heian Period (794-1185)

During the Heian period Inari beliefs began to develop and spread among the populace. The imperial capital moved to Kyoto in 794, causing a great rise in Inari's fortunes. In 823, Emperor Saga presented Tōji, the new temple to protect the nation, to Kūkai (774-835), founder of the esoteric Shingon Buddhist sect in Japan, who thereupon made Inari the temple's local protecting *kami* (Higo 1983:12). In 827, when Emperor Junna became ill, divination revealed the cause to be divine retribution from Inari for using wood from the *kami*'s sacred mountain in the building of the pagoda at Tōji Temple. The court bestowed the lower fifth rank *(jūgoi no ge)* on Inari in an effort to appease the *kami*—a measure that not only seemed to deflect Inari's wrath but also increased Inari's popularity in the capital (Fushimi 1977:80-81; Miyamoto 1984:172).[13]

A number of Buddhist texts describe a separate origin story for Inari, an account in which Kūkai plays a central role. Extant copies date from the Kamakura period but may have been current when the association was taking place.[14] One version tells us that in a previous lifetime, Kūkai and Inari were sitting together in India, listening to a sermon of the Buddha. Kūkai said, "I will be born in an eastern land and will spread Buddhism there, and at that time you will come and be the protective deity of the secret teachings *(hihō)*." Because of this pledge, they indeed met again in 816 at an inn in Japan. Kūkai encountered an old man of very strange appearance: he was almost eight feet tall and very muscular, internally an avatar, externally an ordinary human being. On the thirteenth day of the fourth month of 823, this same old man arrived at the South Gate of Tōji Temple carrying rice over his shoulder and a cedar bough in one hand, accompanied by two women and two children. Kūkai welcomed him, they rejoiced at their reunion, and Inari honored his vow to become the protecting deity of Kūkai's Buddhism (Fushimi 1957:51-54). This image of Inari as an old man carrying rice has become a key element in the iconography.

The Inari shrine's relations with the court continued, and in 927 it was listed in the *Engi shiki* along with 3,100 other important shrines (Fushimi 1977:41; Kuroita 1964, 8:184). The *kami*'s rank was increased in increments until in 942 (Tengyō 5) it reached the top grade, *shōichii*, in thanks from Emperor Suzaku for quelling rebellions in the east and west (Fushimi 1969:11). Another indication of Inari's popularity and importance at this time was its inclusion amoung the top seven of the Twenty-Two Shrines *(nijūni sha)* selected by the court for imperial patronage (Grapard 1988:248; Fushimi 1977:42). The first Inari branch shrine was established in the ninth century; it is the present-day Takekoma Inari in Miyagi prefecture.

By the mid-Heian period, Inari Mountain had become a popular pilgrimage site noted in the literature of the day for attracting men, women, and children and members of all classes (Higo 1983:13; Fushimi 1977:31–37). After 1072, it became a site of imperial pilgrimage as well (Fushimi 1962a:58–62; 1977:42). Pilgrims developed the custom of breaking off a twig of cedar on Inari's mountain as a talisman, particularly on the first horse day of the second month *(nigatsu no hatsuuma)*, Inari's festival day. This twig was called *shirushi no sugi,* souvenir cedar, well known as a poetic convention *(makura kotoba)* of the times.[15] Inari's popularity during the Heian period was due to its status from receiving imperial rank and to its link with the esoteric Shingon sect, which increased followers' expectations for this-worldly benefits. Inari's shrine was a site for popular pilgrimage as well as for elite poetry competitions.[16] Indeed, the appeal to all levels of society was a firmly established part of Inari's reputation by this period.

Medieval Period (1185–1600)

At some point from the end of the twelfth to the thirteenth century, the number of *kami* enshrined at the Inari shrine increased from three to five (Fushimi 1977:46). In 1194 at the time of retired Emperor Gotoba's visit, the shrine received imperial permission to grant Inari's court rank *(shōichii)* to the divided spirit when people wanted to reenshrine Inari (Fushimi 1969:12; 1977:50). The proper rituals for the division of the deity were secret transmissions within the various priestly lineages.

During this period the fortunes of the Inari shrine continued to grow, and the Inari Festival rivaled the Gion Festival in splendor. In 1338, a parade of floats was added to the basic procession of portable shrines; by 1441, these floats numbered forty-six (Fushimi 1977:54). But in the years beginning around 1453, due to great commotion and violence in the capital, the festival was disrupted: the portable shrine was attacked by arrows, the procession was delayed, contributions were insufficient, and for some years there is no information at all (Fushimi 1977:56–58). Finally, in the third month of 1468, during the Ōnin War (1467–1477), the entire shrine complex was burned to the ground. Some of the shrine treasures were moved to Tōji Temple for protection and were returned to the shrine priests later that year (Fushimi 1977:53–58). Rebuilding took about thirty years. Much of the money seems to have been gathered through the solicitations of the Shingon Buddhist priests who were connected with the Inari shrine. For the first time, the five *kami* were enshrined together in one building, which was begun in 1492 and consecrated in 1499.[17] (Previously the three *kami* had each had a separate, contiguous, sanctuary.) A Buddhist temple building *(hongansho)* was also erected in the shrine grounds for the first time, and the system of hereditary priests was expanded to include the Kada lineage in addition to the Hata (Fushimi 1977:63; Ueda and Tsubohara 1984:28).

Toyotomi Hideyoshi (1536–1598), one of the great warlords of this time, had a deep belief in Inari, whom he enshrined in his Fushimi castle as Fulfillment Inari (Manzoku Inari) and in his Kyoto home, Jurakudai, as Worldly Success Inari (Shusse Inari) (Fushimi 1969:30). His name appears often in Fushimi's *Chronology* after his rise to power; he had prayers offered, foxes exorcised, and made generous donations to the shrine. Hideyoshi's pledge of 10,000 *koku* of rice built the two-storied gate *(romon)* (Fushimi 1962b:179). His presence was felt at other Inari centers also. The statue of Fudō Myōō at Toyokawa Inari was a gift from Hideyoshi, and Tamatsukuri Inari in Osaka flourished greatly during his reign, as this shrine was the protector of nearby Osaka Castle.

Early Modern Period (1600–1868)

During the Edo period, a Shingon Buddhist temple was erected within the grounds of the Inari shrine (Ueda and Tsubohara 1984:28). It continued the tradition of the temple *(hongansho)* built after the Ōnin fire, and the Buddhist priests here dispensed divided spirits *(wakemitama)* of Inari as did the fourteen other hereditary (Shinto) priestly lineages. The most famous priest associated with this shrine is Kada Azumamaro (1669–1736), who was born into the Higashi Hagura branch of the Kada priestly line and went on to become one of the four great founding scholars of National Learning *(Kokugaku)*. The house in which he was born and raised was built around 1600 and still exists within the shrine today.[18]

After the medieval period, Inari shrines began to spread all over

Japan, especially into eastern Japan, far from the parent shrine at Fushimi. They were especially numerous in Edo (Tokyo) during this period as the following satiric poem indicates:

> In Edo, shops called "Iseya"
> And Inari shrines
> Are as numerous as dog droppings
>
> *(Chōnai ni iseya Inari ni inu no kuso)*

Inari belief spread with the movement of feudal lords (daimyo), who often took their protective *kami* with them when they relocated. Townspeople were quick to imitate customs of the samurai, flocking to worship these household protectors *(yashikigami)* and also enshrining their own (Iwai 1983:287-297). So many of these *kami* were Inari that in the Kanto area the term "Inari-san" is synonymous with *yashikigami* (Naoe 1983a:114). The large Yūtoku Inari in Saga prefecture was founded in 1687; this Inari was taken along with a bride from Kyoto who went there to marry Nabeshima Chokuasa (Fushimi 1969:30). The large Toyokawa Inari branch temple in Tokyo (Akasaka Mitsuke) was originally the household Inari shrine of a renowned administrator and judge, Ōoka Echizen, who brought the Inari with him from Mikawa to Edo when he took up his post there. Wandering religious specialists and ascetics played a large role in spreading Inari, as well, and there was a popularity boom of the oracular women who gave oracles called *Inari sage* (Naoe 1983a:116). By this time Inari was inextricably associated with the spirit fox that serves as his messenger.

A shrine's sudden boom in popularity for about a year is called the *hayarigami* ("popular *kami*") phenomenon, and there were many such Inari. The spark that ignited a *hayarigami* explosion might be a divine dream, an oracle, or a miraculous occurrence. Miyata (1983:146) gives the following example from his study of the Soma domain. A mountain ascetic named Sogaku, who was sometimes possessed by foxes, died and was buried in an earthen mound *(tsuka)*. Because a white fox was often seen near the mound, people began to call it Sogaku Inari. In 1852, an unbelievably large fish catch was thought to be the result of prayers here, so it was renamed Ōzakana Inari (Abundant Fish Inari). A few years later, someone from that area went to the capital and brought back a divided spirit of Inari from the Fushimi shrine, which was actually the first "official" enshrining of the Inari *kami* there. Prior to that, it was called "Inari" because of the spirit foxes and the white fox associated with the ascetic whose grave was at that spot. The shrine enjoyed a great reputation for a time, and people came from great distances to pray there.

During the sixteenth century Inari had become the protector of warriors, and Inari shrines are found within many castle compounds throughout Japan—often located in the northeast portion of the compound to protect the castle from the inauspicious "devil's gate" *(kimon)* direction. This custom continued into the peaceful years of Edo. Many of the enshrined Inari seem to have been in the Buddhist tradition, for they enshrined Dakiniten as Inari (Gorai 1985:6). In 1611, when Nobuhira came to power, he enshrined an Inari within the grounds of the castle at Hirosaki, Aomori. One of the customs there was to put out offerings for foxes. A 1789 record shows that when foxes did not eat the offerings, this was considered inauspicious, and a special prayer service was held to implore Inari for benevolence (Naoe 1983a:127). Foxes were said to aid warriors as couriers, for in a mere two or three days they could make a trip that took humans ten days (Naoe 1983a:121).[19]

Inari became a fishing *kami* along the coast of Japan from Tōhoku to Hokuriku as wide-net fishing techniques became popular. Inari beliefs probably spread on top of prior beliefs related to the fox, for a number of folk practices—such as divining the size of the fish catch by the type of fox bark heard—were found in the same area (Kameyama 1983:217-223). Urban Inaris took on still new specialties. Inari became famous for fire prevention *(hibuse)* in Edo, and on Hatsuuma, Inari's festival day, it was the custom for people to buy a kite from the Ōji Inari Shrine to prevent fires. Theaters in the Edo period often had an internal shrine to Inari, usually located on the first floor, and there might also be an Inari *kamidana* altar in the greenroom. The lowest-ranking actors were known as "Inari Machi" (Inari Town), because their dressing room was located near the Inari shrine and they themselves served as the priests of Inari during the banquet on Hatsuuma (Leiter 1979:141).

The Inari beliefs that spread in the early modern period were intimately bound up with notions of possessing spirits *(tsukimono)*, lucky deities *(fukugami)*, and miracle-granting *kami (hayarigami)*. In Osaka, a saying summarized the power of Inari to grant one's wishes (Ono 1985:79):

For sickness pray to Kōbō [Daishi],
For desires pray to Inari

(Byō Kōbō, yoku Inari)

These magical Inari beliefs grew out of the esoteric influences that had been absorbed by Inari in the Heian period, developed during the medieval period, and now came into full flower. No longer confined to agricultural beliefs, the Inari *kami* was popular also in urban areas as a luck or prosperity deity (Iwai 1983:288). The varieties of Inari at this time seem endless: there were even millenarian versions of Inari called "World Renewal (Yonaoshi) Inari" at the end of the Tokugawa period (Nishigaki 1983: 165–173).

Modern Period (1868–present)

The government decree that ordered the separation of Buddhism and Shinto attempted to sever two religious systems which had developed symbiotically for many centuries.[20] At Fushimi the structures that were obviously Buddhist, such as the Bishamon Hall, the Monjū Hall, the Daikoku Hall, and Aizenji Temple, were torn down and the Buddhist priests sent away. The names of the *kami* worshiped as Inari were standardized and sanitized, and all imperially related *kami* were removed from the rolls of the shrine. Thus the "divine grandson," Ninigi no Mikoto, was dissociated from formal worship at Fushimi Inari. But at the same time, a form of popular worship developed that continued the more eclectic tradition. Rock altars *(otsuka)* to private manifestations of Inari were secretly set up by believers on the mountain—in direct opposition to the shrine's prohibition—and these altars included the names of various popular Buddhist figures such as Kannon, Jizō, Kōbō Daishi, Emma-ō, and Fudō Myōō. The shrine received the rank of "Great Imperial Shrine" *(kampei taisha)* on May 14, 1871 (Fushimi 1962b:287), and although this rank bestowed great status, the priests were now forced to reconcile popular worship of Inari with government standards. The popularity of the Fushimi Inari Shrine continues today, and details of its current situation are presented in later chapters. My focus on the oldest Inari shrine in no way implies that this shrine is "typical," however. Although some of its traditions and iconography moved to other sites of Inari worship, the features and histories of Inari shrines show great variety and reflect local conditions and particular revelations. The following description of a medium-sized, regionally famous Inari shrine suggests this variability.

Tamatsukuri Inari Shrine in Osaka had a long history before it enshrined Inari and became famous in that regard. Its founding is said to be 12 B.C.E. during the reign of Emperor Suinin when it originally worshiped Shitateru Hime. The name Tamatsukuri, literally "jewel making," is the name of the area around the shrine and refers to a guild of jewel makers (Tamatsukuri-be) that inhabited this area during the Yayoi period (200 B.C.E.–250 C.E.).[21] The jewel here is the comma-shaped *magatama* of great sacred and shamanic power. A tradition associates Shōtoku Taishi (574–622), the first regent of Japan, with this shrine. In 587, when fighting the Mononobe clan over the Buddhism problem, Shōtoku stuck a piece of white chestnut wood (some traditions say a chopstick) into the ground at this shrine and said: "If I will win, let this stick bring forth leaves." It did, and he did, and Buddhism took firm root in Japan (Suzuki 1988:32).

Inari became associated with this shrine sometime in the late Heian period. In the Muromachi period (1392–1568), the *kami* were formally enshrined as the "Inari of Five Happinesses" (Inari Gokō Daimyōjin).[22] A fire during a battle in 1576 destroyed all shrine buildings and records, and when Hideyoshi built Osaka Castle, this shrine became its protector. At this time the shrine was called Toyotsu (Abundant Bay) Inari Shrine and had several Buddhist halls within the precincts. Its Kannon Hall became one of the thirty-three sites for Kannon pilgrimage in this area, made famous by mention in a Chikamatsu play. The shrine burned again during the fall of Osaka Castle in 1615 and was rebuilt only to burn again, two centuries later, in a great city fire in 1863. After rebuilding in 1870, Tamatsukuri received the rank of village shrine *(gosha)* from the government; in 1928 this was raised to the rank of prefectural shrine *(fusha)*. Bombing raids completely destroyed the shrine in 1945, and the present sanctuary of ferroconcrete was completed in 1954 (Suzuki 1988:32–33).

Foxes lived in the area of this shrine from the Edo period up until the end of World War II, and people would put out offerings for them on the road (called Inari-suji) that ran between Osaka Castle and the shrine. As people offered fried tofu and rice with red beans *(sekihan)*, they called out "Nosengyo-ya!"—literally "field alms here" (Suzuki 1988:33). An interesting feature of this shrine is the replacement of the usual wish-fulfilling jewel *(nyoi hōju)* motif found at most Inari shrines with the *magatama* curved jewel. Curved jewels appear on the paper lanterns, roof tiles, and amulets of this shrine, and a necklace of these jewels graces the neck of the female fox statue at one of the subshrines to the right of the main sanctuary. In addition, the shrine has erected a small museum in a *haniwa*-style building of the type in which the jewel-crafting guild would have lived. Inside is a small but detailed exhibit concerning the history and production of *magatama*. To learn about the Korean background and significance of the curved jewels, head priest Suzuki Kazuo traveled to Korea where he met with scholars and purchased objects.

Subtemple of Kenninji dedicated to Buddhist form of Inari, Gion area, Kyoto. The stone sign reads "Dakinisonten"; stone foxes flank the red torii gate before the more traditional temple gate. This is a Zen temple of the Rinzai sect.

Traditions of Buddhist Inari

This part of Inari's history is difficult to reconstruct. What is required is a great deal of archival detective work, unfortunately beyond the scope of this study, for in the reworking of Buddhist Inari traditions, much seems to have been deliberately obscured. When some of this history is recovered, we will understand a great deal more about the condition of pre-Meiji Inari worship as well as the strategies temples employed in the face of government insistence that Inari was a "Shinto" deity. The temples that maintained Inari worship after the separation of Shinto and Buddhism did so by arguing that they had always been worshiping a Buddhist figure which had been perceived by the masses to be Inari. Even if the Buddhist origin story was not entirely false, the popular worship at these religious sites was complexly eclectic. The details of that richness have been lost in the sanitized versions that have become the official histories.

The Case of Toyokawa Inari

Toyokawa Inari is a large Sōtō Zen temple in Toyokawa city, Aichi prefecture. The past history of this famous Inari is still far from clear, and the priests at this temple were not particularly concerned with trying to understand the past. Here is the official history as it currently appears in the temple pamphlet (Toyokawa n.d.):

> This temple, popularly known as Toyokawa Inari, is a well-known Sōtō Zen temple named Toyokawa Kaku Myōgonji. It was founded on November 22, 1441 (Kakitsu 1), by Zen priest Tōkai Gieki. The main figures enshrined are the Thousand-Armed Kannon Bodhisattva transmitted by Priest Kangan Giin and the protective deity of the temple (seen in a vision and carved by Priest Kangan), Dakini Shinten. This deity is the reason why this temple is so widely known as Toyokawa Inari.
>
> Kangan Giin was a famous disciple of Dōgen, the founder of the Sōtō Zen sect and Eiheiji Temple. The third son of the eighty-fourth emperor, Juntoku, he made a great vow to bring salvation to his times and went to China for intensive Buddhist study. Tōkai Gieki (the founder of this temple) was the sixth disciple of Kangan.
>
> Kangan's vision of Dakini Shinten was about seven hundred years ago. In 1264 (Bunei 1) he went to China to study Buddhism, and in 1267, on his return to Japan, he beheld a wondrous appearance: a vision of a deity seated upon a white fox, carrying rice, and bearing a wish-fulfilling jewel in one hand. The figure recited a mystical formula: "On shi ra bat ta ni ri un so wa ka." The meaning of these syllables is: "When this spell is chanted, the faith in me reaches everywhere, and by the true power of the Buddhist precepts, evil and misfortune will be abolished and luck and wisdom attained, suffering removed and comfort achieved, and pain transmitted into delight." This experience moved Kangan deeply. When he returned to Japan, he carved an image of the form he had seen and worshiped it as a protective deity. It was transmitted over the generations and was enshrined and worshiped here at the founding of this temple, Myōgonji.

Since that time, there have been many miraculous occurrences, and today Dakiniten is worshiped widely as a deity of happiness and prosperity who averts suffering and brings relief.[23]

Inari is said to be worshiped here because of the mistaken identification of Dakiniten (who sits upon a white fox) as Inari, but this is almost certainly an "invented tradition" (Hobsbawm and Ranger 1983) from the early Meiji period. The twenty-eighth head priest, Reiryū, and his disciple, Mokudō (the twenty-ninth priest), stubbornly resisted pressures to turn the temple into a Shinto shrine and were consequently afraid of assassination during this volatile period. Through its argument that it had always worshiped Dakiniten, sometimes mistaken as Inari, the temple managed to avoid forced conversion into a shrine. Similarly, they justified the presence of torii within the temple precincts by calling them *kahyō,* the name for the Chinese gates before palaces and mausoleums.

Although there is no study of Toyokawa Inari comparable to Sakamoto's on Chōei Inari (1983), a few clues indicate that similar forces were at work. The origin story from a 1931 pamphlet differs in certain key details from the account in the current pamphlet (Takahashi 1931). A painting of the temple grounds from the Tempō era (1830-1844) provides some evidence that the Inari was originally in the "Shinto" lineage. The Sanmon Gate and other temple buildings are in approximately the same configuration as today. But in the back left corner, where today there is a massive hall to Dakiniten, is a building at the end of a line of red torii labeled "Inari Daimyōjin Gohonsha." Another long line of torii leads away from the Inari shrine into the wooded area to the back and right of the temple. Yet another piece of the puzzle comes from a decrepit, seemingly abandoned, Inari shrine called Nishijima Inari not far from the temple. This Inari is the one that seems to have been incorporated into worship at Toyokawa Inari, but the documentation is incomplete. The Nishijima Shrine existed in the Kamakura period, and Inari worship was added during the Edo period (Yasui 1986:117-118). Then it seems that a fox living within Toyokawa Inari named Heihachi-gitsune—it is unclear if this was a real fox or spirit fox—began to be worshiped as Inari Daimyōjin complete with small shrine building, and this Inari eclipsed the one at Nishijima (Yasui 1986:118). The details of how Inari worship migrated to Toyokawa Inari from Nishijima are fuzzy, but the shift was charmingly expressed by Watanabe Masaka (1776-1840) as a foxes' wedding: around 1750, many hundreds of pine torches were seen along the roads—the wedding procession of the groom fox from Nishijima Inari marrying Hei-hachi Inari and moving to Toyokawa. After this there was said to be no *kami* at Nishijima, and the popularity of Toyokawa Inari continued to grow (Yasui 1986:118).

In the present version of Toyokawa's history, this tradition too seems to have been reworked into one that omits reference to incorporated Inari shrines: now the official story is that Heihachirō was not a fox but an old man with a magic pot who helped in the construction of the Toyokawa temple. It is likely that at this temple too, as in Sakamoto's study of Hon-monji, an Inari was enshrined at some point during the temple's history and that for political reasons the Inari was merged with a Buddhist figure in the early Meiji period. The question that requires further research is whether a Dakiniten was previously worshiped at Myōgonji or whether this came along with the Inari as part of its esoteric Buddhist associations from Fushimi. As Inari had early associations with Dakiniten that contin-ued in the Shingon lineage at Fushimi, I prefer the latter version. Inside the amulet distributed by the Toyokawa temple today are four pictures of deities: Dakiniten, Kannon, Daikoku, and Aizen Myōō. It is especially curious that Aizen Myōō—a deity in the esoteric Buddhist lineage and the main deity worshiped at Fushimi's Aizenji by Shingon priests—is included in this *ofuda* from a Zen temple. The two most obvious explanations are that the Inari in this temple was a *wakemitama* from Fushimi's Buddhist temple, Aizenji, or that the priests deliberately adopted Buddhist imagery from Fushimi's proscribed temple during the Meiji period.

The Case of Saijō Inari

Saijō (Highest, Best) Inari is also known as Takamatsu (Tall Pine) Inari; its formal temple name is Myōkyōji. Located in the outskirts of Okayama city in Okayama prefecture, this Nichiren temple currently worships both Inari and the *Lotus Sutra*. As at Toyokawa, a founding priest had a vision of a figure on a white fox, although this story is purported to be from the eighth century, whereas Toyokawa's is from the thirteenth. Here the tem-ple was said to be founded about twelve hundred years ago after Hōon Daishi beheld a vision of a deity astride a flying white fox when he was praying for the emperor's recovery from illness (Saijō n.d). This deity, almost identical in form to the Dakiniten worshiped at Toyokawa Inari, is here called Saijōi Kyōō Daibosatsu: Great Bodhisattva, Highest-Rank-ing Sutra King. There are subtle differences in the two forms, however: Dakiniten carries rice on her right shoulder and holds a wish-fulfilling jewel in her left hand, while Saijō-sama carries rice on her left shoulder and holds a sickle in her right hand.[24] The parallels between the visions of this eighth-century Tendai priest and the thirteenth-century Sōtō Zen priest are striking and suggest that similar strategies were employed by these temples when Inari had to be explained in a Buddhist way.

A priest at Saijō Inari was certain that the official history presented by the temple was a Meiji-period invention, even though temple publications continue to present it without qualification. "We have three hundred and fifty years of recorded history," he told me, "but we have twelve hundred years of 'history.'" The part of the tradition concerning Hōon Daishi was based on historical evidence; he was said to have had some kind of vision while meditating in the cave at Hachijō-iwa. But the name Saijō-sama did not appear in temple records until the separation of Shinto and Buddhism; before that, the Inari worshiped here was called Inari Daimyōjin. Other widespread traditions were modified as well: the *otsuka* rock altars are here called *hōtō* (treasure towers) and the different names for Inari end in *"tennō"* (Heavenly King) rather than *"ōkami"* (Great Deity). Saijō Inari's history too seems to be an example of the way that some temples dealt with their fame as worship sites of Inari.

Buddhist influences were critical then, in Inari's history and continued development. Nonexclusion was the norm: many Buddhist temples contained an Inari hall within their precincts; Inari shrines often contained halls in which Buddhist figures such as Kōbō Daishi, Kannon, and Daikoku were worshiped. Many of the syncretic associations proscribed by the separation edict returned through popular worship practices. The strategies that the larger temples used to retain both their Buddhist character and Inari worship enabled certain powerful and popular Inari's to survive. Although Inari and its worship have Buddhist forms, many worshipers assume, even when they are within a Buddhist Inari temple, that they are at a Shinto shrine. The survival of the rich eclecticism in Inari worship is due to the efforts of the Buddhist priests at temples like the two described here, but it is also due to the deep roots of Japanese popular religion and its resistance to manipulation and centralization.

2

Priestly Traditions and Shamanic Influences

And it is worthy of remark that although each person present dis-
liked the other, mainly because he or she did belong to the family,
they one and all concurred in hating Mr. Tigg because he didn't.

—Charles Dickens, *The Life and Adventures of Martin Chuzzlewit*

Although this study begins at two famous centers of Inari worship, it soon will be clear that these centers have less power to shape or direct ideas about Inari than their fame might lead one to expect. A person's connection with Inari may not begin at a sacred center, but once established it is likely that the devotee will visit a sacred center as part of his worship practice. The following narrative shows how one devotee literally fell into Inari worship. Even though she makes a monthly pilgrimage to the Fushimi Inari Shrine, her beliefs about Inari are only part of an eclectic and highly individualized set of practices involving Inari, Kannon, and the new religion Tenrikyō.

> I was born in a small Buddhist hermitage in the countryside. It is about 350 years old, and there was said to be an Inari dwelling in the large *sakaki* tree in the grounds. I never paid any attention to it, for I thought that Inari was a fox, and I did not want to worship it. Because I was educated in Christian mission school, I actively disliked *kami* and buddhas, and even incurred the great wrath of my relatives for agreeing to receive Christian baptism, which was a condition for

graduation from that school. So I neglected that Inari because it gave me the creeps. But then something very mysterious happened: the *kami* manifested itself to me, although in a form I could not see, and this changed my attitude completely.

I was in Tokyo during the war, but during the bombing I fled to my hometown in the countryside. My house was completely deserted, but I thought I would be able to live there more safely than amid falling bombs. No one had much food at the time, but when I left Tokyo, friends gave me a little from what they had and tied it up for me in a *furoshiki* wrapping cloth. I returned home in the winter, and there was deep snow all around. From the tiny rural train station, I walked up toward the hermitage but could not find the road in the dark. Finally I saw a lantern in the gate and headed straight for it—only to plunge down into an old well. It was deep and full of water, and it is amazing that it was not full of poisonous gas as old wells often are. Somehow I was able to work my way upward, climbing slowly with feet and hands, and at last I emerged from the well. Now I found the house and went in and dried myself under the heated table.

The next morning, I went outside to look at the scene of my accident. To my total surprise, the *furoshiki* cloth was hanging in the tree, and all its contents were arranged in a neat circle around that *sakaki* tree. And there was not a single footprint in the undisturbed white snow! An old man in the neighborhood told me I had fallen because I had made light of Inari *(Inari o baka ni shita)*. So the next day I apologized profusely, with great fear and trembling, but still felt uncomfortable about it. However, I could not deny that it was the working of something spiritual *(reiteki mono no hataraki)*, and that I was rescued by Inari. This is not a logical matter, but a spiritual one.

Family background, early education, and personal experience are at least as important as priestly teachings in shaping ideas about Inari—and most of the sacred centers are not engaged in a great deal of outreach to their worshipers. The result is a great diversity of ideas about Inari and his worship, a diversity masked by outwardly similar forms for worship. Inari's sacred centers are the shrines and temples where people make pilgrimages, where they request prayer services and talismans, where they worship and communicate with Inari. Although practices tend to be eclectic at the centers, the priests themselves are strongly sectarian. As priests understand their role and Inari in certain ways that may or may not accord with the understandings of worshipers, there are tensions between views of Inari as well as between priestly and shamanistic sources of authority. The issues over which priests and devotees may be in disagreement range from the meaning of the fox symbol to styles of worship, from the question of healing to the role of women. Often there is intense factionalism between and within centers, between centers and worshipers, and between devotees themselves. This chapter describes the characteristics of the centers—including the tensions and factions found there, the similarities and differences between the two large centers, Fushimi Inari and Toyokawa Inari, and the contestations between priestly and shamanic authority within Inari worship.

Shinto priests conduct Hitaki Sai in November to ritually burn the rice straw and return Inari from the rice fields to the mountain for the winter. Fushimi Inari Shrine.

Centers of Inari Worship

Much Inari worship takes place at sites (often including a sacred mountain) that have been centers of Inari worship for centuries. I chose the centers of Fushimi Inari and Toyokawa Inari for my field sites—both well-known and long-standing Inari centers with roughly the same number of employees—in order to contrast Shinto and Buddhist institutions, western and eastern Japan locales, and urban and rural environments.

After describing these two centers, I discuss the rather surprising similarities and differences between them.

Fushimi Inari

Fushimi Inari Shrine is a large Shinto shrine in southeastern Kyoto at the site of the sacred mountain where Inari was first worshiped and where worship has continued since the eighth century. Priests here *(kannushi, shinshoku)* are ritualists who are formally trained in the standardized religious teachings, history, and ritual practices of Shinto.[1] There are roughly fifty Shinto priests, all male,[2] who work in the six main divisions of the shrine: ritual matters, shrine administration, shrine finances, publicity, the pilgrims' inn and wedding hall, and the training and coordination of the approximately six hundred lay worship groups affiliated with this shrine. As in most Japanese institutions, power and responsibility come with seniority and jobs are not necessarily assigned to those who are able or interested. Priests usually rotate jobs every three years, giving each an understanding of the routines of the different offices. Study at one of the Shinto universities is the usual training for this job, but priests may also take a yearlong course for their priest's license if they have a bachelor's degree in a different subject. Most of the priests attended Kokugakuin University in Tokyo; the alternative is Kogakkan University in Ise.[3] A majority of them came from shrine families and will return home to take over the responsibility of their family-run shrine when their fathers retire.[4]

Priests at large shrines tend to lead a life much like a businessman's. They commute to work on crowded trains in business suits, changing into priestly robes after arriving. Once at the office, priests may spend more time doing paperwork than rituals. Unlike small shrines or rural shrines where the priest has a personal relationship with the worshipers, at large shrines the worshipers are often processed through rituals rather mechanically. Priests receive a set salary and benefits package similar to that at a large company.

Many of the priests at Fushimi Inari had an impressive artistic talent that they pursued as a hobby. One was an accomplished potter; another was a painter; other talents included photography, drawing, classical dance, playing musical instruments, and singing. One night as I was eating dinner with two priests who had night duty on the sacred mountain, they burst into the "Ode to Joy" from Beethoven's Ninth Symphony, in harmony, in German, to my astonishment and delight. They also called upon these talents in the performance of certain shrine jobs: playing music on archaic instruments at rituals, photographing the shrine for publications, designing new amulets, carving the large shrine stamp out of stone.

About a dozen shrine priestesses work here. Generically called *miko* (literally "divining woman"), here they are termed *kagura-me* (woman who performs the sacred dance). *Kagura-me* are high school graduates who must retire from this job the day they turn twenty-five, at which point some get married and others switch over to an office job at this shrine or elsewhere. Their main sacred function is to perform the sacred *kagura* dance at shrine rituals and throughout the day for prayer services. They also help the priests with various tasks such as selling talismans and amulets, addressing envelopes for mailing, and bundling thousands of offering sticks for the November fire ritual. Their office operates on a seniority system—reputedly even stricter than that of the priests. Once a week, they take time out from their duties to learn flower arranging and tea ceremony in lessons the shrine provides.

In addition to the priests and priestesses, about one hundred and thirty people work in various capacities at the shrine: guards, maintenance people, cooks, office workers, and a crew who work on the mountain cutting trees and clearing brush. The bright red buildings are large and impeccably maintained. This shrine has an air of solid prosperity about it.[5] Daily offerings to the deities are lavish, extraordinarily so at important rituals; priests and priestesses are resplendent in silk robes; the guards wear crisp, military-style uniforms.

The priests with whom I spoke at Fushimi Inari Shrine were not necessarily of one mind about some issues, but they did have certain concerns in common.[6] They emphasized proper forms of worship: Shinto prayers *(norito),* proper obeisance (bowing and clapping to the deity), correct objects of worship (amulets or divided spirits from this shrine). All priests agreed that worshiping a fox as Inari was incorrect and improper. They were concerned with responding to the changing needs of worshipers while still preserving or at least documenting historical forms. History was stressed here. The shrine was proud of its past because it is here that Inari was first worshiped in the eighth century. Priests considered this shrine to be, not only the origin, but in some sense the center of all Inari worship in Japan, at least in terms of importance. Yet not all the priests knew the details of the shrine's history well. Those who were interested in it read and studied on their own. Knowing the history was not required and the shrine had no formal mechanisms for teaching it.

Toyokawa Inari

Toyokawa Inari, the temple Myōgonji, employs about forty Zen priests, all of whom live in their own home temple in the vicinity. They conduct funeral and memorial services at their home temples for the members of their parish *(danka)*. But this does not usually constitute full-time work, so they also work seven days a week at Myōgonji, taking days off as necessary for their own temple business. (This is possible because their wives are at the home temple to take calls and greet guests.)

The main offices of this temple handle reception of worshipers and guests, personnel and maintenance, finances, furnishings, ritual functions, flowers and interior maintenance, the young priests in training, business of the head priest *(hōjō)*, and food and parishioner business. All worshipers who request a prayer service (minimum cost 2,000 yen, about $16) receive a Buddhist vegetarian meal as a gift from the temple. A huge kitchen prepares the food, served by a staff of lay workers on lacquer trays in various rooms throughout the temple. Besides the hundred or so lay workers who assist in the preparation and serving of food, maintenance people, guards, a carpenter, an electrician, gardeners, office workers, and vendors of prayer flags and amulets work at the temple.[7] Worship is divided between the Zen practices that take place in the dharma hall *(hatto)*, which enshrines the Thousand-Armed Kannon, and the main sanctuary *(honden)*, which enshrines Dakiniten and is the focus of Inari worship.

Myōgonji also functions as a training facility for young men who want to become priests in the Sōtō sect of Zen Buddhism. Living within the temple compound are fifty to sixty priests-in-training. The acolytes— *okozō san* (literally "Honorable Mr. Small Priest")—follow a fairly strict regimen at this temple for four years. High school in Japan is usually a three-year course, but here it takes four years because the *kozō* work during the day at the temple and attend classes in the evening. All live in the dorm, arise at 5 A.M., do *zazen* meditation, perform various functions in the temple throughout the day in addition to their own chores and studying, eat dinner, then go to school from 5:30 to 9 P.M. During the first year they may not return home at all, which means that five or six new boys end up quitting each year. Acolytes may go home once during the second year. After high school, the young priest usually attends a Zen university in Tokyo for the subsequent four years while living and helping out at Toyokawa Inari's branch temple in Akasaka Mitsuke.[8] After this, a novice spends one or more years at Eiheiji, the head temple (with Sojiji) of the Sōtō school, where life is exceedingly strict. Then, like the Shinto priests, the priest may return to his home temple to assist his father,[9] or he may work at a larger temple to gain experience until his father retires. The acolytes were a remarkable group of young men. This was especially apparent during the busy days of the new year, when ordinary high school boys also worked part time at the temple. The contrast between the un-socialized, smoking, giggling, slouching outsiders and the bald, dignified, polite, ritually clad "small priests" was striking.

Priests at Toyokawa were generally more excited about the rituals and teachings of Sōtō Zen than about Inari. A few had read general studies of Inari on their own, but most were not well informed about its origins and history and there was no institutional format to educate them. They were not hostile toward Shinto interpretations and worship, although they them-selves engaged only in Buddhist forms, worshiping Dakiniten and the bo-dhisattva Kannon, the central images of this temple.[10] There was only one teaching they emphasized strongly: Inari is not a fox. They did not sense a great deal of contradiction between the teachings of Zen and Inari wor-ship. Expressing tolerance for different forms of spirituality, they explained that it was a kind of historical aberration that this temple developed as a center of Inari worship. And now that was "just the way it was."

This temple was equipped with a new meditation hall *(zendō)* for practicing *zazen* meditation. It was never used, however, for the *kozō* did their morning meditation in the main hall and the priests thought that meditation was something they had completed during their early training.[11] The temple never opened itself up to the public for meditation even though it had this unused facility. The priests saw their temple as one that focused on prayer services *(kitō)*, rather than a "pure" Zen temple such as Eiheiji, and said, furthermore, that they were too busy to conduct a weekly or monthly hourlong meditation session for laypeople. Some of the smaller branch temples in the area do hold a monthly meditation session for lay-people, however, and the Toyokawa Inari *betsuin* in Tokyo has meditation twice a month, advertised in the newspaper and open to all.

Toyokawa Inari, like Fushimi Inari, was a prosperous religious center. Salaries were generous, buildings and grounds were well maintained, and a new museum *(jihōkan)* to display the temple's historical treasures was under construction while I was there. The buildings were all of unpainted wood. The bright red color, signifying Inari, appeared only in the large paper lantern in front of the *honden* and in the rows of "one thousand" red and white prayer flags *(senbon nobori)* in the area of the inner temple

(okunoin). One priest explained that in keeping with the teachings of
Buddhism, priests should live simply and not flaunt wealth, and the temple should reflect this idea too. But another wisely added that in a temple
famous for this-worldly benefits *(genze riyaku)*—a concept closely tied in
the popular imagination with Inari—a prosperous air was positive advertising that the deity there was responsive to prayers, which in turn attracted more people to the temple.

Paradox at the Centers

The mood of the two sacred centers was very different. On first impression, Fushimi seemed more open and accessible because of the presence
of the mountain, which accommodates itself to any worship style, while
Toyokawa seemed more forbidding and its large buildings restricted of
access. In terms of styles of administration and openness to the anthropologist, however, they were just the opposite. Fushimi priests maintained
a kind of ritual formality even among themselves, while those at
Toyokawa seemed more relaxed and less concerned with appearances in
the temple. A Fushimi priest never left his post until exactly quitting time;
those at Toyokawa felt free to leave if they had something else to do and
it was not busy. The Buddhist priests occasionally took me on a tour of
another temple during working hours; this never happened at Fushimi,
where I had to schedule my formal interview during the priest's private
time after hours. On slow days at Toyokawa, priests played *shōgi* or
watched television; at Fushimi they always seemed to have paperwork to
do. Such variation may derive from the difference between urban and
rural lifestyles, between styles in Kyoto and other geographic regions in
Japan, between Shinto emphasis on ritual and Buddhist emphasis on compassion. Whatever the reason, there was a definite variance in how the
two centers ran, although they both employed about the same number of
people and were both important centers of Inari worship.

    The coexistence of multiple traditions at Fushimi Inari Shrine may
come from the loss of all shrine records in 1468 during the Ōnin War.
Priests can get some idea about the previous configuration of large public
rituals from outside sources, but the history of smaller rituals and internal
traditions has been lost. Of course, the lost traditions too may have been
multiple, but after the Ōnin War and up through the Edo period it seems
that new traditions and priestly lineages were rather freely invented and
interpretations about the meanings of symbols and rituals varied. Para-

doxically, this great destruction may have given birth to new freedoms and possibilities at Fushimi.

Toyokawa Inari faces an even more complex problem regarding its history and authority vis-à-vis Inari. Because its history seems to have been radically rewritten during the early Meiji period—and at the very least the Shinto elements discarded—the priests at Toyokawa do not have as firm a historical ground on which to stand. Priests uncritically cited the facts mentioned in their short history pamphlet about the founding of the temple. No one seemed concerned about ferreting out the actual history at all. They simply were not interested in the question.[12]

Although priests at both ritual centers were tolerant about cases of fervent belief centering on a mistaken notion of Inari, they would try to explain their idea of the correct way if they were conversing with the devotee. A Fushimi priest:

> There are people who worship Inari, and consider themselves to be truly involved in Inari practice, but have never once come to Fushimi Shrine. I think this is a mistake. Of course it is belief, but not proper Inari belief. When someone has a mistaken object of devotion, it is a case of "a sardine's head" and cannot be helped.[13] His faith is good and pure but the object of worship is really incorrect. Of course that person has no idea he is worshiping the wrong symbol, but he really should be worshiping a proper form of Inari's spirit *(mitama)*. Sometimes children put a rock inside a small shrine, and people end up worshiping that, and that is not bad, exactly, because people don't know. Inside small home shrines to Inari that people have brought to this shrine to be ritually burned, I have found statues of Fudō Myōō, snakes, and all manner of other objects, and that is not really very good from our perspective. We are priests, so we want to disseminate the actual spirit of Inari to different sites of worship. Scholars may not think these distinctions are important, but for us they are of the utmost importance.

I had assumed that the Buddhist priests at Toyokawa Inari would feel a sharp contradiction between the teachings of their founder, Dōgen, and the worship of Inari, but they neither expressed concern nor tried to explain Inari in a very Buddhist way.[14] When I asked if this was an example of "expedient means,"[15] a senior priest said my interpretation would be going too far; he did not want to use that term. He explained that although there were no prayer services *(kitō)* in Dōgen's Zen, this form of worship had rather naturally evolved in most Buddhist sects in Japan and now they were even conducted in the sect's head temple of Eiheiji. Their purpose is to pray for people's happiness *(shiawase)*, and this is one method among many for people's salvation. "That is the purpose of religion, to save people, to grant them happiness." What he did not say, but I think implied, is that the practice of Buddhism in Japan is not very different from the practice of other forms of religion. His equation of happiness with salvation shows the this-worldly emphasis that characterizes most forms of Japanese religion.

The lack of centralizing dogma means that, like the devotees, the priests too have differing ideas about Inari and are not consistent as a group or even necessarily as individuals. On the question of the appropriateness of chanting Buddhist sutras to the Inari *kami* at Fushimi, one priest instructed a worshiper: "Japanese *kami* only understand the Japanese language, so *norito* must be chanted to them. If you chant Buddhist sutras, they are in a foreign language, and the *kami* will not be able to hear them." But one of his colleagues commented privately: "Of course any prayers prayed with sincere heart reach the *kami*, who can understand all languages. Why should Sanskrit be an exception?"[16]

At Toyokawa, a similar situation was observed. In talking with various priests at the temple, I learned that they had very different opinions on how this temple had become an Inari sacred center. The currently published position is that Dakiniten, the protector of the temple who rides on a white fox, was mistakenly worshiped as Inari because of the fox, and in this way Dakiniten faith merged with Inari worship. But one priest had a different version: "Both Inari and Dakiniten were worshiped here from long ago, but the Inari was not a divided spirit *(wakemitama)* from Fushimi. It had some other origin. Gradually the Inari gained in popularity, and then this temple became a famous place to worship Inari." (He did not specify where the Inari had come from.) Another priest told me he was quite sure the Inari worshiped at Toyokawa had, in fact, been a divided spirit from Fushimi Inari.[17] This fact was suppressed, he said, during the brutal treatment the temple received from the government during the separation of Buddhism and Shinto. He thought that Dakiniten had been worshiped here, too, but believed that the Inari had deliberately been subsumed into it to save the temple from forced conversion into a Shinto place of worship.

Reminding ourselves that "a man never coincides with himself" (Bakhtin 1984a:59), we note that priests were not always consistent either. Priests who were generally historical or rationalist in most of their pronouncements would sometimes hang up magical charms to rid an old building of centipedes, speak of mysterious deaths after an Inari shrine was unceremoniously dismantled, or relate that when they had a cold it would disappear in record time if they were on duty reading prayers to Inari in the main sanctuary. A Buddhist priest was very surprised that his healing vision of Inari did not take the form of the Buddhist version he prayed to daily. He told me:

> About thirty-five years ago, I had a very serious car accident and was close to death. Although I had been a fervent devotee of the bodhi-sattva Kannon up to that time, it was not she but Inari who came to me. When I saw the figure of Inari, I laughed, because I thought I was dead. It was not in the form of Dakiniten, however, but a figure in a colored robe, coming toward me, hair blown back. I could not tell if it was male or female, but this Inari had a very gentle face and was probably female. I seemed to lose consciousness again, but when I came to I tasted something delicious in my mouth, like Calpis [a yogurt drink], and saw a *hyōtan* gourd floating in space from which this delicious medicine poured right into my mouth. This continued for three days and two nights, and within a month I was completely healed, to the doctors' amazement. After this experience, I strongly believed in Inari. I think that because I had spent so much time in the main sanctuary, chanting sutras to Inari, she came and gave me the medicine when I was in a life-threatening situation.

Shamans

In addition to Shinto priests and Buddhist priests, who conduct formal rituals at their respective shrines and temples, a third type of religious functionary plays an important role in Inari worship. Held in great esteem as religious specialists by their followers, these people are nonclerical, shamanic ritualists. The shaman, shamanic healer, or spiritualist *(odaisan, ogamiyasan)* is someone who has direct access to spirits and deities, the source of important information not usually available to human beings about healing, the otherworld, the fate of the dead, and the future. "Sha-manism" comes from a Siberian term for phenomena connected by his-torical transmission. It does not constitute a single complex throughout the world, however, but it is an analytical category that may include disparate phenomena. Anthropologists today prefer to speak of shaman-isms in the plural; they are more interested in particular manifestations than in universal generalizations (Atkinson 1992). Although the concept of shamanism overlaps with that of spirit possession in many studies, the term "shaman" implies the ability to control access to the spirits, whereas spirit mediums may be the vessels for spirits but have little control (Lewis 1971, 1986; Bourguinon 1976; Turner 1972).

In Japan, shamanism has a long and complex history—including the shamanic Queen Himiko of the third century; the early empresses who served as mediums for the oracles of the *kami;* the arrival of Buddhism in the sixth century, which gave rise to the mountain asceticism later called Shugendō; the medieval teams of female medium *(miko)* and male ascetic *(yamabushi);* the government suppression of Shugendō and shamans during the Meiji period; and the reemergence of shamanic forms with post-World War II religious freedom, especially in the context of the new religions. (See Blacker 1975; Hori 1968; Sakurai 1974-1977.) There are a number of surviving local variations of shamanic traditions, from the blind *itako* of Tohoku to the *nuru* and *yuta* of Okinawa. Contemporary Japanese shamanism differs from the dramatic forms in neighboring Korea in various ways: it is far more subdued in expression, costume, and music (Blacker 1975; Kendall 1985).

Among the Inari shamans, possession by a *kami*—or, more likely, communication with a *kami*—is indicated not by violent seizures or wild dancing but by subtle changes of pitch in the shaman's voice, her eye movements, or the rhythm of her voice. Charismatic religious specialists played a major role in the spread of Inari worship, especially during the Edo period (Naoe 1983a:116). New Inari shrines were often started as the result of a divine dream of a shaman or even an ordinary person, for messages from the *kami* were taken very seriously. In a study of Inari shrines in Tsugaru (Aomori), the northernmost tip of Japan's main island, Naoe (1983a:123-130) found there were three Inari shrines on the sand dunes in Shariki village. Only Takayama Inari is still thriving today, however, although they were all roughly the same size and all had shamans, there called *gomiso,* living in the vicinity. It turns out that only Takayama Inari granted a license to the *gomiso,* who lived not just in that area but in Akita and Hokkaido as well. Those who received the license felt a deep tie to this shrine and spread its reputation in other areas by organizing group pilgrimages back to this Inari shrine, keeping its popularity alive.

The shamans who practiced on Inari Mountain had varying backgrounds. About half had parents or close relatives who were shamanic and in whose paths they followed; the others came to this role through the classic pattern called shamanic initiation.[18] In this scenario, the person suffers terrible problems, often including debilitating illness, until finally the *kami* spontaneously speaks to her or through her. One of my informants, Yoshiba-san, had had a fairly normal childhood, for example, although she later learned that her mother had done the waterfall austerity while she was pregnant,[19] which gave the child a connection to Inari from the beginning. She married, had three children, and was leading a fairly typical life until things began to fall apart when she reached forty—triggered, perhaps, by her husband's blatant affairs with other women. Yoshiba-san began to think she was crazy because she could see dead people's shapes, so she went to various shrines and temples looking for help. Finally a shamaness told her that one of Inari's spirit fox helpers was "attached" to her. She needed to enshrine and worship this spirit, she was told, thereby transforming it from a possessing to a protecting one. She performed arduous rituals, including the hundred-day waterfall austerity, learned to control her spiritual abilities, and moved out of her husband's house. Now, like the shamaness who helped her, she makes her living helping other troubled people. She lives in a small house at the foot of Inari Mountain in Kyoto and has a number of loyal clients all over Japan. Like most of the other shamanesses I knew, she is dedicated primarily to Inari but also serves other deities including Buddhist ones. She receives direct revelations from Inari in the form of voices, dreams, and mysterious signs.

Unlike the priests, who often perform rituals for people they do not know, the shamanesses usually have a deeply personal relationship with their clients. They travel to see them, share their troubles, weep with them, and admonish them when necessary. While the priests' credentials include educational achievement and certain licenses, the shamans' credentials are their reputations, usually spread by word of mouth. Their income is highly erratic: most on principle will not charge a set fee but trust the client to give what she can. Yoshiba-san had no money at all one day; the next day, a satisfied client arrived with a gift of 1 million yen ($8,000 at that time). The money was soon gone, however, for she made generous donations to the offering boxes of the *kami* at the shrine in thanks for this boon. She trusted that her *kami* would take care of her and that when she was again reduced to nothing, someone else would come through—and this did seem to happen. Shamans usually had an elaborate altar in their home in the main room, and the constant arrival of clients made their abode more like a religious establishment than a private home. Most of the shamans I met during this study were female. They ranged widely in age, degree of spiritual prowess, institutional affiliation, ritual style, and background. Although there are male shamans,

Buddhist Inari worship, Sōtō Zen sect, in hall to Muei Inari within Eijūji, Shinshiro, Aichi prefecture.

I met far fewer of them during my year at the sacred mountain than women.[20]

Two Sources of Authority: Priestly and Shamanic

Early forms of Japanese religiosity seem to have been based on two types of *kami* and the communities that worshiped them. The clan *(uji)* had its own tutelary spirit, a deified ancestor *(ujigami)*, while the other kind of religiosity was directed toward an outside deity *(hitogami)* who was "accessed" through a shaman and worshiped by people unrelated to one another. The clan deity, the *ujigami*, protected its group, that is, blood relatives and those who married in; the functions of the *hitogami* were more specialized and anyone could pray to it (Hori 1968:30-33). In the analysis of Ellwood and Pilgrim, these two tendencies solidify into religious communities as the natural (into which one is born) and the intentional (deliberately chosen); their forms of leadership are the institutional and the charismatic (shamanic); their two functions are expression of communal cohesion and vehicle for innovation and individual vision (1985:19 and 127-129). Hori notes that neither the *ujigami* nor *hitogami* forms of worship remained pure: they were mutually influential (1968:34). Often cited as prototypes of the two basic patterns into which Japanese religions tend to fall, they are more useful in distinguishing worship patterns than types of deity, most of whom could be worshiped in either fashion.

From as early as the seventh century in Japan there has been tension between priestly and shamanic religious authority, a tension played out between institutions and inspired individuals. Prior to this time, religion/government took the form of direct transmissions from the *kami* through oracles spoken by shamanic females—sometimes interpreted by males (as in the example of Queen Himiko of the third century)—as well as the organization of groups under regional or clan *kami* in the *ujigami* system. The system of charismatic leadership was abandoned in favor of centralized bureaucratic control around the seventh century, when Prince Shōtoku began "to rule the nation with the help of his bureaucratic officials, and not on the basis of the unpredictable divine oracles transmitted through shamanic diviners" (Kitagawa 1966:25). The centralization of the state following Chinese models required the "institutionalization of the charisma of the Shinto priesthood" (Kitagawa 1966:32).[21] The new Buddhist institution also had close ties with the state. But the shamanic forms continued to thrive and developed into an eclectic mountain religion that came to be called Shugendō. Solitary ascetics *(ubasoku, hijiri)* versed in a mixture of Shinto, Buddhist, and Taoist notions spent time practicing austerities in the mountains, developing spiritual powers, which they then used to heal and to perform miracles. These figures were threatening to the orthodox Buddhist priesthood and to the state, which banished the founder of Shugendō and issued edicts four times during the eighth century about the proper conduct of Buddhist clerics in an effort to control these powerful ascetics (Kitagawa 1966:40–41). In time the clan-based worship group was replaced by the residential group. People began to worship the *kami* of the area in which they were born *(ubusuna no kami),* and by the middle ages the *ujigami,* no longer confined to one bloodline, came to be seen as the protecting deity of the area in which one lived (Kokugakuin University 1985:71). From the early centuries, these tensions have continued in Japanese religions, and periodically religious institutions or the government attempts to suppress the power of the shamanic element. Many of the new religions follow the pattern of revelatory shamanic origins that develop into a vast institutional structure, sometimes splintering into rival factions or new sects by new revelations.[22]

Authority in Inari Worship

Inari is usually considered to be the *hitogami* type of deity (Hori 1968:35) but also serves in some cases as an *ujigami*. The part of the Hata clan that settled at Inari Mountain probably considered this *kami* to be their pro- tecting deity (*Nihon rekishi daijiten* 1970:405), and for many centuries the Fushimi Inari Shrine has served as the *ujigami* for a large part of the south of Kyoto.[23] Some of the divided spirits that left large Inari shrines to be reenshrined in people's households grew in local popularity and finally became village shrines (Naoe 1983a; Miyata 1988). When Inari was reenshrined in a local shrine along with ancestral spirits that pro- tected the village, Inari developed that character also, although it is not technically an ancestral *kami*.

Both priestly and shamanic claims to authority coexist throughout the world of Inari in Japan, sometimes in tension, sometimes in creative har- mony.[24] The Shinto priests emphasize the history of their sacred center, proper transmission of traditions, priestly lineages, the study and licensing of ritualists. The ethos of the priesthood at Fushimi is one of quiet dignity, ritual elegance, precision of performance. Worship style is based on de- tailed traditions, as intricate as the tea ceremony, with minute directions about which foot to move first, how many degrees to bow, the number of offering trays to be used. These priests tend not to emphasize mystical experiences and pride themselves on carrying out their tasks with formal- ity and solemnity. This does not mean they do not have personal experi- ences of the *kami*, but this is not stressed in their role as priest. They delight in the knowledge and use of the shrine's historical traditions: the calligraphy on the tag hanging from the arrow talismans *(hamaya)* sold at the New Year, for example, was copied from a two-hundred-year-old document. The priestly ethos includes a fierce loyalty to the shrine and the *kami*—an ethos exemplified in a story the head priest tells at the training session each year. During the occupation, he says, some American soldiers wanted the antique sword that was the temporary repository *(goshintai)* of the deity at his shrine. The priests did not know what to do—they did not have the language skills to explain what the sword meant to the shrine and, moreover, they were young and inexperienced, for the older men had died in the war. Eventually they agreed to hand it over, but wanted to pray first. They prayed the same *norito* over and over, not wanting to stop because they did not want to give away the seat of the *kami* and symbol of their shrine. They prayed fervently, tears running down their faces, and finally the soldiers left without the sword.

Most of the Buddhist priests at Toyokawa Inari were quite interested in Sōtō Zen ideas and rituals and enjoyed teaching me about them. About Inari they were not so well informed, or particularly interested, and several apologized for having so little information. They calmly accepted their role as caretakers of a religious tradition they had not trained for; they neither promoted it nor subverted it. The ethos of the Buddhist priests was one of relaxed diligence. Although the priests had a busy ritual calendar, fed and housed thousands of guests, conducted prayer services throughout the day, saw to the education and training of the acolytes, and managed their own home temples as well, they managed to maintain a calm atmosphere at the temple. Even during the New Year, when they were frantically busy, their body language was agitated but their faces serene. They chatted easily with each other and with guests around a hibachi charcoal fire, cooked up wonderful snacks of roasted rice cakes and seaweed or grilled shiitake mushrooms with soy sauce over the hot coals, and did not seem particularly concerned if a guest witnessed this. When one of their exhausted number fell asleep while sitting among them, they joked that he was in a state of *sokushin jōbutsu*, enlightenment in this very body.

The shamans, in sharp contrast to Shinto and Buddhist priests, derive their authority from direct experience of the *kami* and may engage in various austerities to increase their spiritual powers. Their ethos was eclectic. Each had a constellation of deities and practices garnered from a wide range of possibilities—practically the whole spectrum of religion in Japan. In addition to a connection with the Inari *kami*, shamans were associated with other religious centers (Mount Kōya, Mount Ontake, Tenrikyō), Buddhist figures (Kōbō Daishi, Jizō, Kannon), other *kami* (Sarutahiko, Ebisu, Benten), and various other spirits and beings from the otherworld (ancestors, the unhappy dead, the spirits of miscarried or aborted fetuses *(mizuko)*, spirit foxes, dragons, snakes). Personal experience and training were more important than institutional or doctrinal consistency in determining the sources of a shaman's powers and her hermeneutical stance. One woman told me that she thought she really should not chant sutras to the Buddhist figures, because she had a Shinto license and not a Buddhist one. But she really had no choice, she said, as she hears the voices of Jizō and Kōbō Daishi speaking to her and must therefore worship them properly. Her own experience is thus more important than any formal rules. Within this eclecticism, however, some shamans were constantly innovative and open to new ideas while others were rooted firmly to a set of traditions. Although the shamans' authority comes from their connection to the otherworld, this does not mean they are totally mystical or irrational. Their work involves performing rituals, but it is not limited to only religious means: they serve as advocates and confidants, as well, and may know physical therapies such as massage. Solving a client's problems usually involves not only intercession with the beings of the otherworld but some very practical work in this one.

Shamanic healers often worked across institutional boundaries, praying to both Shinto and Buddhist deities. Even in *kō* worship groups that followed the prescribed institutional patterns fairly closely, syncretic elements managed to slip in. One Fushimi *kō* included a Buddhist sutra in its official prayerbook; another group instructed members in the use of the esoteric Buddhist *kuji* purification method.[25] One leader of a Toyokawa *kō* told me that Toyokawa Inari consisted of a Shinto shrine within the temple—a notion, unsupported by visual evidence, that has been untrue for at least the last century (although a common assumption for many). The priests at Fushimi seemed more concerned with keeping the two religions separate than did those at Toyokawa. One Shinto priest, in reply to a woman's question about worshiping Inari and Fudō Myōō together, responded that it was not a good idea: "The two should be treated in different ways, rather like two sets of guests, one who smokes and the other who does not." A great deal of syncretism can be seen at most Inari centers, but it is just these elements that are systematically excluded from the booklets of glossy photographs sold at the sacred centers.

Claims to priestly and shamanic authority clashed, in one case at Fushimi, over the matter of offerings *(shinsen)* to the Inari *kami*. The food offerings presented daily and at rituals to the deity by the priest vary a good deal from shrine to shrine but follow historical traditions at each shrine. Devotees sometimes gave food offerings to the shrine on a monthly basis, but this usually took the form of a large bottle of sake. (Most people simply made monetary offerings.) One shamaness was instructed directly by Inari each month concerning the offering to be made, and she would take that item to the shrine—a huge fish, sake, rice, whatever Inari instructed. One month, Inari told her to offer Chinese cabbage *(hakusai)*,[26] for which she received some negative comments from the priests. One asked if she had really been instructed to do this by Inari, implying that he doubted her shamanic authority. Although she felt hurt and angered by this treatment, the priests did have trouble with unsolicited perishable offerings, for there were problems with storage and it complicated their routines to some degree.

Much worship on the sacred mountain at Fushimi (and other mountain centers) is of a personal nature and may not involve the priests at all. Worshipers with a direct and personal connection to Inari do not treat the priests or their rituals in a particularly deferential manner and may simply ignore them. During official rituals in the main sanctuary, it was sometimes impossible to hear the words of the priest because of the impetuous bell-ringing, hand-clapping, and chanted prayers of individual worshipers who made no concession to the service in progress. A man carrying a miniature torii walked right through the middle of a priestly fire ritual on the mountain to get to his own rock altar. And the guards usually had to clear a path for the priests when they filed into the main sanctuary for a special service, for the bustling crowds of worshipers, intent on their own business, paid them no heed. I asked a priest about this, wondering if perhaps I was projecting my own notions of politeness here, but he agreed that such behaviors struck him as rude also. Although all manner of people are said to worship Inari, he thought that perhaps this behavior revealed a preponderance of "low-class" types. Buddhist priests too reported that their temple was often the locus for worship by shamanic *kō* about which they knew nothing. They would see the leader instructing her group, but their activities were private and did not include worship conducted by the priests.

Not that priests merely preserve the old while shamans create the new. New rituals are created by priestly and shamanic religious leaders alike, but in different ways. Priests at the Fushimi Inari Shrine try to be responsive to the needs of worshipers in the creation of new rituals or festivals *(matsuri)*. In 1957 and 1963, the Industry Festival (Sangyō Sai) and Industrial Safety Festival (Sangyō Anzen Sai), respectively, were created. Although they seemed relevant at the time, they have not proved popular in the long term. A priest observed: "In the creation and maintenance of festivals, at base are human needs and human wants. But if these are too narrowly construed, the result is not successful and finally no one will attend them." Their creation of Motomiya Sai (Original Shrine Festival), however, has been a success. It came into being in 1951 when the priests thought there should be a summer festival at the shrine. Today they send postcards to every person who has received a divided spirit *(wake-mitama)* of the *kami* inviting them to participate. The current mailing list has 80,000 names, and about 60,000 people will either donate a *chochin* lantern (thousands of these are hung throughout the grounds) or request a prayer service during the festival. There are strong parallels in this festival to practices related to the Obon Festival of the dead. The Moto-miya Sai takes place on July 22 and 23, Obon on the thirteenth to six-teenth of the old seventh month, now celebrated in either July or August in different parts of Japan. The decoration of the shrine precincts with lanterns recalls the special lanterns used to honor the visiting dead and the custom of welcoming the dead back from the mountains with fire; two groups of devotees perform a circle dance similar to the Bon Odori. A priest insisted there was no connection to these Buddhist customs: the lanterns are merely an offering to the *kami,* he said, the dance merely two examples of folk dances (from Shiga and Osaka). Whether or not it was their intention, the fact that similar customs are familiar to Japanese peo-ple at this time of year makes this festival appealing. And it has special meaning to people who have enshrined a divided spirit of Inari in their homes—this is its shrine of origin and they return to the center during the hot summer and enjoy a festival of light. Although the priests gave the festival a particular meaning related to the Inari shrine and its *kami,* they used a number of familiar forms that resonated with other seasonal tra-ditions in Japan.

Yūzū Inari, a new version of the Buddhist Inari, was recently installed at the branch Toyokawa Inari temple in Tokyo, where people call on the power of the wish-fulfilling jewel held by Dakiniten to increase their wealth. In this case, the priests developed the idea in response to what they perceived to be believers' needs, built the new shrine building, and posted a sign explaining the characteristics of this form of Inari. They took a symbol from the repertoire associated with the Dakiniten form of Inari and then elaborated it in a new way, but a way that resonates with the character this deity has had for centuries.

Shamanism gives birth to new traditions, too, but in ways that may be more disjunctive. A new shrine came into existence when a shamaness I knew received an oracle from a divine snake *(ryūjin)* living in Amakusa, resulting in a new tradition unrelated to previous local ones. Summoned from Kyoto through a referral to a small town in Nagasaki prefecture, once there she sensed a snake spirit calling to her. Her client drove her around until she discovered an old pond, completely overgrown with weeds, where the snake still lived. Realizing that this snake had been instrumental in bringing her to this area and giving her work, she thenceforth took large bottles of distilled spirits *(shōchū)* and ten eggs to feed this spirit in thanks. One night, months after she first met this spirit snake, it possessed her in her Kyoto home and related its history, which she recorded in automatic writing. She detailed this experience in a letter to the town council, which debated the matter and decided to set up a shrine to the snake spirit as it had requested, even though the snake's message to the shamaness was quite different from the story that local folklorists had recorded earlier. Although the story given by the shamaness did not accord with local tradition, the people took the neglected snake spirit's message seriously and built it a new shrine at great expense. The shamaness's authority was more persuasive to them than their own local history.[27]

New traditions came into being, in the first two cases, through a deliberate, rational extension of associated symbols into a new function; in the last case a divine oracle, transmitted through a shamaness, replaced an older tradition. This tolerance for new religious content in old forms, coupled with the respect for shamanic authority, makes the evolution of popular religious ideas fascinating but almost impossible to trace historically. As in the case of the rock altar tradition (Chapters 1 and 5), when a popular or shamanic tradition first comes to a sacred center it may be resisted or ignored by the priests, who may eventually come to accept it. Some traditions, however, are studiously avoided by the priests. Although fried tofu is the main popular offering at Inari shrines, the priests never seem to include it in their daily offerings to the *kami*. This seems to be a recent aversion, however, for Toyokawa sold *oage* within the precincts before the war for the convenience of believers (the branch temple in Tokyo continues to do so), and old Fushimi records indicate that fried tofu was sometimes part of ritual fare for the *kami*.

Authority to take action in matters regarding Inari may come from divine dreams rather than an institutional directive. Embree (1939:253) describes a case in which an Inari shrine was established by a mother after a message in a dream. Her son neglected the shrine after her death—until another dream and signs from Inari persuaded him to restore it. Even if a priest saw a decrepit Inari shrine, he would have no jurisdiction to restore it or order it repaired. The centers themselves have had to submit to government control in earlier times, especially intense during the separation of Shinto and Buddhism and in the prewar years. As a result of these pressures, the centers lost their authority to preserve traditions, and some practices were eliminated or totally reinterpreted. The priests were then in the position of trying to preserve popular worship while pleasing the government. Shamanic sources of authority can undermine priestly traditions, but they can also maintain or increase the popularity of a sacred center; the same can be said for individual practices and government pressures.

Masculine vs. Feminine

Although it would be wrong to equate the priestly with the male and the shamanic with the female without qualification, the tensions between the two sources of religious authority often play themselves out in just this way. For most of Japanese history, the priesthood has been a male bastion and shamanic healers have often, though not always, been women. The two roles and genders united in creative cooperation in the terms of female medium *(miko)* and the male priest-healer *(yamabushi)* that worked together to exorcise and heal (Blacker 1975). The priest would chant the appropriate prayers to induce the spirit to descend into the medium's body; he would then interrogate it as it spoke through her mouth, either banishing it through his superior power or negotiating a compromise mutually beneficial to the spirit and the host. In my observations of Inari shamans, I never saw this kind of teamwork. But in the priestly referral of certain possessed or troubled believers to shamanesses, we can still see the indirect acknowledgment that both types of religious functionary are necessary.

Instead of cooperation I often saw tension and lack of mutual respect between these two religious figures, especially when they crossed gender lines. In other words, I heard more criticism of female than male shamans from the Fushimi priests. The shamanesses ranged from those who conformed in most ways to dominant cultural norms in Japan about acting female to those who acted idiosyncratically by avoiding what they saw as unimportant trappings that hindered their spiritual development. The shamanesses who seemed to be respected by the priests were those who maintained their culturally defined female roles and extended their caretaking into the spiritual realm. The others—those who considered themselves to be more male than female or described themselves as man-haters *(otokogirai)*—seemed less interested in conforming to the priests' expectations of them and were not much liked by the priests.[28] A priest once told me that he really could not understand the idea of possession, an admission that led us to the topic of women who sometimes became shamanesses after a physical or psychological crisis (see Blacker 1975; Eliade 1964). Regarding the shamaness whose crisis was described earlier, he said that her husband's affairs and lack of loyalty to the family were her own fault because she did not try to be "charming" for him. He had no sympathy for her side of the story at all.

Whereas the ritual behavior of the priests followed prescribed channels, that of the shamans took very individual forms, including powerful anger. On one occasion a shamaness was called by concerned relatives to help straighten out a family consisting of an older woman and her two grown sons who had gotten the family into serious debt through gambling. The shamaness spent hours chanting the *Perfection of Wisdom Sutra* in front of their family Buddhist altar, but she insisted that the family members all sit in that room or the adjoining one, some writing their names on the hundreds of prayer sticks she would later burn in a purificatory fire. She interrupted her prayers often to exhort them to discuss how they planned to get themselves out of this financial mess. With tears running down her face, she told them that the dead father of the household was worried and frustrated that he was unable to help them. Finally, she stood over the brothers, lecturing and scolding, crying and shouting, that they should not simply get the money from relatives but should work at any job they could get and pay off the money through their own honest labor. Although she is a short woman, she seemed to fill the room with her anger and power, and the men were almost cowering before her on the tatami mats, eyes cast down, not meeting hers. In the next room the women were all weeping. Here we do not have a possession per se or a priestly interrogator. But the shamaness does derive status from her affiliation with Inari Mountain and the shrine. And her use of various techniques—ritualistic, psychological, emotional—to break the impasse was very effective. A priest would not, in general, go this far.

Lay Worship Groups

Priests and shamans (or lay leaders) come together in a formal manner in the case of *kō* that are granted official status by the sacred centers. *Kō* are lay worship groups that focus on a specific deity or sacred site and may include pilgrimage or certain ritual activities at specified times of the year. Not all Inari *kō* in Japan have an official tie to a particular shrine or temple, and the centers do not grant automatic status to every *kō*. Roughly six hundred *kō* are officially recognized by Fushimi Inari, three hundred by Toyokawa Inari. Fushimi has a fairly rigorous procedure for admitting worship groups to the official ranks; Toyokawa has no procedures at all but simply keeps a record of the groups. Perhaps Toyokawa preserves an older pattern of *kō* association, for at Fushimi shrine, until the Meiji period, *kō* were focused in narrow service-oriented ways, donating money and assistance for specific rituals. One earlier *kō* was exclusively focused on the donation and maintenance of the handwashing basin *(temizu sha)*. At Toyokawa during the spring and fall festivals this pattern is still apparent, although the temple now handles most of the details required for the festival. A group called the *Shoei kō* is responsible for carrying the sacred palanquin; the *Ongaku kō* provides the ritual music. In past days *kō* also existed to provide festival robes, prayerbooks, divine children *(ochigo san)*, and the like for the large festivals. The newer pattern of *kō* is that of a communal worship group, broadly focused on the deity Inari, traveling together to some sacred center for periodic worship on a monthly or yearly basis. Toyokawa has both kinds of groups, while Fushimi seems to have shifted to the newer pattern. In general, at Fushimi *kō* tend to focus more on their own group, rock altar, and leader than on the shrine as a whole. Two exceptions of which I am aware are a *kō* from Hikone, which comes to Fushimi every month and picks up all the litter on the mountain as a service to the shrine, and a *kō* that presents folk dances at the shrine during the Motomiya Sai in July.

Organization of *Kō* at Fushimi Inari

There are three types of *kō* at Fushimi Inari Shrine: the *dantai,* a group with a leader and from five to fifty members; the *atsukaisho,* which has a leader and at least thirty people; and the *shibu,*[29] which has at least one hundred members, a leader *(chō),* and an assistant leader *(fukuchō).* It is also possible to be a *kō* member without a group *(chokuzoku kōin).* Members of all these groups are divided into three categories by the yearly donation they make to the shrine:[30] regular *kō* members *(sei kōin)* give 1,000 yen; special *kō* members give 2,000 yen and up; and honorary members *(meio kōin)* give 5,000 yen or more.[31] For this financial support, the shrine gives a return gift to every *kō* member and a subscription to the quarterly publication *O-Inari* with articles about the history of the shrine, believers' testimonials, and notices of upcoming rituals and events.[32]

　Kō that become officially affiliated with Fushimi begin in various

Monthly fire ritual *(hitaki)* at home of shamanic leader of Inari
lay worship group *(kō)*.

ways: a strong devotee may pull a group together to form a *kō*, or perhaps
an Inari *kō* in some local area decides to make an official connection with
the Fushimi shrine.[33] In the priests' estimation, roughly half of the *kō*
leaders are shamanic and have some sort of direct communication with
Inari; the majority are women. This proportion changes, however, for the
successor to a *kō* shamanic leader may not have this talent. It is fairly easy
to become a *kō* at the first level, but to become an *atsukaisho* or *shibu*
requires the leader (and assistants) to attend the weeklong training course
(kōshūkai) offered by the shrine (up to three times); it also involves

observation of the leader's rituals at her home altar by priests from Fushimi Shrine and a fairly long association with the shrine (usually seven years). The priests want these lay groups spreading the worship of Inari, but they do not want to grant official status to groups that do not conform to certain key ideas of the shrine.

So long as the worship of Inari is conducted in a proper fashion and the role of the fox is correctly understood, the Fushimi priests tolerate a great amount of diversity within the *kō*. Some are run by Buddhist priests; some are involved in the worship of Kōbō Daishi as well as Inari. Most conduct monthly rituals in the leader's home and in this way function almost as satellite shrines. As in the smaller, private religious establishments on Inari Mountain, there is considerable personal contact between the leader and members of the group. Apart from conducting the rituals usually performed by a Shinto priest (such as a ground purification ceremony before building a house), the leader may engage in healing, geomancy, and personal counseling—functions that many priests at large shrines no longer perform. In a *kō* that was highly regarded by the shrine, the leader, a woman in her forties, had taken over from her husband's mother who had become too ill to continue. The mother did have shamanic talents; the daughter-in-law does not, however, and in fact only half-believed when she began the job. But strange things have happened that are pulling her deeper into the job and into Inari beliefs. She was asked to pray for a dying person for whom all hope had been given up; unaccountably, he recovered a week later. Doctors told him he would never work again because of his bad heart; he now works every day. This kind of experience shows her the mysterious powers of Inari, she says, and she is becoming more confident in her job.

The following account of a monthly fire ritual at an Inari *kō* gives the flavor of these satellite Inari communities. The largest *kō* formally associated with Fushimi Inari Shrine has over seven hundred members and is located about three hours by train from Fushimi. This *kō* has its own worship hall in the home of the *kō* leader, Kawashima-san, a woman in her fifties. Her spacious living room houses a large altar, and believers come and go as if it were a public shrine rather than a private home. The room has a bell to announce the worshiper's presence to Inari, votive plaques and offering sticks for sale like the shrine, and even an *omokaru ishi,* the heavy/light rock for divination (here in the shape of a wish-fulfilling jewel of polished granite). Every month Kawashima-san conducts a number of worship services, the most dramatic of which is the *hitaki* fire ritual.

Kawashima-san and her two female assistants, attired in the formal robes of Shinto priests, conduct a standard service before the altar, exactly following the procedures taught to them at Fushimi Inari Shrine. A male member of the group announces the different parts of the ritual to those assembled. While the assistants are carrying out the ritual, the head of the group sometimes nods her head and moves her mouth silently, indicating that she is in communication with Inari. At the end of this part of the ritual, there are about twenty people in the room, half of whom trickled in after the start of the service. The assistants, helped by members of the group, suspend a white cut-paper hanging *(hitaki gohei)* from the middle of the ceiling and to each corner attach long lacy paper streamers that they stretch to the four corners of the room. A low round metal pan (about three feet in diameter) constructed of silver-colored metal with a golden jewel decorating the sides is positioned under the hanging. One of the assistants carefully lays some of the wooden offering sticks in a square configuration in the center of the pan. These *hitakigushi* have been purchased by believers who write their name and age on them before offering them to be burned, believing that thereby their prayers are carried up in the smoke to Inari.

At 8 P.M. the fire ritual begins. The fire is lit in the freestanding fireplace, and offering sticks are piled up and burned until several hundred have been consumed. The Shinto Great Purification Prayer *(Ōharae kotoba)* is chanted over and over by the whole group during this ceremony. As this is basically an ordinary living room, the smoke and heat become intense and sweat pours down the faces of those seated close to the fire. Four-foot-high tongues of flame reach hungrily for the paper decoration, which flutters in the heat and seems to pull away from the fire. Sparks shoot out, but somehow the paper never bursts into flame. When the fire gets too high, the chanting voices of the key women get louder as if they are imploring it to stay under control. Their eyes focus on the top of the flame, and together they move their eyes—and the flame—down to a safer level. Three of the more spiritually advanced assist with symbolic hand gestures (mudra; Jap. *inzō*) to compel the fire to obey their will. The pattern repeats over and over: they arrange the sticks, the fire leaps up and threatens the ceiling, they bring it under control, it burns down, they add more sticks. Finally, all the prayers have been sent and the fire dies down to coals. All bow and clap toward the fire, then turn and do the same toward the altar.

The head of the group thanks everyone for coming, and the man who did the announcing gives a short inspirational speech. People tear off bits of the paper decoration as a protective talisman for the next month and burn the one they have carried in their wallets the past month. Several stand near the hot coals and rub the heat from the sacred fire into sore or troublesome places on their bodies. The sacred meal *(naorai),* always served in some form after a Shinto ritual, consists of a tiny cup of *sake* and small slice each of dried squid and seaweed. People begin to say their farewells and make their way home; those remaining sit around enjoying an informal snack of tea and rice crackers. As plans are discussed for the big spring festival next week, each guest receives two bananas from the altar offerings to take home. The lingering heat and smoke feel like tangible symbols of the goodwill and cooperation that prevail in this group.

The most direct mechanism by which the Fushimi priests try to shape the *kō's* ideas and practices is the Kōshūkai. This training session takes place for one week in June, and from fifty to seventy people usually attend. Priests provide instruction in Shinto styles of worship along with the history of the Fushimi shrine and the Inari *kami.* Although this is a constructive way for the priests to influence the form and content of the Inari *kō,* there is no guarantee that *kō* leaders will agree with the teachings or particularly respect the priests. One shamaness was bitter that status among *kō* leaders in the priests' eyes depended, as within the shrine itself, on seniority, not spiritual achievement. A shaman who took the course to receive the certificate thought the priests cold and bureaucratic; although he lived close by, he had nothing to do with them afterward. But others are glad for the opportunity to learn from priests and take pride in being thought proper *(majime)* by the shrine. They remain close to the priests who were their instructors during the course and make it a point to see them when they return to the shrine, often with gifts from their local area. For the religious specialists who officially associate with the shrine, there are a number of benefits. The most important is probably the high status they receive from a formal affiliation with Fushimi Inari Shrine. When they have reached a certain rank in the *kō* hierarchy, they receive a signboard to hang outside their home indicating that the *kō* is officially designated by the shrine. High-ranking priests from the shrine may journey to the *kō* to attend a ritual; when the head priest *(gūji)* himself attends, it is a special honor. The leader, and sometimes all the members, may be invited to participate in one of the elaborate rituals at the shrine or to raise the rank of their *kō*. Association with the shrine and its priests may be a helpful check on "spiritual inflation" by helping to focus the shaman's attention. Even the complainers gain much from the experience: although *kō* leaders must attend the training session at least once and no more than three times, most attend the maximum rather than the minimum number of sessions.

Organization of *Kō* at Toyokawa Inari

The *kō* at Toyokawa Inari are not managed by the temple. The priests keep a list of these groups, but there is no process of approval, no training session for leaders, no yearly festival for members, no fee to the temple. *Kō* here have from thirty to five hundred members, and about three hundred *kō* are listed with the temple. Those with a shamanic leader are rare. Although the priests sometimes see shaman-led groups worshiping at both Toyokawa's main temple and at the Tokyo branch, those groups are not formally affiliated with the temple. Leaders tend to be male, while women often serve as secretary or treasurer for the group. In contrast to the main pattern of Fushimi's *kō*, the groups do not usually meet in the leader's home for monthly worship; when they meet as a group it is at the temple for worship or to help out during a busy time.

Whether the *kō* is a neighborhood group, an occupational group, or a group led by a shamanic religious specialist, those in the Kantō area tend to worship at the Tokyo branch temple at the New Year and make an overnight pilgrimage to the main temple in May. Participants may pray for personal benefits, but the emphasis is on service to the temple. Although the membership has changed from mostly male to mostly female, the pattern of male leadership (passed down to a son) is still generally followed and is said to be the most stable in preserving the group. The priests said that the peak of worship by *kō* was from 1955 to 1970, when huge groups of up to seven hundred worshiped and stayed at the temple. Since then the number of *kō* has not fallen off, but the size of many *kō* is shrinking; many *kō* leaders and members were concerned that membership is increasingly constituted by the elderly and that younger people are not joining.

One hugely successful *kō*, organized differently from the typical pattern, is located in Nagoya. It was founded by businessmen and runs like a well-oiled machine. About two hundred of the five hundred members attend the monthly pilgrimage to Toyokawa Inari, riding from Nagoya on a train expressly run for them by the Meitetsu Company on this day. Over the years they have donated a number of items to the temple, and on their five-hundredth monthly visit they dedicated a small rest house they had built at the back of the temple. This *kō* has no shamans, possession, or healing; it focuses on business prosperity. Some people may simply be praying for their own financial success, but I spent some time with one of the key leaders, a remarkable man who devotes a great deal of time and energy to community service. In addition to all the work he does for the *kō* and temple, he raised enough money to rebuild a shrine in his neighborhood, works with local drug addicts and a group that looks after elderly people living alone, and takes turns serving on a neighborhood safety patrol he helped to establish. He feels that he has benefited from the blessings of "Toyokawa-sama" (Inari) and should therefore do what he can to help others. This *kō* seemed fairly unusual in being so active, well run, and innovative concerning ways to help the temple.

Without a sacred mountain and personalized forms of Inari at Toyokawa, most worship took standard forms and focused on the temple. The group arrived, had a prayer service, partook of a vegetarian meal afterward, then usually broke up for individual worship. At this time, people might offer a personal prayer flag, or pray at the main hall to Kannon (or at one of the small buildings to Kōbō Daishi, Daikoku, Binzuru, Fudō, Shōtoku Taishi, or Jizō), or wander back to the Spirit Fox Mound (Reikozuka). But without a mountain, there was really no austerity to be performed and no waterfalls in which to chant. Worship here, although perhaps no less sincere, had more the appearance of a casual visit to a temple than the intense mountain pilgrimage of Fushimi and other Inari sites with mountains.[34]

Although neither religious center was severely restrictive, priests at both sites had concerns about extreme variations in beliefs. Priests at Fushimi worried that the *kō* leader, sometimes considered to be a *kami* herself by her followers, would be the focus of the group rather than Inari and the main shrine. A Buddhist priest said that often the beliefs and practices of the *kō* were closer to some kind of idiosyncratic new religion than to traditional Inari worship, and this was difficult to control. As we shall see in the final chapter, priests tend not to confront believers directly but try to influence them in indirect ways. At Fushimi, one mechanism is the training session where *kō* leaders are taught correct ritual forms by Shinto priests. Toyokawa, however, relies on restricting the iconographic forms at the temple to the ones of which they approve—a kind of insistence on proper forms through the absence of inappropriate ones. This restriction of form may not be a clearly articulated policy, but the priests' reluctance to encourage popular forms of Inari worship and the relatively small and contained space they manage (compared with the large mountain at Fushimi, not all of which is the shrine's property) give them far greater control over how the temple's space is used by worshipers.

Inari *kō*, whether or not they are led by a shamanic figure, play an important role in maintaining and spreading Inari beliefs and practices. They may be closely tied to the sacred center and try conscientiously to practice in ways consistent with priestly ideas; but they may also conform only in surface ways to the centers, the leader more influenced by instruction she received from a parent or teacher. Priests were astonished by the variety of new ideas that seemed to creep into even the most traditional groups. At one Buddhist worship service at the main temple itself, each member of the *kō* received a pinch of incense from a priest as a symbolic purificatory agent to rub on her body. Those sitting near me instructed me to taste it three times, then rub my hands together and pat down my body. When I later complained to the priests about the horrible taste in my mouth from the incense, they were flabbergasted that worshipers were using it in this way.

Foxes and Fox Possession

Priests were united in their denunciation of the idea that Inari is a fox. They stress that the fox is the *kami*'s assistant, or messenger, and it is a serious mistake to worship a fox as Inari or vice versa.[35] This position was clearly adopted by some of the *kō* leaders after hearing the priests' comments during the training session. On an overnight pilgrimage with one group, I happened to mention that I was going to participate in the folk custom of fox feeding *(kitsune segyō)* the next evening. From the assistant leader of the group I got a clear and strong message that such a custom had nothing to do with Inari worship but was a folk custom that had slipped in through the association of the fox as Inari's messenger. Another Fushimi *kō* leader, however, was more temperate in his understanding of the fox. He did not conflate the *kami* and the fox but did think that this vulpine assistant of Inari was an exceedingly important figure for many believers. Having grown up in the countryside where people paid attention to the barking of real foxes as omens, he felt his understanding was different from the majority of priests who were college graduates and perhaps committed to upholding the reputation of a high-ranking shrine. He thinks of the spirit fox as something like a dog that always follows one around; this spirit is the working of the Inari deity. Worshiping the animal (or spirit animal) directly is wrong he thought, but he fully believes that an invisible fox spirit follows Inari believers at all times. In addition to these thoughtful positions, numerous people simply equate Inari and the fox. The *Dictionary of Shinto* lists Inari without censure as an example of a *kami*'s assistant *(shinshi)* becoming the main *kami (shūjin)* itself (Ono 1985:395).

The Toyokawa Zen priests also felt that Inari was not a fox and that the fox symbol should not be stressed. One priest told me he was shocked when the temple established the Spirit Fox Mound (Reikozuka) a few years ago—in direct contradiction to their deliberate policy not to emphasize the fox. When the area and new stone shrine were first dedicated there was a ceremony *(kaigen shiki)*, but the priests otherwise never pray there and no rituals take place there, even though Dakiniten is enshrined at the center of the fox mound. (Yet an inner courtyard of the Okunoin, to which no one except priests is admitted, is ringed with 301 white porcelain fox statues, the spirit assistants of Dakiniten.)

Most fox statues are adorned with votive "bibs" *(yodarekake)* and sometimes hats as well. In response to my question about this, a Fushimi priest said that priests never tie the bibs on or assist others in doing so. But to the worshipers the offering of a bib has meaning, so they tie them on with great reverence and enthusiasm, even though they sometimes have to step on the altar surface to do so. He said the priests rather frown on the practice, but then shrugged and philosophically added, "But what can we do? We cannot have a priest follow every devotee who goes up the sacred mountain." Ambivalence about the fox was described by a priest from Saijō Inari: although the main sanctuary itself is devoid of any fox imagery, fox symbols clutter the mini-pilgrimage *massha* area and mountain. He said he had no problem with the fox symbol per se but thought that the fox was often understood *as* the deity by believers. Because this Inari center emphasizes Buddhist teachings concerning the *Lotus Sutra,* priests were particularly concerned that the fox be understood properly. They did not even give the fox the status of a messenger or assistant of the deity. Rather, they said it was simply the animal vehicle on which deity rides.

Fox possession is a spiritual/psychological malady that has been associated with Inari for centuries. Although priests at major sacred centers did perform exorcism rituals in the past, today this function is left mostly to the shamanic religious specialists. Priests today deal with the problem quietly: performing a prayer service *(gokitō)* or ritual purification *(oharai)* or advising the family or person what to do next. Although the number of cases brought to shrines and temples is decreasing yearly as the interpretive idiom shifts from spiritual to psychological, priests still considered the idea a "dormant volcano" *(kyūkazan)*: it seems to be sleeping but is still very much alive, especially in rural areas. Most priests admitted that a religious cure often worked, but they seemed uneasy with the idea of fox possession because it represented a superstitious level of popular belief from which they wanted to distance themselves and the sacred centers.

Interpretative Frames: Magical vs. Rational

Generally speaking, priests used a more "rational" way of talking about matters that shamans described in "magical" terms: what shamans took to be religiously significant, priests tended to regard as coincidental.[36] For example, the steaming rice cooker *(kama, narigama, meido)* was understood differently by the two. Some shamans believe it to be divinatory—holding that the quality and duration of the sounds it emits represent a message from the *kami*—while the priests emphasize its use as one method of purification, noting that there is a scientific explanation for the production of sound when heat is applied to the wooden steamer. Of course priests too believed in the power of Inari to effect changes in the world, but in general they were more cautious about the assignment of religious significance. Shamanic healers paid a great deal of attention to meaningful coincidences, which are often helpful in tracing the etiology of an ailment. "The headaches started after my grandfather died" or "We saw a snake on the gravestone"—such comments give the healer key information in ridding the patient of his troubles. Healers pay attention during a religious service to the way wax drips off a candle, the color and direction of incense smoke, even the quality of the shamanesss voice during her chanting. But a priest said this kind of thinking was too superstitious. If an offering tipped over or a priest collapsed during a ritual, he said, it would just be "one of those things" and they would carry on with the service.

Near the end of my first year of fieldwork, I had a fascinating talk with a Fushimi priest who separated the Shinto priests at that shrine into the categories "hot" and "cold" (he used the English words), by which he meant those with a more mystical (hot) bent compared with those who were more rational (cold). Of the fifty priests at Fushimi, he could only think of five "hot" ones. He explained that the status of priests is higher than that of shamanic healers *(odaisan),* and while priests must have some faith *(shinkōshin),* they should not be too fervent. The Buddhist priests too made some distinctions between doctrinal interpretations and magical ones, but they tended not to dismiss the significance of certain strange happenings, particularly those they had experienced firsthand. Most of the Toyokawa priests told me privately of some strange experience that had affected them deeply. Although the Fushimi priests tended to deny or downplay this kind of occurrence in our conversations, one priest indicated that he had had such an experience but declined to share it with me.

But the Buddhist priests represented a spectrum of positions. One evening, as I was eating dinner in the temple with the two priests assigned to night duty, I heard a fascinating exchange concerning their opinions on the reality of the otherworld *(ano yō).* One said it was his job as a Buddhist priest to conduct memorial services for the dead because this is a custom in the Buddhism of Japan, not necessarily because the spirit world *(reikai)* actually exists. He thinks Buddhism is a religion of everyday life and the living. The other politely disagreed: even though he was a Zen priest, he had been raised in a Shingon sect temple and his father had taught him that all religions must deal with the unseen world. Even though both priests had undergone virtually the same formal training in a religion with concrete teachings, they had very different ideas about this core issue.

In both sacred centers, devotees attributed magical or healing properties to symbolic items used during rituals. After the Ohitaki Sai fire rituals during November at Fushimi, devotees dismantled the fireplaces and took home singed cedar boughs and lumps of charcoal, which they said had magical and medicinal uses such as curing colds and cancer. Priests knew of these practices but did not encourage them, saying the purpose of the sacred fire is to burn the rice straw and release the spirit of the *kami* so it can return to the mountain for the winter. Nevertheless, the notion that the fire's remains *(hitaki no ato)* have sacred power is one of the Seven Mysterious Traditions of Inari Mountain, of which many priests tend not to approve.[37] To discourage the taking of the burnt leftovers, priests devised a way for participants to keep a *tamagushi* offering bough as a symbolic representation of the deity. The same thing happens during the summer purification ritual, Nagoshi no Ōharae, when the priests and

worshipers pass through a large miscanthus reed ring *(chi no wa)*. As soon
as the formal ceremony is over, the people dismantle the ritual ring and
take home the reeds that lined the sides. In response to my question, an
elderly woman said, "If I put this reed in my entryway, it will prevent
robbers and other bad influences from entering my home." This phenomenon occurs at Toyokawa Inari also, particularly concerning the flower
petals scattered by the priests during ritual processions as a symbolic
purification. Some ladies told me they deliberately sat at the back of the
hall during one service because they knew they had a better chance of
getting these lucky petals—in fact, this was why they had come to the
service. They were more interested in obtaining these paper amulets than
in observing the ritual or listening to the chanted sutras.

Fire was used differently by priests and shamans. Priests esteemed fire
for its power as a purifying agent in Shinto and for the symbolism of
destroying the passions in Buddhism. Shamans are known for their mas-
tery of fire (Eliade 1964:470), and those involved in Inari worship often
demonstrated this skill. Shamans conducted *goma* (or *hitaki*) fire rituals
in their homes, commanding the flames not to touch the fluttering paper
streamers or burn the house down. Dozens of candles burned on the altar
of one woman, and she even slept while they burned—unthinkable to
most people in fire-conscious Japan.

Shamanic healers believed they had certain powers that they could
impart into objects. An elderly lady refused the tiny cup of sake after a
ritual on Inari Mountain, worrying that it would make her drunk. A male
shaman made some elaborate esoteric hand gestures (mudra) over the cup,
then emitted a sharp shout, and then told the lady that he had removed
the alcoholic content and now she could safely drink it. One of the *kō*
leaders, believed to be almost a *kami* herself by her followers, always ran
two fingers down the front of each amulet she distributed to her group,
in order to transfer some of her power into the object. The priestly notion,
however, was that amulets are the outward symbols of an inward attitude
and the objects themselves have no inherent magical powers. Sometimes
believers wanted to pay for a prayer service and then go off to the mountain while it was in progress. But the priests explained that without the
person's participation, the ritual had no meaning: for it to work, the
person had to be present.

It is not that the priests are iconoclasts who deny the need for symbolic expression (Turner and Turner 1978:xiv). Rather, they tend to inter-
pret symbols metaphorically, or historically, while shamans (and some

devotees) favor literal meanings. But because there are no clear dogmas in Inari worship, the priests are not as far removed from the shamans as they might be if they were propagating a doctrinal message. In other words, the symbol (fox, jewel, cedar bough) does not stand for an abstract concept that suggested it in the first place. Rather than deriving from a central and unifying narrative, an orthodox interpretation, the symbols came to be used in Inari practices or associated with the Inari deity in various ways.

Two Dangers: Coldness at the Center and Spiritual Inflation

It is not surprising that outsiders view large, complex institutions as being cold. In contrast to the small local shrine or temple where one can meet the priest raking the garden or drop in for a cup of tea, the larger institutions develop hierarchies that make direct access to the top priests almost impossible. An institution can circumvent this impression of coldness by certain public relations techniques, but Fushimi Inari Shrine chooses not to do so. Although many devotees and *kō* members and leaders had warm and close relationships with certain priests, they spoke of the institution itself as exceedingly cold and unnecessarily bureaucratic. Some *kō* leaders were laughing uproariously (in private) after the comments of a priest who had come to a ritual in the *kō* leader's home as a representative of the shrine. After making a brief speech to the assembled group of worshipers, he sincerely invited them to "stop by and say hello next time you visit the Fushimi Shrine. We can't do much besides offer you a cup of tea, but we would love to see you." Because his office was known as being particularly unfriendly, even to people who had legitimate business there, the notion of a devotee just stopping by for tea really made the women laugh. There was sometimes an assembly-line feeling to the prayer services, especially when the shrine was very busy, and people sometimes felt slighted or embarrassed when their question was answered by priests in a rude or dismissive way. Problems that priests did not wish to deal with got lost in the bureaucracy.

Priests at Fushimi themselves sometimes spoke to me of this coldness, which they acknowledged. They said there was a big difference between "family shrines" and "company shrines." The family shrine was not necessarily a hereditary shrine, but one small enough that the group related to one another like a family.[38] A company shrine, on the other hand, was one whose size required hierarchy and a division of labor for smooth functioning. Even though priests performed most of the jobs, few of these jobs related to the actual worship of the *kami*; the rest were essentially the paper-pushing tasks one finds at any company. They claimed a long history for this coldness, and one priest believed it was found here even before the Meiji period. During the Edo period (1600–1868), there were great pressures from the government to keep practices rational and focused on a Confucian-derived ethic of morality. The shrine expelled one of its renters who became possessed; shamans were forbidden but worked in secret. But at the same time, it should be noted, priests (at least at the Buddhist temple Aizenji within the shrine precincts) were using an esoteric ritual to exorcise possessing foxes from their victims (Fushimi 1957:43 and 137).

The main reason for the shrine's cold image was not size or organization but a deliberate ethos. The priests felt they had certain appearances to keep up—a kind of detached dignity. This was apparently not a new phenomenon, one priest explained, but one with some historical depth. He was not sure why it had happened. His novel explanation: "It's like being a car salesman—if you are too friendly, it seems phony to the customer and you can't sell the car." A *kō* leader thought that perhaps because this shrine had received such a high prewar rank (Kampei Taisha) and all of its priests are college graduates, they had an extremely high image to uphold and could not risk losing face in any way. Another way to see this phenomenon of coldness is in reaction to the extreme individualization and diversification of Inari beliefs in Japan (Chapter 5). By following prescribed forms, conducting set rituals, preserving historical patterns in somewhat rigid ways, the priests provide a counterweight to the centrifugal forces that have been so strong in the history of Inari worship.[39]

But coldness was not the only danger. The shamans could sometimes stray into the other extreme from the priests' coldness—into what I call spiritual inflation, an exaggerated sense of one's own spiritual powers and loss of self-restraint. Most shamanesses tended to be rather modest: their pronouncements were made in ambiguous terms in appropriate settings. But one shamaness began giving people gratuitous advice from the otherworld concerning illnesses that would afflict their families if they did not have her perform certain rituals for them. When she gave advice of this sort to one of the more conservative priests at the shrine, it made him furious. On a pilgrimage to Ise Shrine, she strode up to a wheelchair-bound woman and told her she knew the reason for this woman's handicap and could make her well. Moreover, this shamaness believed that her moods directly affected the weather. Finally, in demanding 1 million yen ($8,000) to cure someone, she went too far and angered even the priest who had sometimes referred people to her. She had gotten too greedy, he said, and refused to recommend her anymore. In a cultural setting where even priests were quite restrained about pronouncing whether a person's beliefs and worship style were correct or not, this intrusive manipulation of people's personal affairs was highly offensive.

Toyokawa Inari was not, to my knowledge, considered cold by devotees. But the temple had far fewer systematic dealings with *kō,* and generally the relationship seemed a genial one of priests as hosts and worshipers as guests. As a center of Inari worship, however, Toyokawa took a passive, even distant, role: it engaged in little outreach or advertising, developed no new festivals, but rather relied on its famous name to draw crowds. Unlike its branch temple in Tokyo, which has a deep connection with Inari traditions, the main temple almost completely ignores Hatsuuma, Inari's most important holiday. Pilgrims often arrived in huge tour groups, and whatever history and tradition they learned came from the professional tour guides, not from the priests. The priests at this center were curiously detached from the Inari phenomenon and carried on with Buddhist routines and worship even though they realized that the reason most people came was to worship Inari.

Factions in the World of Inari

When I began to study Inari worship, I assumed that it was all somehow related if not quite a seamless unity. Even for the first few months of intensive fieldwork, although I knew there were differences between some of the sacred centers, especially the Shinto and Buddhist sites, it seemed there was a coherence, even harmony, within each center. But gradually, as people became more candid with me about their ideas and opinions, I discovered an enormous amount of underlying factionalism within centers, between centers and their worshipers, between different lay groups, and between different centers.[40] This tension was not acted out in obvious ways. I only learned of it as people from different groups described their views of other groups to me in private.

Within the centers, groups of priests were allied over certain issues and opposed to other priests over questions of Inari, styles of worship, or the meaning of being a priest. Some Fushimi priests thought others "too fervent"; the opposing faction, in turn, called them "salaryman priests, not real Shinto priests." I got some sense of the differences between these two types in their comments about my participation with some pilgrims in the waterfall austerity. The group that invited me to join them in this practice was not an official *kō;* their rock altar was located in an area not presently belonging to the shrine. A day or two later, one priest lectured me about my lack of professionalism: I was a scholar, not a worshiper, and I would lose my objectivity, he scolded. My description of the value of participant observation did not seem to mollify him. But other priests were impressed and praised me for my attitude of interest and sympathy rather than cold detachment.

There were tensions, too, between lay workers and priests at both main centers. In both cases the issue was status. The workers thought the priests were condescending to them, and the two groups did not mingle freely. Even when workers and priests both spent the night in the shrine or temple for security reasons, they ate and fraternized in separate rooms. Of course there was a huge differential in salary as well. One of the female lay workers wondered if the distinction between workers and priests was because the priests were college educated and the workers were not. But she also thought that age should count for something, too, and said that the older workers should get more respect even if they are doing unskilled jobs.

Members of *kō* often described their group as being unique for reasons that turned out not to be particularly unique at all. Workers at certain teahouses on Inari Mountain disparaged other teahouses; religious healers could be exceedingly competitive. A shamaness told me that she met another female healer on the sacred mountain and was asked by the older woman how often she did the waterfall austerity. When she replied, "Every day," the older shamaness looked taken aback and said that she used to do austerities every day when she was younger, but that she had graduated *(sotsugyō shita).* "Can you imagine?" my informant repeated to me (and the small audience in the teahouse) over and over in a sarcastic voice, "she thought she had graduated! One never completes austerities, but continues them for one's whole life." Another shamaness was totally dismissive of all male religious healers: no matter how hard they worked, she said, no matter how long they did austerities, they never made much spiritual progress because they can never eradicate their sexual desire for women. And I heard far nastier comments than these.

Tensions between priests and shamans occur over issues of authority and propriety. Each group feels some measure of superiority vis à vis the other: priests think they are of higher status than healers, while some healers claim they have direct access to the *kami,* which is more important than any amount of study. One priest said he felt that priests were altruistic, for they worshiped the *kami* for the sake of other people, whereas devotees on the mountain tend to pray for themselves—and although shamans pray for others, they do so as a kind of business. But a man from one of the religious establishments on the mountain not connected with the shrine thought the priests got so absorbed in their office duties that they really had little time for people. Not all alliances were among similar types of people: certain shamanesses and priests were in agreement about some issues such as the efficacy of healing with crystals or respect for mystical experiences. And sometimes priests were very fond of worshipers whose ideas they did not particularly condone. Thus there was no single pattern that determined how alliances formed—they were based on friendship, similar ideas, respect, occupational solidarity, a shared training session. Even though there were divisions among the priests, they presented a united front to some degree. This was not the case for the shamans, however, who did not usually know each other and seemed guarded and competitive with other healers.

The different centers of Inari worship had almost no contact with each other, and with only a few notable exceptions, the priests had no desire to learn more about the other centers. There was no coordinating body, no loose cooperation between shrines, and the gap between shrines and temples was even wider. Even if Fushimi Inari Shrine once had a clear historical connection with another Inari shrine, it has no particular connection with that shrine today. The exception to the pattern of total separation was the informal network of Shinto priests who might have studied together at the same time or worked at Fushimi before moving to their home Inari shrine (although most priests' home shrines were not Inari shrines).

If Buddhist and Shinto priests did visit each other's sacred Inari centers, it was only in an informal way during a sightseeing trip or out of curiosity. They did not introduce themselves and compare notes about Inari. The priest from Tamatsukuri Inari Shrine was interested in visiting me at Toyokawa and in traveling to other Inari shrines, but his interest was exceptional. The one time I did introduce priests from Shinto and Buddhist Inari centers to each other was not very successful. Everyone spoke stiff, formal Japanese, and it was a particularly uncomfortable meeting. Before the meeting took place, a priest at the host institution emphasized that although he would extend hospitality to the other priests because they were friends of mine, he had absolutely no desire to meet priests from another Inari institution.

It was when I was beginning to make arrangements to move to my second fieldwork site, after having been almost a year at Fushimi, that I encountered strong objections to shifting to another Inari center. Male and female shamans who worked in the Fushimi area told me I would incur divine retribution from Inari if I went to a Buddhist center. A *kō* leader said that Toyokawa was Buddhist "and not a real Inari." A Fushimi priest concurred that it was "not a real Inari" and added that it was probably "very boring." A shamaness predicted that there would not be enough to study there and I would leave early—and in any case would become quite ill if I went. Many people assured me there would be no housing available. I asked for a letter of introduction from the Fushimi shrine I could take to Toyokawa—the content simply declaring that I was a legitimate American researcher studying Inari—but the shrine was unable to write one for me because "they are Buddhist and we have no connection to them." The great suspicion toward another center of Inari worship (which most of these people had never visited) was telling. The issue seemed less a matter of Shinto versus Buddhism than one of loyalty to a particular Inari and, perhaps more important, to a particular sacred center.

Priestly vs. Shamanic Authority: A Delicate Balance

The age-old tension between historical transmission and divine inspiration persists in the world of Inari. Priests at Fushimi Inari, the oldest Inari shrine in Japan, value the shrine's long history and try to document and preserve proper historical transmissions of symbols, rituals, and priestly authority. But priests who are well versed in the history of this Inari shrine paradoxically understand that this very history is constituted by change, development, dispersal, and reinterpretation. Although priests had their own strong opinions on correct practice, most realized that Inari is a complex world of beliefs in which they are an important but not a controlling part.

Buddhist priests at Toyokawa were open to learning about Inari but did not focus on this aspect of their institution. Some assumed that their temple's historical connections to Inari worship were different from the version in the present "history," but to my knowledge no one was working on this issue. They accepted great diversity in the style and content of worship of devotees, and even though Zen Buddhism interested them far more than Inari worship, they did not try to channel people's devotions into more Buddhist forms. The priests at the branch temple in Tokyo were much more involved in Inari and Zen outreach—creating a new form of the deity, Yūzū Inari, and offering laypeople the opportunity for *zazen* meditation.

Shamans have the certainty of their own religious experience, which gives them much status—even quasi divinity—in the eyes of their followers. They have direct access to the *kami*, or his messengers, and may also have gifts of healing and prophecy bestowed on them by the deity or resulting from long years of painful austerities. Loyalty to a parent or teacher's instructions is more important than following the doctrinal formulas of a sacred center. The shamans' reputation is critical in continuing their work—not only do they have to uphold a certain level of propriety in the eyes of their followers, they must also accumulate impressive success stories about their powers. Yet they must maintain a delicate balance between narrating these stories and still acting humble. Shamans tend to continue performing austerities even after they have a channel of communication with the *kami*, who may periodically require of them certain difficult tasks, punishing them if they do not comply.

The sacred centers of Inari worship are not particularly centered or central. Although they present a fairly unified face to the outside, they contain a great diversity of opinions: factions are rife and authority is contested, both within the center and from without, along the age-old split between historical transmission and divine inspiration. And because there are many centers in nonhierarchical relation to one another, there is no unanimously accepted "Center of Inari Worship." What constitutes "orthodoxy" or "heterodoxy," therefore, depends on where one is situated. Each center has certain positions it holds to be correct or proper. But these doctrines are not clearly propagated, and people continue to harbor personal opinions greatly at odds with those positions.

The irony at the heart of the orthodoxy/heterodoxy divide is that they are mutually supportive and corrective. For the priests, the shamanic activity, even if not entirely condoned, keeps Inari continually vital and personally meaningful to new constituencies. The highly personalized style of the shamans adds a warm human dimension to a sacred center that can be cold and bureaucratic or perhaps, hospitable but not particularly enthusiastic about Inari worship. The enormous revenues the centers receive from these popular energies allow the priests to conduct splendid rituals with all the proper robes and implements of the highest quality. They can afford to maintain the buildings, grounds, and gardens and upgrade the facilities. And, in circular fashion, it is this institutional splendor that signifies the power and benevolence of Inari to grant individual prayers which thus, in turn, attracts more people to the shrines and temples. The priests, by working with the *kō*, deal with devotees who are doing a kind of outreach service. And what they learn from these shamans keeps them in touch with the ideas and concerns of contemporary devotees.

The various constituencies involved in the worship of Inari have rather different worldviews where the *kami* is concerned. The negative extremes create some tensions: priests wince at shamans spreading strange ideas about Inari; shamans chafe at being scolded for something Inari instructed them to do. But there are genuinely affectionate and respectful relationships between some of the priests and shamans, who look forward to seeing each other at pilgrimages or annual rituals. Overall, I see the tension between the two religious orientations as a healthy one. The priestly adherence to tradition stabilizes, the shamanic innovation revitalizes, and this balance is what keeps Inari worship deeply rooted and ever growing.

3
Symbolizing Inari: The Fox

He said, softly:
   "You are only a man-made idol, but you stand as a symbol of
what man cannot know, and is not destined to know. As such, I
make my humble bow to you."

—Robert van Gulick, *The Emperor's*
Pearl—A Chinese Detective Story

The earliest extant fox story in Japan also purports to explain the etymology of the word for fox, *"kitsune."*[1] A sixth-century man from Mino one day met a woman in the fields. She agreed to marry him, and soon they had a son, and at the same time, their dog had puppies. Life was peaceful, except for the incessant barking of their puppy at the wife. She begged her husband to kill it, but he felt compassion for it and could not bring himself to do so. One day the dog startled the wife with its barking, and suddenly she reverted to her true fox shape, perched upon a rough fence. Although the husband was surprised, his love for his wife was deep, and he told her that he would never forget her, and that she should come back to sleep with him, which she did, nightly. Her name, and the name of all subsequent foxes in Japan, was therefore Kitsune, "come and sleep."[2]

   The fox in this story is a good wife and mother, but another kind of fox-woman in Japanese stories seduces men and makes fools of them. Foxes in human form may play harmless pranks, or they may possess people against their will. Spirit foxes were employed to nefarious ends by sorcerers; mediums and healers may be assisted in their tasks by white spirit foxes even today. Fox stories in the *rakugo* and Kyōgen traditions are hilarious; the more macabre tales can be nauseatingly gruesome. Foxes are associated with the earth where they make their homes, with fire, with sexuality; they can fly, change shape, cause mirages. They range from villainous to saintly.

How much of this range of folklore has relevance to the worship of Inari? Are fox traditions quaint survivals from previous ages, or are they still powerful and meaningful in present-day Japan? I shall try to answer both questions by describing of the range of themes and symbols associated with foxes. This is impossible to do in a very concise fashion, as there is much overlap, mirroring, and inversion. Within each thematic discussion I indicate historical depth, connections with Inari beliefs, and continued existence. This last aspect represents an important addition to the English-language materials on fox folklore in Japan, which tend, in unfortunate Orientalist style (Said 1978), to borrow liberally from older sources without concern for how ideas may have changed, disappeared, or come into being in new circumstances. Simply because I did not hear about some aspect of fox lore does not mean it has disappeared, of course, but I indicate which ideas are still discussed and which my informants had never encountered. Exact historical development and direct causal relationships can only be suggested. I also mention, when appropriate, relevant information about real foxes, which may help us to see where the animal itself leaves off and the cultural symbol begins. Although the fox has stronger popular associations with Inari, the jewel is the more ubiquitous symbol. The topic of sexuality and foxes involves jewels, and in the next chapter we will find connections with fire, treasure, and light, clusters of three jewels, and punning parallels between jewels and souls. Buddhist and Shinto meanings flow together in this magical jewel of transformative power. This chapter focuses on Inari's foxes and the main associations that cluster around them.

Inari and the Fox: Theories of the Association

How the fox came to be associated with Inari is the knottiest problem in Inari studies. Although theories abound, no firm textually grounded answer exists. Many scholars do not even realize this is a problem and assume that the fox was always associated with Inari, a premise that early

Fox statues at Inari shrines. From top left, clockwise: (1) Mother and cub, Hanazono Shrine, Shinjuku (Tokyo). (2) Fox and fellow shape-shifter badger statues at
Inari shrine in ruins of Nagashino Castle, Aichi. (3) Mother and cub at Tamatsukuri Inari Shrine, Osaka. Note that mother fox wears a necklace of curved jewels,
the main motif at this shrine built on the site of an ancient jewel-making guild.
(Photo courtesy of Suzuki Kazuo.) (4) Fox with red votive bib and offering of fried
tofu between front paws at the Spirit Fox Mound, Toyokawa Inari.

documents do not seem to support. Perhaps the fox was indeed always there, at the popular level, but in that case surely the fox would have been mentioned in written sources for the first three to five centuries of Inari's existence. Here I want to review briefly the main arguments in the secondary literature for the association of the fox with the deity Inari and indicate their relative merits. But with additional investigation of primary sources, new information may well come to light—not only in terms of a fine-tuned chronology of fox and Inari references but perhaps even new sources of information suppressed during the Meiji-period separation of Shinto and Buddhism.

Early records of the Inari shrine do not mention the fox. In the *Yamashiro fudoki* origin story of the eighth century, we find the spirit of rice in animal form, but this is a white bird and not a fox. In a contemporary publication, the Fushimi Inari Shrine explains that other *kami* in Japan have animal assistants (the pigeon of Hachiman, the deer of Kasuga, the crow of Kumano), and in similar fashion, rather naturally and "unnoticed" *(itsu no ma ni ka)*, the fox became the messenger of Inari (Fushimi 1969:36–37). But if the fox association were part of the shrine's own traditions, would there not be some sort of narrative explaining the origins or significance of their animal messenger as at the other shrines (Shimonaka 1937, I:139–140)? The absence of such a document, or even a folk narrative, may point to an outside or later association.[3]

Indigenous Associations of the Fox with Rice

Japanese folklorists emphasize the connection of the fox with the *ta no kami* field deity (Yanagita 1962; Iwai 1983; Naoe 1983a). Two main reasons are hypothesized for the association. First, foxes may have seemed to be outrunners *(misaki, osaki)* for the arrival of the field deity. It is thought that foxes were particularly visible around the first horse day of the second lunar month *(nigatsu no hatsuuma)*, when the mountain deity descends into the fields, and were therefore seen as servants of the rice field *kami,* announcing its imminent arrival. The specifics of this argument do not seem to correspond exactly with the agricultural calendar or the behavior of foxes (Miyata 1988:119), but there are other reasons the association between rice and foxes might have been made. The most reasonable one is that foxes would have been seen around rice fields, where they fed on rodents that ate the rice, and were thus seen as its protectors. Other visual associations include the fox's color, close to that of ripened rice, and the observation that the fox's tail resembles a full sheaf of rice.[4] The second hypothesis of the folklorists is the association of foxes with the places of worship of the field *kami* (Yanagita 1962). The place-name Kitsune-zuka (fox mound) is found all over Japan; these originally seem to have been natural or artificial mounds near the rice fields where the rice deity was worshiped. And when places called Kitsune-zuka are excavated, they often turn out to contain *kofun* burial chambers, which connect them with the ancestral nature of the mountain *kami* (the winter form of the field *kami*).

It is now widely accepted that the fox is the messenger of the field deity. Because the earliest worship of Inari seems to have been related to rice and the yearly changing of the guard of the field and mountain *kami*, it is possible that the fox association entered Inari worship this way. But why only at Inari Mountain? Other *kami* were associated with rice but do not seem to have developed any particular connection with the fox. Conversely, the sacred nature or even divinity of the fox was sometimes asserted, but this was not only in connection with Inari. And although fox appearances were taken as omens, they were not necessarily positive omens.

The two earliest extant fox references are in the *Nihon shoki* (720), both during the reign of the Empress Saimei (r. 655–661). The first mentions that in 657 the people of Ihami saw a white fox, and this was probably taken as a good omen (Aston 1972, II:252). In 659, however, the fox omen was inauspicious: "A fox bit off the end of a creeper which a labourer of the district of Ou held in his hand, and went off with it" (p. 263). Aston notes that this omen, in combination with another in which a dog carried a human hand and arm to a shrine, was interpreted to mean that the empress was going to die (p. 263).

In the eighth and ninth centuries, records imply that foxes were numerous within the capital and even strayed inside the imperial palace. There was no fixed pattern of interpretation of their sightings as auspicious or inauspicious, and no connection yet to Inari or even rice. Of the nine foxes mentioned in the 797 *Shoku Nihongi*, the ones that were presented to the emperor were auspicious, regardless of color, as was the one that appeared outside the palace gate. But the foxes that howled at a temple and entered the palace were taken as bad omens (De Visser 1908a: 16–17). The two foxes that had the misfortune to run into the palace in 833 and 849 were clubbed to death and killed by a dog, respectively, and the emperor shot the one that wandered in in 855 (De Visser 1908a:17).

Foxes must have been very bold in the latter half of the ninth century, for records describe repeated vulpine defecation on the general's seat in the guards' barracks—the fox even urinated directly on the night watchman sent to protect the barracks—and howling on the palace roof even in the daytime (De Visser 1908a:18). The 927 *Engi shiki,* "Procedures of the Engi Era," lists three types of foxes as very lucky omens: white foxes, black foxes, and nine-tailed foxes (Kuroita 1964, 9:528).[5] But ordinary foxes still invaded the palace and caused mischief at this time (De Visser 1908a:13 and 18-19).

The first fox deity appears in a curious incident in 1031 at Ise Shrine. Fujiwara no Sanesuke (957-1046), minister of the right, records and condemns this in his diary, the *Ouki.* De Visser's translation reads as follows:

> On the fourth day of the eighth month of the fourth year of the Chōgen era (1031), the Saigū [imperial priestess] called with a loud voice, not to be compared with other (human) voices. A god (namely, a fox) spoke through her mouth. She was mad and built two Shintō temples which she dedicated to the gods of the Naigū and Gegū. Thereupon she summoned all kinds of worthless people and made them dance the kagura [sacred dance] and perform other frantic dances night and day. Then the sorceresses of the capital began to worship a fox (imitating the Saigū) and to declare this animal to be the great divinity of Ise. Such things are very wicked. [De Visser 1908a:25; parentheses in original, brackets added.][6]

De Visser says this was the first reference in the Japanese texts to a fox god (1908a:129), and one notes that it is not at an Inari shrine, but rather at Ise, the seat of the sun goddess. The deity enshrined in the outer shrine is Toyouke, who as the *kami* of food, clothing, and shelter would later be worshiped as Inari in many settings. But here the fox seems to have no particular connection with agriculture. Even by the early twelfth century, Oe no Masafusa's treatise, "A Record of Fox Spirits," chronicles fox mischief in the capital during the year 1101 without any reference to Inari. Foxes were seen as sacred, however, under the protection of an unnamed deity (Ury 1988; Smits 1996). The important point at this juncture is to note that manifestations of divine foxes were not necessarily related to Inari at this time in the early eleventh century.

The folkloric argument has a fairly wide popular circulation. A number of my informants described the origin of the fox in Inari worship as due to the presence of real foxes around rice fields; I never heard reference to Yanagita's "fox-mound" argument, which is a little obscure. A Ginza bar hostess thought the foxes were catching mice. An antiques dealer in Kyoto told me that foxes came out of the woods to the fields at precisely the time when the rice ripened. He had a variation on this story that I never encountered in other sources: the fox originally *ate* the ripened rice, and the people were troubled; angry Inari transformed the fox into the protector of rice from that time forward, and that is how the fox came to be the messenger of Inari.

But the argument that the fox was the messenger of the field deity and naturally became the assistant of Inari as rice deity has a weakness: not all food *kami* had foxes as messengers, and not all fox divinities were seen as Inari. So something else must have contributed to the specific linking of the two. More important, even if it took centuries for the Inari–fox association to develop, why was it not systematically incorporated into the shrine's traditions?

Etymological Explanations

Probably the most often cited explanation for the fox association with Inari is a play on words. One of the several food *kami* identified as Inari is Miketsu no Kami ("honorable food deity"). In some dialects, *"kitsune"* is pronounced *"ketsune"* (Gorai 1985:11), so *"miketsu"* is a homonym for "three foxes" and people therefore began to think of Inari as a fox deity or as related to foxes (Iwai 1983:289; Miyata 1988:119) (see the glossary). It is not a recent invention; De Visser cites records from 1776 and 1799 that mention this pun (1908a:138). It is not clear whether the wordplay had been developed yet or not, but in the late-thirteenth-century *Shinto Gobusho* there is an entry that mentions the Three Fox *kami* (Gorai 1985:23), though this may simply describe the Akomachi tradition described below. A similar pun occurs when the name of another *kami* connected with food, Ōgetsu Hime, is written with the characters for "big fox" *(ō-getsu)* (Kusano 1953:114).

A more recent suggestion in the same vein has been proposed by Gorai Shigeru (1985). He searches for the origin of Inari and locates it in a primitive religious complex he takes to be older than Inari. According to Gorai this primitive base, from which all later religious development in Japan grew, consisted of four main ideas directly concerned with human needs: the food spirit, spirits of the dead, nature spirits, and magic and prophecy. Before rice cultivation, people would have subsisted by hunting and gathering, and he thinks the food spirit worshiped then was *ketsune,* which can be written "root (spirit) of food" (p. 11). This name is close to that of one of the *kami* mentioned in the classics as giving food to humans from her dead body, Ketsu Hime, and its manifestation would have been often seen in the form of foxes, *kitsune/ketsune* (p. 12). Except for the name of the goddess of food, Gorai offers no textual support for his hypothesis that *ketsune* was the original food spirit in Japan. This *ketsune* hypothesis has been picked up uncritically by a number of subsequent writers (Ōmori 1989:94; Miyata 1988:116); I have not seen it debated in the literature.

Puns and wordplay do have a special power in Japanese, where homophones abound, and religious practices are often linked to a significant pun. In Heian-period poetry, punning was "probably the single most common rhetorical device." (Seidensticker 1976:xii). Puns may indeed account for the fox association, but again we must wonder about the chronology and the particular relation to Inari. Both of the *ketsu* explanations relate foxes to the deities of food. But it is not clear when these particular *kami* named in the *Kojiki* and *Nihon shoki* began to be worshiped as Inari. It seems that, at the beginning, a deity called Inari was worshiped at three sites on Inari Mountain and was not identified as other *kami* until perhaps the Kamakura period (1185–1392). As with the first explanation—that the fox was the messenger of the field *kami*—we find no particular reason why the fox should have settled with Inari. After all, the food deities with whom it was associated either visually (fox in the rice fields) or verbally (in puns on the words for fox and food) existed before Inari and were probably not worshiped as Inari until the late twelfth century.

Buddhist Origin of Inari's Fox

A Buddhist text describes the origin of foxes at Inari Mountain. This text probably dates from 1332 (Fushimi 1957:3) but describes events that were supposed to have occurred between 810 and 823:

> In olden days, at Funaoka Mountain to the north of the capital, lived a pair of old foxes. The husband had white fur on his body like rows of silver needles and the tip of his tail glowed and looked like a five-pronged *vajra* [a Buddhist ritual implement]. The wife had the

head of a deer and the body of a fox, and led five cubs, each of different appearance. Around the year 816, the two foxes and their five cubs went to Inari Mountain and all knelt in front of the shrine and prayed fervently to the *kami:* "Although we have the bodies of brute animals, we are naturally endowed with wisdom. We sincerely wish to protect the world but this wish is difficult to achieve in these [animal] bodies. We respectfully ask to become the sacred assistants *(gokenzoku)* of this shrine from this day forth."

When the deity granted this prayer there was suddenly a stirring from the altar and Inari spoke: "I have skillfully manifested various forms, employing expedient means to teach and benefit sentient beings. Your original vow is also mysterious. From this moment onward, you will be the attendants *(shisha)* of this shrine, compassionately assisting worshipers and devotees. The husband fox shall serve in the upper shrine and shall be called Osusuki; the wife fox shall be in the lower shrine and shall be called Akomachi."

In accordance with this, they made ten vows. They grant people's desires, so people who believe in this shrine see them in dreams as oracular foxes.[7]

As there is a reference to "Akomachi of Inari Mountain" in the *Shin-sarugakuki* (De Visser 1908a:140), written between 1058 and 1065, the tradition may be as early as the mid-eleventh century if the name "Akomachi" originated with this particular story.[8]

These Buddhist texts (perhaps oral traditions at first) had a lasting impact on the Inari tradition: the image of Inari as an old man carrying rice is now taken as the standard "Shinto" anthropomorphic representation of the *kami;* few know it derives from a Buddhist story in which Kūkai met Inari (described in Chapter 1). It is entirely possible that the story of the Funaoka foxes was the tradition that linked Inari with the fox. Higo speculates both historically and theologically about the rice and fox connections to Inari. The political ties between the Tōji Temple and Inari shrine had practical benefits: the former gained lumber and popular acceptance; the latter received imperial recognition and increased popularity from the association. The emphasis on rice may have facilitated the benefits to the Inari shrine—for as the capital grew, the demand for rice would also have increased, and Inari as the *kami* who protected rice would thereby have gained the patronage of all who depended on this staple crop (Higo 1983:13). Moreover, Higo wonders if the fox was deliberately chosen as a counterweight to the sacred monkey messenger of the *kami* of Mount Hiei, the location of the Tendai sect, the main rival of the Shingon sect. He admits this is only speculation but finds it intriguing that, in parallel fashion to Shingon's construal of Tendai as exoteric compared with Shingon's esoteric doctrines, the monkey is a yang and the fox a yin animal (p. 14). Again it is unclear if these were deliberate strategies or fortuitous coincidences. And there is always the possibility that just as there were great numbers of monkeys living on Mount Hiei, the fox was the most visible denizen of Inari Mountain. Perhaps the Buddhist thinkers wove this natural symbol into their syncretic doctrines.

A related tradition involves the term "Myōbu," which refers both to Inari's attendant foxes and to the subshrine in which they are worshiped. The word is actually the rank of a court lady, and a number of traditions explain the term's use here. "Myōbu" does not appear in the main text of the *Inari Daimyōjin ryūki* in which the Funaoka fox story occurs, but it does appear as a chapter heading and later at the end of the document (a seventeenth-century copy) in a different hand, noting that Myōbu are the white fox messengers of Inari (Fushimi 1957:42). A publication of the Fushimi Inari Shrine (1969:40) says they have two traditions about the name Myōbu. In one, when Emperor Gosanjō made a pilgrimage to the shrine in 1071,[9] he bestowed the rank. It does not say if he bestowed it on a shrine, however, or on a fox. A more elaborated tradition has it that during the earlier reign of Emperor Ichijō (986–1011), a noblewoman called Shin no Myōbu undertook a seven-day seclusion at the Inari shrine and received the protection of the spirit fox there. She subsequently had a successful career and in gratitude bestowed her court rank on the spirit fox Akomachi (Fushimi 1969:40). If this tradition was indeed from the tenth century and not projected back from a later date, then spirit foxes were in place by the late tenth century at the Inari shrine.

It is clear that, at least for some people, the foxes were not simply messengers of the *kami* but *kami* themselves. In a Muromachi-period (1392–1568) tradition that describes the original buddhas *(honji)*, which were equivalent to the culture-specific manifestations *(suijaku)* in Japan, along with the five main deities of the Inari shrine and their original buddhas it lists Buddhist equivalents for the three spirit foxes of the Myōbu shrine. In this tradition, at least, the three sacred foxes themselves were seen as divinities. In my conversations with contemporary devotees, I never heard the Funaoka fox story or the Myōbu tradition cited as the reason why the fox became the assistant of Inari. Priests sometimes mentioned historical influences from esoteric Buddhism, but they did not focus on any particular text as critical.

The Link with Dakiniten

A promising argument advanced by people with some knowledge of the
Buddhist syncretism in Inari is that the fox came in with the worship of
Dakiniten. This deity, later worshiped as Inari in certain lineages of transmission, came to be depicted as a female bodhisattva astride a flying white
fox. If Dakiniten was definitely associated with a fox before it entered
Inari beliefs, our problem would be solved. But of course it was not that
simple. As in much of the scholarship relating to Inari, arguments are
associational and evince little interest in even a tentative chronology. The
two critical questions are: how did Dakiniten come to be worshiped as
Inari, and was Dakiniten in fact associated with a fox before it entered
Inari beliefs?

The answer to the first question is, not surprisingly, through syncretism of Shingon with earlier indigenous beliefs. The most direct connections are two Buddhist traditions subsequently cited in Inari shrine documents as a set even though they are centuries apart. The first, the Records
of Emperor Junna (*Tenchō gyoki*; 824-833), says there are divine guard-
ians *(ten)* in Tōji Temple, the assistants of Inari Myōjin, and these deities
have great bodhi-mind. The second record was written by the Shingon
priest Shukaku Hoshin no Ō (1150-1202), the second son of Emperor
Goshirakawa. In his *Shūyōshu* he notes that when Kūkai died his words
were recalled by a disciple and included the following information: In this
temple is a deity called Madarajin, which has three faces and six arms.
The middle face of Shōten is gold,[10] the left face of Dakiniten is white,
and the right face of Benzaiten is red. This is the assistant *(shisha)* of Inari
Myōjin (Kida 1976:318).[11] In the earlier text, Inari's assistants within Tōji
are demigods (Jap. *yasha;* Skt. *yakṣa*) but *dakini* are not mentioned; in the
later text, the form of Inari's assistant has been consolidated into a *yasha*
that combines three devas, including Dakiniten.

The figure of Dakiniten is a Japanese transformation of an Indian
demon called *dakini*. In India *dakini* were female demons who ate people's
hearts, but they were converted to Buddhism by Vairocana (Dainichi, the
central Buddha of the Shingon sect) and became protecting deities
(zenshin). In the Womb Mandala *(Taizōkai mandara),*[12] a group of three
dakini occupy a space in the border area called *Saigaiin* at the lower right.
They sit before a dead human body, eating human flesh (Furuta 1988:639).
In the *Commentary on the Dainichi Sutra (Dainichi kyō sho),*[13] we learn
that the *dakini* know the date of a person's death six months before it

happens and arrive to eat the *nin-o,* human bezoar, a magical substance in the human heart (Gorai 1985:123–125).

Although a definite chronology of Dakiniten iconography has not been establshed, Murai Ichirō believes that the earliest depictions were probably in the form of complex mandalas.[14] Extant examples vary, but they usually include a composite figure at the center, with multiple heads and arms, seated upon one or more white (sometimes winged) foxes. A number of figures may surround the central deity—such as the Four Great Princes *(shidai ōji)* or attendant children *(dōji)* similar to those who serve Benten. All the figures hold symbolic or ritual implements, such as a jewel, sword, incense box, rope, bell, or "diamond pounder" *(vajra);* snakes coil around their wrists, ankles, or necks. Gradually the representation probably simplified into a single figure sitting astride a white flying fox. But in neither the depiction of the *dakini* in the Womb Mandala nor in Kūkai's description of Madarajin (the text linking Inari with Dakiniten) do we find a fox.

If in fact the fox was introduced as a part of Dakiniten imagery and was thereby connected with Inari, how did it happen? Two avenues of possibility exist. First we must consider Chinese influence, for Kūkai studied in China for two years (804–806) and may have found the image there before he was given Tōji Temple. On this topic I have seen no firm evidence, but several hints are tantalizing. Watters tells us that in T'ang China (618–907) the fox was worshiped everywhere; people said there was not "an inch of ground without this elf" (Watters 1874:55). This seems to have been a popular form of belief, however, and perhaps the learned monk would not have encountered it on his quest for higher religious forms. In more recent days, we note, the Chinese fox or fox deity manifests himself as an old man with a white beard (Krappe 1944:126; Giles 1926:436)—the form in which the Inari deity appeared to Kūkai outside the temple gates in the Buddhist origin story of Inari worship.[15] Foxes in China, moreover, were ridden by spirits: "When men are dead, their ghosts often go to reside in foxes, or use these animals as hacks, riding on them through the air and over land and water for enormous distances and with lightning speed" (Watters 1874:58). This last belief has great antiquity. A Han-dynasty (206 b.c.e.–220 c.e.) writer, Hu Shen, states: "Foxes are spook-beasts on which the demons ride" (De Visser 1908a:9).

It is unlikely that we shall ever know if these Chinese images influenced the positioning of Dakiniten on a fox. A second and more direct possibility is that the fox was substituted for the Indian jackal.[16] Again the idea seems simple at first but turns out to be more indirect than some scholars claim. In India, the *dakini* were associated with a jackal. When this animal was described in sutras, the characters pronounced *"yakan"* in Japanese were used and sometimes glossed with *"kitsune"* (fox) (De Visser 1908a:56–57).[17] Although Sasama claims that *dakini* in India rode on jackals (1988b:144), he provides an illustration only of a jackal lurking near Kali, on whom *dakini* attended (p. 147). Apparently he assumes the fox was already the messenger of Inari when *dakini* ideas were incorporated and therefore thinks the fox simply replaced the jackal (p. 144). Although *dakini* may not have ridden on jackals, both jackals and *dakini* fed on dead bodies, were said to frequent graveyards, and thus were associated images.

It is reasonably clear that *dakini* did not ride on foxes (or jackals) in China (De Visser 1908a:118). Rather than direct iconographic transmission, perhaps it was sorcery that connected foxes and *dakini* in Japan.[18] De Visser speculates that when the Shingon priests began the *dakini* cult (which included sorcery) in Japan, indigenous fox sorcery was already well established (1908a:118). Gorai agrees and moreover, argues that "employing foxes" *(kitsune tsukai)* emerged before *dakini* sorcery developed. The former arose from Shugendō mountain ascetic practices combining yin-yang magic and esoteric Buddhism (Gorai 1985:85). It is possible that the connection was made from the following series of associations: Dakiniten sorcery strongly resembled fox sorcery and the two became identified; the fox thereby became an element in Dakiniten sorcery; because Dakiniten had been identified by Shingon priests as the assistant of Inari, Dakiniten's fox also became Inari's fox. In 1107, Lord Tadazane had a monk perform the Dakini Rite *(dakini no hō)* to ensure his promotion to regent. After a week, one of his representatives saw a fox. After two weeks of the rite, Tadazane dreamed he met a fantastically beautiful woman with long hair. He grabbed her hair and awoke to find a fox tail in his hand. He was promoted and enshrined the fox tail on Mount Hiei.[19] By 1107 (or 1254, the date the tales were collected), therefore, Dakiniten sorcery was clearly associated with foxes. The *Dakiniten hō* was used as a magic spell by both Shingon and Tendai esoteric schools (Sasama 1988b:142). Taira no Kiyomori is described in the *Genpei seisuiki* from around 1250 as realizing the value of Dakiniten sorcery after meeting a fox-woman while hunting. The fox he was chasing turned into a "yellow woman" who promised him a wish if he spared her life. She called herself King in the Midst of Seventy-

Four Roads *(Shichijūshi michi no naka no ō)*; he identified this with the
Deva-King Venerable Fox *(Kiko tennō)*, one of the names of Benten, and
concluded that to become rich he could practice *Da-ten hō*, Dakiniten
sorcery (De Visser 1908a:42–43). In the *Shūyōshu* record described earlier,
another name for Dakiniten is Hakushinkoō Bosatsu (White Dragon Fox
King Bodhisattva). The author of *Shioshiri*, a mid-Edo period text, asserts
that Dakiniten, Izuna, and Akiba are all versions of the same "foreign"
deity (Daigo 1977:805). The multiplicity and permeability of forms involving foxes began early and continues today.

Fox as the Original Deity of Inari Mountain

I mention this final theory only briefly because it seems to be suggested
exclusively by foreign writers following Frazer regarding animal forms of
the "corn spirit" and is not based on Japanese historical and textual
traditions. After De Visser works his way through numerous historical
sources concerning Inari and the fox, he concludes that the fox was the
original divine form on the sacred mountain, replaced in time by an anthropomorphic form, even though his laborious textual research does not
seem to support such a conclusion. Primarily he wants to fit Inari into the
"universal pattern" in which it is "the human shape which in the course
of time conquers the original animal form of the gods and converts the
animals into servants of the anthropomorphic deities" (1908a:142–143).
As evidence De Visser uses a nineteenth-century text that refers to foxes
being worshiped on Inari Mountain "in olden times" in a shrine called
the Tōume Sha; *"tōme"* as a word for fox was used in *Genji monogatari*
dating from 1004 (1908a:56).

Again we can ask, as with the first two arguments described here: if
the fox was always connected with Inari Mountain, why was it not mentioned in earlier records? De Visser offers a rather lame explanation: "The
silence of old books regarding their connection with Mount Inari was
probably due to the fact that the fox cult on that mountain had been united
with the anthropomorphic cult and was hidden behind the general name
of 'Gods of Inari'" (1908a:144). It is likely that the notion of a fox-*kami*
existed in Japan before the advent of Inari, but this does not explain the
reason for the association of the two. In later works in English, Buchanan
(1935:33) and Krappe (1944:136) follow De Visser in the assertion that
foxes were the original deities of Inari Mountain. Not all Western writers

blindly follow his lead, however. Kamstra takes the opposite position—that "the lady preceded the fox," that is, a female goddess was prior to the fox association (1989:181).

If I have been able to demonstrate nothing besides the complexity of the problem of the origin of the fox connection to Inari, at least we have gotten some feeling for the rich syncretism, iconographic creativity, and permeability of forms during the early centuries when Inari beliefs were developing. And I think it likely that there was not one cause but a confluence of several. The Buddhist texts were certainly influential. But whether they in fact gave rise to the image of the fox, or merely attempted to give Buddhist significance to an already developing image, is not certain. It may have been purely an accident: perhaps a Buddhist artist was crafting an image of Dakiniten and wanted to seat it upon an animal in the manner of Indian and Chinese depictions that placed divinities on tigers, elephants, peacocks, and other majestic animals. In searching for a native carrier for the deity in Japan, where none of these animals exists, he may have come up with the fox as the most mysterious and dignified representative of the local fauna. But this, of course, is no more than speculation.

Two factors connecting Inari with foxes seem to have been paramount: Buddhist esoteric influences and the indigenous associations of the fox with rice. After these factors coalesced into the idea of the fox as Inari's assistant, that image was colored by notions of fox sorcery, shape-shifting foxes, tricking foxes—a complex range of associations that grew around the fox in Japan. Various influences came together to create the Inari fox, which was probably in place by the eleventh century, certainly by the thirteenth. What is certain is this: after the connection was made, Inari and the fox were inextricably associated, so that even today the mention of one calls the other to mind. Priests try to persuade people that Inari is not a fox. That this is still a major problem for them shows that it is still a widespread belief.

Merger of Inari's Fox with Other Fox Traditions

In the following sections I pay less strict attention to chronological development. My aim, rather, is to indicate the range of ideas, images, and associations that have been linked with Inari's fox over the centuries and in the present. Most foxes in Japan—real, imaginary, or folkloric—soon had some relation to the Inari fox, usually a simple identification, so that two things seem to have happened. In a two-way flow, folk practices involving foxes became incorporated into Inari worship while Inari beliefs spread quickly throughout Japan on top of the layer of fox beliefs.

Real Foxes and Inari

The fox is a member of the canid family. Of the twenty-one different species of fox, the most widespread and well known is the red fox *(Vulpes vulpes)*, which lives over a wider geographical range than any other carnivore on earth (Macdonald 1987:10-15). Although they live almost everywhere, often quite close to humans, foxes can be "elusive to the point of invisibility" (Macdonald 1987:13). But when they are in fact visible to their human neighbors, they prove to be fascinating, intelligent, infinitely adaptable, playful, and mysterious. Foxes do funny things: Henry describes a fox who chased airplanes at the Minneapolis airport and tells of generations of foxes discovering the pleasures of running and sliding on winter ice (1986:13-14 and 133-134). A fox living in a noisy factory in Oxford, England, developed the habit of chasing bicycles (Macdonald 1987:185-186). Israeli foxes in the desert teased and tormented striped hyenas, wearing what Macdonald could only describe as an "impudent expression": "Foxes would seem to be prey to an irresistible and rather churlish desire to make these amiable goofs the butts of their quick wit" (1987:77-78).

Foxes lived throughout Japan, except for some islands,[20] until extreme urbanization in recent decades drove them from the centers of human habitation (Yoshino 1980:3; Koizuka 1982:22). Because foxes prefer to live on boundaries between cultivated and wild habitats (Henry 1986:35), they were often visible and sometimes so tame that people called them by human names (Naoe 1983a:122; Nozaki 1961:143).[21] Foxes develop survival behavior in response to threats: Macdonald was astounded by the differences between the elusive, almost invisible foxes in England, where they are destroyed by farmers and hunted for sport, and the bold foxes on a protected reserve in Israel (1987:71). The Japanese fox was not, to my knowledge, subjected to systematic persecution and thus would not have been overly shy about human contact. Macdonald also reports that rabies has never spread to Japan (1987:192), which helps to account for the good relations between the vulpine and human cohabitants.

The Inari *kami* was thought to have responsibility, not just for her own spirit fox attendants, but also for the behavior of real foxes at least by the Edo period (1600-1868) and probably earlier. In the third month of 1673, beginning on the twenty-fifth day and continuing for seventeen days, prayers were offered by priests at the Fushimi Inari Shrine because foxes or badgers had caused mysterious occurrences at the imperial palace (Fushimi 1962a:200).[22] A story with wide distribution in the Edo and Meiji periods described human threats against Inari for the behavior of real foxes.[23] The same story appears in the memoirs of Meiji statesman Satō Naotake (1882-1971) as an actual memory of a boyhood occurrence in Saga in which he and a stableboy went to the Inari shrine and beat on it with sticks while uttering abusive language so that the fox would return a chicken it had stolen—which it did (Gubler 1974:126). Sometimes Inari shrines were built over a fox den or after a real fox had performed a strange act or useful service. In fact, the Fushimi Inari Shrine developed its official policy of reenshrinement *(kanjō)* in 1792 in response to inquiries from the magistrate's office because a farmer found a fox hole in his thicket and built an Inari shrine there (Fushimi 1977:50-51; 1962b:250). Similarly, because a fox lived in the shrine that protected the dike at Kaname Jinja (now Haneda Airport), the shrine acquired the appellation Anamori ("Hole Protection") Inari (Nomura and Abe 1982:afterword). According to shrine tradition, one night in 1779 (Meiwa 7), a white fox sat on top of a boulder within the grounds of Tomoe Shrine next to the castle at Tahara (Aichi prefecture) and gave oracles to the people there. The fox told them to build an Inari shrine at that site, and even now it is believed that touching the rock will bring great happiness. As recently as 1923 a fox was deified in gratitude for discovering the murder weapon in a grisly case in Kobe: the fox was set up in a new Inari shrine, where police and detectives were among the devotees (Casal 1959:18-19).

At other Inari shrines, too, live foxes were fed and venerated. People actually brought foxes from all over Japan and released them on Inari Mountain in Kyoto to be protectors of the mountain (Naoe 1983b:304). They seem to have been numerous there until the 1930s. Residents of the sacred mountain told me that as more people began keeping dogs, the foxes disappeared. One of the teahouse owners on the mountain showed me an old photograph of one of the last foxes, a bedraggled, lonely looking fellow. The grandfather said that when he lived there as a young boy, foxes were much in evidence and would sometimes curl up and nap on the tatami matting in the shop and take food right from his hand. The teahouse family was excited to report that they had seen a fox on the mountain just that year, so perhaps they have returned. At one time, a fox was kept in a stone room at Hyōtan Yama Inari in Osaka (Iwai 1983: 289). A late-nineteenth-century missionary account gives a remarkable description of the priests' ritual feeding of the foxes at the Takekoma Inari Shrine in Sendai (Hartshorne 1902, I:316–317). To my knowledge, no Inari shrines keep live foxes at the present time. From time to time, however, a mounted stuffed fox is presented to a shrine or temple by a devotee. Toyokawa Inari has two of these rather unpleasant items: a mangy looking red fox hidden away in a storeroom and a white fox that was presented after I had left. They never become objects of worship, or even decorations (the way a scroll painting or carving of a fox might), perhaps because of a fear of retribution. The idea that dire retribution comes after killing a fox is found throughout Japan. A related folk taboo has it that one should never wear mufflers or jackets made of fox fur to an Inari shrine (Suzuki 1982:191–194).

A form of divination that has become a children's game called *kokkuri* is associated by many with Inari—perhaps because it is sometimes written with the characters for fox, dog, and badger. It works something like a Ouija board,[24] using a tripod of sticks with tray on top (a coin or pencil can also be used), and requires three people lightly touching the tray with their right hands. A question is posed, and slight movement of the sticks indicates the answer. (Often "yes," "no," and so on are written beforehand on a piece of paper.) Although the entry in *Nihon minzoku jiten* (1978:259) does not mention Inari, I was repeatedly told during fieldwork that I should look into this Inari-related phenomenon. A folklore scholar told me there was a *kokkuri* boom after World War II, in the 1970s, and it was again very popular in 1990, along with many other forms of divination. His understanding was that after performing the divination, one had to be sure to visit an Inari shrine and offer fried tofu at midnight. A Japanese anthropologist told me that Kokkuri-san is a fox, and one must never open a south-facing window during the game or a fox will come in. But after the questions are finished, fried tofu must be offered at the southern window. A person born in the year of the dog must never ask the questions, as foxes hate dogs. A group of high school girls told me *kokkuri* was scary—they said some boys were doing it and the one who did not believe got his finger burned. But they said no offerings were necessary, as the fox or badger spirit that comes is of fairly low status. An Inari priest thought it was just a game and said that Kokkuri-san was a badger.

Fox Possession and Fox Bewitchment

Fox possession *(kitsune tsuki)* is a phenomenon often associated with
Inari because of the fox connection and because people believed to be
suffering from this malady used to be taken to Inari shrines to be cured
(Naoe 1983b:304).[25] Fox possession may derive from the practice called
Inari sage or *Inari oroshi* (Inari's descent), a religious ritual through which
Inari's oracles were deliberately sought (Iwai 1983:290). But the term
usually implies the more insidious type of uninvited possession in which
a spirit fox takes over the host's body or personality. Fox possession may
appear in very dramatic forms—as when the person crawls on the floor,
eats directly from the dish without using his hands, and even barks like a
fox (Hearn 1974; De Visser 1908a; Casal 1959; Blacker 1975)—or in
milder forms such as vague physical discomforts.

　　Although the concept is still very much alive—some people still go to
Inari shrines when they believe themselves or a relative to be possessed by
a fox—the numbers appear to be declining yearly. Priests are in general
quite uneasy with the idea. They say it derives from fox-related superstitions and really has nothing to do with Inari (which is not true historically) and should be handled by medical specialists. Shinto shrines will
perform a general *oharai* purification if requested, however, or a more
elaborate prayer service *(gokitō)* in which a special *norito* called *magamono-barai* (purification of the distortion) is read. The Buddhist equivalent at Toyokawa Inari is called *shogitaisan* (drive away the interference).
Although the fox is the spirit animal most often associated with this type
of possession, cases of badger possession also find their way to Inari
shrines. And religious specialists may find their clients troubled by spirit
snakes or dragons as well as foxes.

　　Fox bewitchment *(kitsune damashi)* is sometimes spoken of as a kind
of possession, but it generally refers to a more lighthearted type of trick
played by a fox. The fox can trick *(damasu)* people into seeing things that
are not really there—such as processions or battles (Naoe 1983a:123;
Nozaki 1961:190 and 196)—or it can change shape *(bakeru)* so that it
appears to be a lovely woman or Buddhist priest. The classic example of
shape shifting is the seduction of men by foxes in the form of irresistibly
beautiful women.[26] There is no consensus on how these mischievous foxes
relate to Inari. All fox folklore becomes linked with Inari through the fox
association to some extent, but shape-shifting foxes seem to have a deeper
connection to Inari than tricking foxes, for the shape-shifters are seen as
manifestations *(keshin)* of Inari or his messengers.

Detail from Meiji-period woodblock print by Toyohara set at the Ōji Inari Shrine. Foxes change themselves into mail carriers, gentlemen and ladies, a lamp post, and Buddhist priest. Note that fox at bottom right sees his transformed reflection in the water as he places duckweed on his head to effect his shape shifting. (Author's collection.)

The Fox in Inari Worship

With the long historical connection and numerous cultural associations, it is not surprising that Inari is associated with the fox to such an extent that the fox is often seen as Inari and vice versa. Images of the deity Inari occasionally depict a fox, in Shinto or Buddhist priest's robes, carrying rice or a jewel. Devotees who had been influenced by priestly attitudes were usually careful to tell me they did not worship a fox, which after all was merely the messenger of Inari. But others—perhaps no less fervent but less aware of the priests' attitude toward the fox—clearly worshiped the fox as Inari. One day a man brought two dusty old fox statues to an Inari shrine to be burned with other retired sacred paraphernalia and rather loudly announced that he had been worshiping them as Inari. The priest grimaced, explained in a rather curt fashion that Inari was not a fox, but said that he should have a prayer service anyway for the retirement of these sacred objects. The man seemed confused and embarrassed. Miyata notes that in the countryside, at smaller, less institutionalized Inari shrines, Inari's true form is often thought to be that of a fox, and it is in these areas that the barks and habits of foxes are observed carefully for their oracular meanings (1988:116). And much of what is called "Inari beliefs" in the Tsugaru district of Aomori turn out to be older beliefs and practices concerning the sacred fox itself (Naoe 1983b:305).

In addition to being a complex religious symbol, the fox, usually in combination with the jewel, has become a signifier for Inari. On any street leading to an Inari shrine, the fox logo will be prominently displayed on shop signs, bags, wrapping paper, and items offered for sale. One of the famous local products *(meibutsu)* on the road leading to the Fushimi Inari Shrine is a *miso*-flavored rice cracker in the shape of a fox mask. The Toyokawa Inari equivalent emphasizes the jewel in its delicious *hōjū manjū* bean cakes, but fox-face crackers are a popular item too. At the shops, two kinds of fox representations are for sale: Inari's guardian foxes of pottery, stone, and metal, used in home shrines, come in pairs and are characterized by erect tails ending in a jewel; in addition, there may be cute foxes in the form of plush toys, keychains, coin purses, and decorations on handkerchiefs and notebooks. The cute type is regarded as Inari's "mascot" *(masukotto)* and is not considered sacred. Many tourist maps use a fox to signify the presence of an Inari shrine, often in combination with a red torii. Even the shrine uses this mascot image sometimes: one year Fushimi's office of lay worship groups gave, as a gift to *kō* members for their financial contributions, a drawstring cloth bag picturing two cartoonlike foxes with big eyes and the words "Fushimi Inari" in roman letters. Clearly this image signifies Inari, but it is not taken as a representation of the *kami* or even the sacred foxes.[27]

Although fox statues almost always flank the altar and guard the front of an Inari shrine, the fox image is never directly manipulated or addressed by priests during formal worship. Even so, foxes usually are iconographically ubiquitous and many practices at Inari shrines involve foxes. In general, these are popular rather than priestly, part of the local lore about Inari and not necessarily condoned by the priests. An Inari shrine, no matter how small, will usually have a pair of guardian fox statues in front of the main sanctuary or on the altar. But this number usually multiplies as worshipers offer additional statues—ranging from cheap mass-produced porcelain sets to handcarved stone images—inscribed on the base with the donor's name. Inari's foxes (like other guardian animals of Japanese temples) usually come in pairs representing male and female.[28] Each holds a symbolic item in its mouth or under a front paw: most often this is a jewel and key, but it may be any combination of jewel, key, rice sheaf, scroll, or fox cub. Realistic fox statues evoke the mystery of the animal, but they are rare. Representations of the fox at Inari shrines, although infinitely varied, are also somewhat stylized: they are usually seated with heads looking forward and tails pointing straight up, ending in a wish-fulfilling jewel at the tip.[29] Zoologist David Macdonald says that in all his hundreds of hours of observing foxes, he never saw one hold its tail in this manner (although cats frequently do).[30]

Fox statues are not just given to temples; sometimes they are borrowed from them. At Toyokawa Inari in Tokyo, the petitioner takes a set of small seated white foxes from the worship hall and places them in her Inari shrine at home, where she prays to them until her request has been granted. Then she returns the set to the temple, purchases a new set from one of the teahouses there, and adds that set to the collection in the worship hall (Toyokawa 1978:62). Lafcadio Hearn described the same custom at the Oba Shrine at the turn of the century, but in that case only one clay fox was used (1974:314). And on Inari Mountain in Kyoto, at Araki Ōkami, a religious establishment that is not part of Fushimi Inari proper, there is a variation called *kuchiire shinkō*—literally, "the religious practice for adding a mouth." The mouth refers to that of a bride or an employee, who traditionally would have entered the household as "another mouth to feed," and this practice is used specifically when one wishes to marry or find a job. A set of three foxes is purchased from the shrine office, taken home, and must be devoutly worshiped every day until the desired employment or marriage is achieved. The priest cautioned that one must not bring them back too hastily but must wait until the new situation seems stable. The foxes are dressed as a head clerk *(bantō),* a bride, and a groom.

Another popular practice—not restricted to fox statues but occurring with most religious statuary in Japan—is their use in folk healing. The devotee rubs his hand on the part of the statue that corresponds with his own pain, then rubs that part of his own body. Tarō Inari at the Tokyo branch of Toyokawa Inari is said to be particularly good at curing sickness, and people vigorously rub the fox statue in front of this shrine. Devotees bring bibs and hats for the foxes—as they do in fact for many other religous statues in Japan—as offerings in either petition or gratitude. Often layers of hats and bibs from numerous donors almost obscure the fox's form. A fox statue that gets broken portends bad luck in the eyes of some believers, who then take it to an Inari shrine or temple for ritual disposal. But others believe the opposite: that fox, they believe, will thenceforth represent the power of the *kami* to heal that particular illness. If the fox's leg is cracked or broken, for example, it represents the ability of that Inari to cure leg problems.

Most shrines and temples in Japan offer amulets, votive plaques, small statues, and such items for sale. At Inari shrines and temples, these may take the form of the sacred fox. At Fushimi, at the main shrine at the foot of the mountain, the only fox object for sale when I was in the field was a small metal charm that looked like it was made of origami folded paper. But at the Okusha, the shrine situated partway up the mountain, a number of fox objects were available.[31] Here items for sale included votive plaques in the shape of fox faces, ceramic representations of an *otsuka* rock altar with a fox in relief on the front, a small metal bell depicting a pair of foxes, ceramic bells in the shape of a fox, and a credit-card-style plastic amulet for good marriages showing a white fox couple. It is probably not coincidental that this subshrine is located in "Myōbu Valley" (related to the worship of the spirit fox Akomachi) and that real foxes used to live in this area.

At Toyokawa Inari too, regarding fox representations for sale, there was a similar division between formal and popular religious items available at the main temple in Aichi prefecture and the branch in Tokyo at Akasaka Mitsuke. The main temple offered no religious objects depicting a fox, but the branch temple in Tokyo had a number: small foxes on the end of a keychain, a pressed metal representation of Dakiniten on a fox, a keychain with a small plastic gourd inside which Dakiniten rode on a fox, and small ceramic foxes. Priests explained that probably the reason for the difference was that belief in Inari had been particularly fervent in Edo and the temple there had created new amulets in response to worshipers' requests.

The food offering most popular at Inari shrines is fried tofu *(oage, abura-age)*, and it is commonly agreed that foxes are said to like this particular food. Priests do not usually include this item in the daily food offerings to the deity, but the stores that line the approach to Inari shrines and temples almost always sell fried tofu for the devotees to offer. Before the war, the Toyokawa Inari Temple sold *oage* within the temple precincts to worshipers as a popular offering. Some shrines even have a fox feeding station where offerings can be made to Inari's spirit foxes. At Fushimi this station is called the Gokujo, a red building just above the main buildings on the way up the mountain. No sign identifies its name or function (though all the other subshrines have wooden signs), and the priests never make formal offerings there as they do at the other subshrines. Many people have no idea of its function and pray to it as if it were an ordinary subshrine. Others do know the tradition, however, for I sometimes saw a pile of *oage* left on the stand in front. Taikodani Inari in Suwano, which is modeled directly on Fushimi Inari, has a fox feeding station called Myōbu-sha. There, too, there is no *kami* enshrined within, but two circular holes in the bottom of the altar platform allow the spirit foxes entrance and egress.

At Toyokawa Inari, it was unclear to me for a long time whether fried tofu was part of the temple offerings to Dakiniten or not. Some priests told me it was; others insisted it was not; still others said it was, but only on festival days. One day, after the prayer services were completed, a young priest and I went to the main altar and looked very carefully at the offerings and saw there was no tofu at all. But another priest said that it was not offered at the main hall but at the Okunoin inner hall. I finally solved the mystery on Hatsuuma,[32] Inari's festival day, when a priest took me to see some fox statues in the Okunoin, not usually open to the public. We asked the elderly layman in charge about the *oage*, and he told us a big basket of it was sent over from the kitchen every day as an offering to Dakiniten. So here the temple did continue the tradition, but the priests were not particularly aware of it because it was not offered in a ritualistic fashion but by the lay workers continuing an older temple custom.

Why fried tofu is said to be the favorite food of foxes is another great mystery. Clearly this is not what foxes eat in the wild,[33] and no clear tradition links it with the fox or Inari worship. One religious specialist speculated that it is associated because it is the same color as the fox. At the Tokyo Toyokawa Inari Temple I was told that unlike today, when one can simply buy fried tofu, it took a great deal of time and effort to prepare from scratch in the old days and thus was a suitable offering for the *kami*. Gorai, taking us back to forgotten Buddhist traditions, gives the most reasonable solution: he says that although Shinto *kami* never receive fried foods, fried foods are offered to the deva *(ten)*, in esoteric Buddhism, and *oage* quite possibly entered Inari worship this way—originally as a Buddhist offering to Dakiniten (Gorai 1985:41–42 and 131). It should be noted in passing that the reason why one kind of sushi and two kinds of noodles are called *"Inari-zushi"* and *"Kitsune soba/udon"* is because all of these dishes contain fried tofu—hence the Inari and fox associations. And completing the circle on the association, this kind of sushi is commonly offered to Inari.

Certain Inari shrines have traditions concerning the spirit foxes of that area. During the coldest time of the year *(daikan)*, between the Ōyama Ritual and Hatsuuma, folk tradition has it that all of Inari's assistant foxes come to the sacred mountain in Fushimi.[34] Human pilgrims are numerous then, too, because people who undertake the circumambulation of the mountain at this time (and also at the hottest time) gain more benefit than at other times of the year. During this period of great cold, pilgrims leave offerings for the spirit foxes by the side of the path all over the mountain in a custom called *segyō* (Fushimi 1969:46). The foxes in the eastern part of Japan all went to the Ōji Inari Shrine on New Year's Eve, where their ranks were decided for the coming year (Amino 1959:15). And in the north, many foxes attended the Hatsuuma Festival at the Takekoma Inari Shrine in Sendai—and on that night the ferryman carried all passengers without charge, because most of the fine gentlemen needing passage were thought to be Inari's servants in human shape (Hartshorne 1902, I:317). Although these spirit foxes may not be visible to the eye of the average person, a resident of the sacred mountain told Buchanan in the 1930s that he could smell them: "Theirs is a divine, fragrant, faint, burnt-flesh odor. . . . It is easily recognized but very difficult to explain and describe" (1935:36). Although I never heard about the smell of foxes, a teahouse owner told me she had seen photographs taken on Inari's sacred mountain in which spirit foxes or dragons could be seen hovering in the background. At Toyokawa Inari, a priest said that tradition has it that if one sees a white fox in the candlelight, it portends a good year.

Given the strong popular association of Inari and the fox over the centuries, it is difficult to imagine Inari worship without its attendant fox customs. The priest's resistance against excessive emphasis on the fox seems to have been a fairly recent development. Apparently it began in the Edo period among the National Learning scholars and continued during the Meiji-period sanitization of Shinto, when its superstitious, "primitive," animistic elements were disavowed. Traditionally any mysterious natural phenomenon could be a manifestation of *kami,* and Motoori Norinaga's famous definition of *kami* specifically mentions foxes as an example of *kami* (Earhart 1974:10-11). This sanitized attitude did not permeate very deeply into popular thinking, however, and the association of Inari with the fox remains a cultural given for most Japanese. Without the fox, Inari might have been just another agricultural *kami* unable to adapt to the changes in Japanese society.

Taming the Fox? Natural and Cultural Symbols

Foxes refuse to be domesticated. A badger *(tanuki)* makes a pet something like a dog—it can even be walked on a leash—but a fox, even raised from birth by humans, never relaxes and hates being touched (Koizuka 1982:44). Macdonald, who hand-reared foxes in the course of his studies of fox behavior, describes how Niff, one of his foxes, slept in his bed with her nose in his ear when she was tiny but changed as she got older. She would trust only the humans who had raised her and "became hysterical with fear" if a stranger appeared (Macdonald 1987:61). Someone brought a live fox to Fushimi Inari about twenty years ago, according to the local shrine carpenter *(miya daiku),* who built an exceedingly strong cage for it. But the fox escaped by tunneling out. The natural enemy of the fox is the *domesticated* canine, the dog. This mutual antagonism forms the rationale for a number of traditional folk cures and talismans against fox possession and dog sorcery. The character for "dog," written on the forehead of a child, protects it from foxes (Buchanan 1935:53). Fish paste smeared over the body of a fox-possessed person and licked off by a dog is so abhorrent that the fox leaves (Koizuka 1982:29). Conversely, carrying a fox tooth keeps one safe from dog sorcery (De Visser 1908a:121).

Because of its qualities of independence and wildness, the fox is associated with the mystery and fundamental unruliness of nature. Strange happenings in nature are attributed to foxes and badgers: rain from a sunny sky, strange lights at night, rocks that emit sulfuric fumes, and even volcanic eruptions. What unites these phenomena is not that they are necessarily bad or violent, but unexpected and uncontrollable. Like the power of nature, the original Japanese *kami* were amoral—potentially beneficial or destructive depending on proper propitiation by humans. To some degree they were synonymous with the powers of nature, or at least had these powers at their control. The sacred fox, similarly, cannot be controlled by humans. Even the seventy-five tiny foxes "owned" by a family are not trustworthy: although they bring the family its initial wealth, they may also make public the family's secrets or trick a neighbor and make it appear that the deed was done by a member of the family (Hearn 1974:326-327).[35] If the sorcerers who employed foxes to magical ends used them to further their own lust or greed, the fox never came to assist them again (Koizuka 1982:34). And spirit foxes can possess a person against his will and bring retribution for some slight. As with the Japanese *kami*, the proper attitude of respect toward sacred foxes is required to avoid misfortune.

A variation on the "scissors, rock, and paper" hand game was played by geisha and their customers from the late Tokugawa to Meiji periods. In this game, called Fox Fist *(kitsune ken),* two people play and the three roles are fox, headman, and hunter—symbolized by hands cupped behind head as ears, hands on thighs, and hands holding gun, respectively. The headman loses to the fox, who bewitches him; the fox loses to the hunter, who shoots him; and the hunter loses to the headman, who outranks him. (See Koizuka 1982:195; Hartshorne 1902, I:147; Joya 1963:223.)[36] The interesting point is that the fox plays a dual role as the real fox, which can be shot, and the spirit fox, which can bewitch. The fox can bewitch the headman, but not the hunter, who kills his natural form—perhaps obliquely indicating the importance of both the natural and spirit forms.

There are a number of fox stories in Japan in which humans take delight in killing or hurting the fox. The single fox reference in the *Manyōshū* (Nippon Gakujutsu Shinkōkai 1965:62),[37] Japan's earliest extant poetry collection (mostly from the Nara and Heian periods), is in a poem that expresses rather cruel delight in hurting a fox doing nothing more than crossing a bridge:

> Boil water, my lads
>   In the kettle with a spout!
> We will dash it on the fox,
> Coming from the Ichihi Ford
> Over the log-bridge of cypress

The danger from real foxes does not seem great, but the *Tsure-zure gusa* of around 1337–1339 mentions incidents of foxes biting people (they get stabbed by swords) (Yoshida 1974:164). The tricks of spirit foxes are usually harmless, but one horrifying tale describes a fox animating the corpse of an old woman (it gets beaten to death) (Yanagita 1975:71–72). Mayer has a subgenre of folktales under "Cleverness at Work" called "Destroying the Fox" (1986:149)—but this is often more difficult than it looks, for there is another category called "Failing to Destroy the Fox" (p. 201). These sometimes jarringly brutal stories remind us that it is dangerous to romanticize wild animals. They may also show us a few things about our own skills for survival, not all of which are morally or aesthetically pleasing. In the woodblock print of a foxes' wedding by Hiroshige (Fukuda 1975:86–87), the foxes in the foreground are walking erect and dressed like Japanese. But in the background are six real foxes, sitting on their haunches, grooming themselves, again calling attention to the distinction between real foxes and cultural fantasies about them.

In many stories, the fox in disguise is killed immediately when it is discovered to be a fox, even if it has done nothing wrong. One type of story mediates this stark choice of killing the fox or being tricked by it. In the famous Kabuki play *Yoshitsune senbon zakura,* a fox has changed itself into Yoshitsune's loyal retainer, Tadanobu, in order to be near the drum, Hatsune, made from the skin of his parents. Tadanobu accompanies Yoshitsune's mistress, Shizuka Gozen, to Yoshino because she has the drum. In Act VII, confusion arises when the real Tadanobu and the fox-Tadanobu both arrive, and we learn the story of the fox who hears the voice of his parents every time the drum is struck. He apologizes for causing trouble and, bowing to the drum in tears, says he will leave. Yoshitsune hears all of this from a concealed place and is moved by the great family loyalty exhibited by the fox, which makes his own treatment by his brother all the more unbearable. He presents the drum to the fox, who is overjoyed. As a return gift, the fox provides information about traitors and magical protection for Yoshitsune and his party (Halford and

Halford 1956:370-372).[38] Considering the complexities of the fox's situation, and noting parallels with his own, Yoshitsune exercises compassion rather than killing the fox simply because it is a fox.

Foxes and Nature

Foxes can thrive in urban centers such as Oxford, England, "living off the offal of academia" (Macdonald 1987:176), especially in areas with gardens, but Japanese cities can be so devoid of accessible earth that it is unlikely foxes are still living in them. One writer says that foxes cannot be seen outside a zoo today, "for we've destroyed the nature they lived in" (Hiraiwa 1989:5). And it seems that to some degree, real foxes helped to foster fox folklore. A Japanese diplomat, returning to his boyhood village after thirty years in Europe, was pleased that foxes and foxlore disappeared when houses replaced their groves (Gubler 1974:131). Gubler gives other reasons besides human population expansion for what he terms "the eclipse of the once widespread tradition": the commercial raising of foxes for their pelts, which began in 1915 and by the 1930s had spread to twenty-one prefectures (plus occupied Korea and Manchuria), as well as education, secularization, and the loss of faith in the indigenous religion after defeat in the war (Gubler 1974:133).

The fox is still associated with images of unspoiled nature, however. Advertising encouraging people to come to the northern island of Hokkaido often features a fox. Usually the posters depict a lone fox frolicking in the snow, and this northern fox *(kita kitsune)* has become a trademark of Hokkaido. Souvenirs from Hokkaido are likely to feature cute versions of the northern fox, and if the tourist looks carefully, a postcard or two featuring a real fox may come to hand. In all of this the fox has become a mere sign, signifying Hokkaido or nature, and has lost much of its mystery and majesty. The foxes I saw in the Sapporo zoo looked nothing like the magnificent pictures of foxes in the wild: they were mangy, bedraggled, and some were missing one or more legs. An attendant explained that these foxes had lost their limbs in attempts to escape.

For Japanese people not directly involved in Inari practices or folklore studies, the main sources for learning about the fox are children's books. Older people learned fox folklore from their parents and grandparents—usually in the form of stories that really happened to people they knew—but have not, for the most part, transmitted these stories to their children. So the younger the person, the more likely she will have learned what she knows about spirit foxes from books and not from her forebears. Even shrines and temples may transmit their fox tale, not in their history pamphlet, but in a separately published children's book.[39] Even serious scholars turn to children's books to get information about foxes. To write about the methods of shape-shifting foxes, Komatsu got some material from his second-grade daughter's bookcase and from animated Japanese fairy tales on television (Komatsu 1990:46). But these sources may be problematic, as stories are often bowdlerized, sanitized, and prettied up before publication as children's literature.

But juvenile foxes may lack precisely the qualities that make the fox such a powerful religious symbol—its fundamental otherness, impossible to domesticate. In a fascinating experiment, Soviet biologists bred foxes that were somewhat docile toward humans—and after twenty generations (twenty years) had created a new animal, a kind of dog-fox:

> The transformed fox now approached humans rather than fleeing from them, and greeted them with tail-wagging, face-sniffing and licking. But it was more than a docile silver fox—the animal had also changed physically. Some of Belyaev's foxes now sported floppy ears rather than the prick-ears of an adult fox. [Coppinger and Feinstein 1991:127]

The reason this happened, Coppinger and Feinstein argue, is that "tameness is a general characteristic of juvenile animals" (p. 127). The experiment lead to the "juvenilization" of the foxes' growth patterns; effectively these foxes are "perpetually young" (p. 128). Belyaev did biologically what infantilized fox traditions do culturally. And although the product may be easier for humans to relate to, it has lost the power and mystery that come from its wildness.

Outside the Inari context, the fox in present-day Japan has two faces: on the one hand are the cute fox toys and protagonists in sweet fairy tales; on the other is the fox as an image of swindler and extortionist. In 1986, a nationwide search was on for a man involved in the kidnapping of the president of the Glico confectionery company: his main distinguishing feature was his "foxy eyes" (*Mainichi Daily News* February 28, 1986). Around that same time in Tokyo I came across a poster warning elderly people not to be taken in by the slick sales pitch of door-to-door salespeople, for there had been a rash of fraudulent schemes targeted on the elderly. The poster depicted a lone old man, peeping out from behind his door with chain lock still fastened; on his doorstep stood a fox and badger in human shape. The fox was shown as a rather buxom female, resonating with stories of fox tricks as a kind of seduction.

The real fox is not an endangered species, although its numbers sustain great slaughter yearly. Macdonald garners some gruesome statistics. He reports: "Together they add up to one of the largest onslaughts on any mammalian species: in one year rabies controllers in Alberta killed 50,000 red foxes, sheep farmers and gamekeepers in Scotland killed 9,000, fur trappers in the USA killed 356,000. Worldwide the annual toll of foxes is astronomical"(1987:207). But in spite of all this, the worldwide fox population is not threatened and attempts to reduce their numbers actually end up increasing them (p. 207).

Is the folkloric fox a living symbol in Japan? Western writers have been predicting its doom for the last hundred years. At the turn of the century, Lafcadio Hearn was convinced that Western forms of education, particularly science, would soon eradicate fox superstitions in Japan (1974:341-342). Three-quarters of a century later, Gubler was again consigning this symbol to history (1974:133-134). Western writers often succumb to romanticization and exoticization when describing foreign cultures and tend to regard change as a one-way, linear process in which the new necessarily replaces the old. Recent reflexive essays on one of the most romanticized of "island paradises," Bali, have implications for the Japanese case as well. Like Bali with its "demonstrated capacity . . . for continuous and creative self-renewal" (Hanna 1976:xii), Japan too has long been famous for its ability to take on new foreign elements, reshaping and reinterpreting them to its particular cultural needs.[40]

Reminding ourselves that it is precisely those people who doubt the fox's power who get tricked—and that the salient characteristic of real and spirit foxes is their continual adaptability—let us see how foxes dealt with the tremendous social and cultural changes that occurred during the Meiji period, when Japan abandoned three centuries of virtual isolation and suddenly faced the technology of the West. In fact, foxes seem to have had no trouble reworking their tricks to include the wonders of the Western world. Foxes now delivered telegrams (Yanagita 1957:311), took the shape of railway trains (Chamberlain 1971:115), and turned into phantom cars (Buchanan 1935:48-49). Spirit foxes in the twentieth century did not abandon their traditional pranks even as they developed new styles. In 1875, people living in Kobe made a loud procession, banging drums, ringing bells, and beseeching the fox to return a man who had been missing for three days (Casal 1959:3-4). In 1932 the *Japan Chronicle* of

Kobe attributed two accidents involving twelve injured jockeys to the killing of a fox on the racetrack that morning (Casal 1959:27). When Embree did his fieldwork in Kyushu in 1935-1936, his informants reported the frequent sighting of a fox-train on the railroad tracks—a long row of lights at night—at the place where fox dens had been destroyed to build the railroad (1939:258). A wind near the Ōji Inari Shrine in Tokyo in 1957 was so strong it bent the camphor and cypress trees to the ground but did not disturb even a needle on the pine trees (Casal 1959:14). I never heard of any computer-related mischief of foxes, but surely they are working on it.[41]

Thirty years ago Casal seemed to have no trouble finding actual narratives of fox trickery (Casal 1959:2), but during my fieldwork I did not hear any stories of fox tricks related as contemporary narratives. Informants told me about things that happened to them as children or things that happened to their parents and grandparents. It is hard to decide if the idiom is disappearing as a meaningful cultural category—or, rather, if narratives were deliberately edited before being told to a foreign researcher in the 1990s. Total adherence to belief has never been a defining characteristic of Japanese religious attitudes. Perhaps the person who would never admit to having any personal experience with foxes, because the whole business is superstitious and backward, may still react to the power of the fox symbol with its centuries of cultural meanings. Like other cultural forms that seem to die out or go underground, but turn up again in the new religions, the exorcism of possessing foxes is an important activity in some of these religions, notably Mahikari (Davis 1980).

Gifts from the Fox

If we lose the ability to relate to the fox, we also lose the gifts the fox may bestow on us. These gifts are very special: they have a strong connection to the power of nature and almost an inverse relation to money. The fox gift is quite separate from fox payment, which is in human currency and ends up being only partially real. Foxes who must pay for food or services do so in money, for example, but the next morning at least half of it turns to grass or dead leaves (Hearn 1974:332-333; Manabe and Vidaeus 1975:11-12). In one report, a payment of gold, silver, and silk the next day was "tattered straw sandals, old shoes, tiles, pebbles, bones and antlers" (Ury 1988:192). But a fox gift is not concerned with piles of minted metal but, rather, with instinct, the cyclical bounty of nature, knowledge of nature's patterns and how to read them, animal communication, protection from fire, and, most valuable, the gift of life—none of which money can buy.

There are three types of fox gifts. First, the children who are born of a fox mother and human father inherit certain qualities from their fox mother. In the story that opened this chapter, the child born of such a union, "famous for his enormous strength, could run as fast as a bird flies" (Nakamura 1973:105; *NKBT* 70:69). The fourth-generation descendant of this same union was a woman called "the Fox of Mino" who was very strong and tall, with the strength of one hundred men.[42] The offspring of the fox-woman Kuzunoha of Shinoda Woods and husband Abe no Yasuna was Abe no Seimei—a famous sorcerer and astrologer who was blessed with "divine wisdom and the precious gift of prognosticating and foretelling things to come" (Buchanan 1935:40). Even in Korea, where the fox has such a negative image, the child of a fox and human turned out to be a great general with supernatural powers, fair judgment, the ability to unmask bad foxes, and powers to calm nature (Zong 1982:56-58). These children of fox mothers have inherited the animal and spiritual qualities associated with foxes—which makes them supernatural, superhuman, by their very natures. Not only do the animal qualities make them physically superior to humans but their animal awareness about powers and patterns in the universe gives them knowledge beyond human ways of knowing.

The second type of fox gift is that given by a fox-woman to her human husband or half-human son. The fox mother may give her child the ability to understand the ways of the human world and the speech of birds and animals—a secret that is sometimes contained within a book, a box from the Dragon Palace under the sea, or a shining jewel (Komatsu 1990:54; Nozaki 1961:103 and 111).[43] Or she may plant the rice in such a way that when it grows it looks unfruitful to the tax assessors but actually yields a bountiful harvest (Yanagita 1952:57; Dorson 1962:132-134). She gives them the wisdom and bounty of nature.

The third type of fox gift, which requires no actual kinship with foxes, is the gift bestowed in gratitude for kindness from humans. After a samurai returned a fox's jewel, which he had snatched away from a possessed woman, the fox became his protecting spirit and used its superior senses to guide him through robber-infested woods at night and other dangerous situations (*NKBT* 25:533-535).[44] The grateful fox will warn of fire or military attack, change into a beautiful woman and sell herself to a brothel to raise money for the indigent benefactor (Mayer 1986:127-

128), and even sacrifice her own cub to repay the debt owed to a human (Volker 1950:84).

Negative fox gifts are only an inversion of this. For they never come without reason and almost always exactly "fit the crime." In a very early story in the *Nihon ryōiki,* a man cruelly skewers some fox cubs, so the mother fox skewers the man's baby (Nakamura 1973:212–213; *NKBT* 70:291); in the *Uji shūi monogatari,* a man shoots at a fox, which runs to the man's house and sets it on fire (Mills 1970:218; Tyler 1987:298–299; *NKBT* 27:152). Possession by the famous Otora-gitsune results in an oozing left eye and lame left leg because two stray bullets during a battle wounded the fox in these places (Manabe and Vidaeus 1975:16). Fox revenge may have contributed to the strong image of retribution associated with Inari, for even today people are loath to move an Inari shrine for fear of the dire consequences. It is not always the case, as Gubler (1974) suggests, that the Inari fox is good and the folk fox is evil, for traditionally Inari sometimes took revenge through foxes (De Visser 1908a:75).

These gifts from the fox are received from mating with the fox or treating the fox with consideration and respect. If the fox is associated with the powers and unpredictability of nature, then it would seem that a positive relationship with the natural forces without and the instinctual forces within, neither of which can be brought under total human control, will bring wonderful and useful gifts that cannot be purchased for mere money. If the relationship is negative, retributive "gifts" will surely result. But even negative gifts send a message: they can instruct the receiver and others about natural powers and forming healthier relationships with them.

Contemporary Encounters

Everybody in Japan seems to know something about foxes. Older people related stories about bewitching foxes as experiences that actually happened to them or their acquaintances; younger people knew about them from fairy tales they had heard or read as children. References to shapeshifting foxes turn up in classical literature and in Kabuki and No plays. People would sometimes tell me a famous fox story but mix up elements from two or more tales. Only folklorists had a systematic understanding of the fox traditions in Japan, but most people had some awareness of the basic ideas.

Most people with whom I spoke had seen real foxes, but usually in a zoo or on television. Few people today have the opportunity to encounter

a fox in the wild. Even people who live in the countryside see foxes only
in the glow of their car headlights and do not venture into the dense
mountain woods at night. A man in his late fifties related his terror at
meeting a real fox in the woods when he was a boy:

> When I was a junior high school student, my parents sent me out to
> buy some rice. We lived up on a mountain in Hikone [on Lake
> Biwa], so I had to walk down the mountain to the store. Suddenly,
> facing me in the opposite direction was a fox. We both stopped and
> stared at each other. I felt as if I had lost all my thoughts—my head
> was muddled and I couldn't think. I had heard stories of fox be-
> witchment and was worried this would happen to me, so I slowly
> backed away from the fox. The fox continued to stare at me until I
> got out of sight. I took another path down to the store.[45]

This same man said that his uncle had actually been tricked by a fox
about fifty years ago in the following manner:

> My uncle was at a party, and had quite a bit to drink. The host
> wrapped up some *Inari-zushi* for him to take home to his wife as a
> present. He set off, on the same mountain road on which I met that
> fox. Suddenly, a beautiful woman appeared, and invited him into her
> house. He agreed, being a rather lecherous fellow, and she invited
> him to take a bath. He took off all his clothes and sank into the
> steaming hot water—but the next thing he knew, he was naked in a
> rice paddy and the sushi was gone! He concluded that he had been
> tricked by either a fox or a badger.

Devotees of Inari were not necessarily more familiar with fox traditions and held a great spectrum of interpretations about the fox's meaning
in Inari worship. But devotees did tend to have positive feelings about the
fox—in contrast to those with no contact with Inari who sometimes expressed a sort of unease about this animal. One woman who has been
coming to the Fushimi Inari Shrine for over fifty years said that her friends
tell her she may be possessed by a fox. She does not believe this. On the
contrary, she says, she feels calm and refreshed when she sees Inari's fox
statues or a famous scroll painting of foxes displayed in the tearoom on
special festival days. The spirit foxes of Inari continue to be active in the
dreams, religious experiences, and hermeneutical orientations of some
devotees. Most of the people who had an active relationship with spirit
foxes were shamans or followers of that tradition. That is, they believed

in direct communication from Inari—unmediated by Shinto or Buddhist institutions—which sometimes took the form of encounters with her messenger foxes. The following are some representative narratives that devotees told me.

A lady I met at the Toyokawa Inari Betsuin in Tokyo said that when she was a young mother, her daughter was playing on the second floor of their home and fell out the window. The mother was not even aware that anything had happened until a neighbor rushed over to tell her. She ran into the yard and saw the child standing, unhurt, amid a broken window frame and shattered glass. Years later, an ascetic *(gyōja)* who knew nothing of this story told her that Inari had once saved her daughter by taking her in its mouth. She finally understood that this was why the daughter had been unharmed: a spirit fox had caught her in its mouth and set her down on the ground gently. The mother was profoundly grateful, for, she explained, if the daughter had been crippled, she would not have been able to marry.

Machida-san, a male healer whose father also had spiritual abilities, is a businessman in Osaka who leads a lay worship group. Three years ago, he was at Fushimi Inari Shrine and suddenly was overcome by a feeling of tremendous loneliness. He quickly returned home to find that his father was dying. On his way to the funeral a few days later, Machida-san's younger brother saw a dead fox in the road. The family realized that because the father had been such a strong Inari devotee, this fox had died when the father did, to be his psychopomp, guiding him on the road in the otherworld.

Revered as a living *kami* by her followers, Makino-san is a seventy-eight-year-old shamaness who has supported herself as a healer and religious leader since she was a young woman. Her home is in Tokyo, and when she prays two *byakko* (Inari's white foxes) carry her prayers to the *kami* at Inari Mountain in Kyoto and return to her, in the blink of an eye, with the *kami*'s response. When I accompanied this woman and her *kō* on the pilgrimage up Inari Mountain, she climbed the long mountain path spryly for her seventy-eight years. When I commented on this to members of the group, they told me that under her feet, unseen by spiritually undeveloped people such as ourselves, were her two white fox helpers lifting her effortlessly up the path. And most mysterious of all, they said, white hairs sometimes appear on her clothing and on the curtain near her altar. They are about an inch and a half long and can only be from the messenger foxes, as they have no pets at all in the house. When such a hair appears, it is placed in a box on a black felt cloth and treated reverently. When I saw the box, there were about fifteen white hairs in it.

One day a call came to the Fushimi Inari Shrine while I was sitting in the shrine office. I heard the priest who took the call say, over and over, "But Inari is not a fox." Later I asked him what it had all been about, and he said that a person living in Shizuoka prefecture recently moved into a new house across the street from an Inari shrine. He has a dog, and the neighborhood people came to him and asked him to get rid of it. They explained that dogs are the worst enemy of foxes, so keeping a dog is exceedingly disrespectful to the Inari shrine. The priest told him that from the point of view of the Fushimi Inari Shrine, there is no problem at all: since Inari is not a fox, keeping a dog has nothing to do with Inari. But he qualified his remarks by telling the man: "Even though I think the villagers are totally incorrect in this, for the sake of village harmony and your acceptance there as a new family, you may have to give in to their mistaken beliefs."

Clearly the idea of Inari's spirit foxes is still alive to some extent in present-day Japan, even though narratives like these are probably less numerous than they once were. And it is by no means the dominant discourse: many Japanese people regard this kind of talk as old-fashioned and superstitious. But the figure of the fox still retains much of its sacred and dangerous aura—at least to judge by the comments I heard when I told people about my study or showed them my extensive collection of fox statues. The idea that I was in such close touch with all those foxes seemed to make otherwise rational people rather nervous.

Feeding the Foxes

Although the symbol of the fox was of far greater interest to me than to most of my informants, I think it has a great deal of significance in Japanese culture. Unlike cherry blossoms and Mount Fuji, however, the meaning of the fox has not crystalized into pat formulas that can be neatly articulated. The fox in Japan is characterized by negative and positive associations. It is the sacred messenger of Inari; yet it may humiliate and trick people. In possession the fox may deliver sacred oracles; or it may take over one's very personality. It represents the fertility necessary for the continuity of life; but also destructive unbridled sexuality. The fox steals things, especially food, but it may bring supernatural gifts. Sacred and demonic, divine and bestial, it repays human treatment appropriately with reward or revenge.

During the winter of 1990 I accompanied a group of people in a town near Lake Biwa as they fed the foxes during the coldest time of the year. This custom, called *kitsune segyō*,[46] was originally practiced in farming communities around the Kinki and Chūbu districts (Naoe 1983a:121; Miyata 1988:117). A related custom around Hyōgo was called *kitsune-gari*. In this case small boys put a straw fox on top of a green bamboo pole and walked around the village, beating a drum, shaking a sacred wand, and chanting a song to drive out the poor foxes and welcome the lucky foxes (Miyata 1988:117).[47] The custom was absorbed into Inari practices and became a lively annual custom in the entertainment districts, where people made offerings to Inari's spirit foxes in a procession with bell, drum, and samisen (Ui 1976:45). During the coldest time of the year, in a continuation of this custom, I observed hundreds of small piles of food by the side of the path at Inari Mountain. The village where I observed fox feeding had a population of under 9,000. It was a lovely, traditional-style rural village, increasingly rare in contemporary Japan, and seems to have kept its charm through the efforts of a wealthy resident who has used his influence to maintain the old-fashioned elegance. Among the rice fields, large, stately homes behind plastered walls faced impossibly narrow paved roads. In wooded groves stood weathered shrines and temples, including three small Inari shrines.

When I arrived with Miura Hiroko, a student of Japanese folklore who was studying the customs of this village and had invited me along, the family had already arranged the food offerings in two baskets. They consisted of fried tofu, rice balls made with red beans (*sekihan*),[48] and flat shiny green leaves that were used as plates. (They said it would be rude to place the offerings directly on the ground.) Responsibility for the ritual circulates among three households, and this year it fell to the Hirota family. The grandmother had prepared all the offerings at her brother's house, and her son and his children were the principal participants in the event. At this time of year, they said, there is usually snow on the ground and it is very difficult for foxes to find food, so they put out food to help them.

The main Inari shrine is a small red building without resident priest on the side of a mountain. On the two sides of the building at ground level are "fox hole" openings marked by small red torii. The Senior Citizens Club of the village takes responsibility for cleaning and maintaining the shrine. One day when the grandmother was sweeping the grounds, she saw a fox run by, so they know there are still some living in the area. Her son is very proud of their local *kitsune segyō*, which he practiced as a boy with his father. He never gave the custom much thought until one day, when reading a children's book to his son and daughter, he encountered a description of fox feeding and realized this custom probably existed throughout Japan. Now he feels a greater significance to his actions. But he also worries that if his children leave for the cities, as young people are wont to do these days, the custom will die out in his village.

We left the house at 6:30 after sitting around the kitchen drinking tea and chatting. It was a cold, crisp night, although a little overcast. The group included Hirota-san and his two children, the mother from one of the other households, an elderly man, the folklorist, and myself. (Hirota-san's mother did not come along.) It was already getting dark, and they used three flashlights. As we walked through rice fields and into the forest up the mountain to the path leading to the Inari shrine, the group shouted *"Sengyō, sengyō"* in a singsongy manner reminiscent of the cries of old-fashioned street vendors. This cry alerts the foxes that the food is coming, they said, as well as protects the participants from fox possession. And there is a strict taboo about looking back: one must only look forward or risk possession by the fox following behind.

The first stop was the Inari shrine. They put food on a rock near the natural spring, then at the subshrine to the left of the main shrine, the shrine proper, and the two fox holes at the base of the building. They got very excited because some of the food that had been left there by others had been gnawed at, presumably by foxes. Next we went to the shrine of the field deity *(nogami)* and put food in front of each religious statue and small shrine building. It took about one hour to make the full circuit of stops. Hirota-san kept teasing the children: tickling the back of their necks, barking *"kon kon"* like a fox, and telling them he thought they had sprouted a fox tail. It was lighthearted and fun. He told us that when he was a child, only boys and men were allowed to feed the foxes because of taboos about women's pollution (although the women, of course, prepared the food for them to take). These days they do not discriminate by sex, he said. During his childhood, they set out later and took no lights at all, so it was pitch black and quite terrifying. Even with our flashlights, it was dark in the mountains and the road along the rice field was not lighted.

There was a curious ambivalence about the fox. These people were feeding and revering the fox, but they were also afraid of it and protecting themselves against it. Somehow the fox was both Inari's spirit fox and the wild fox in the forest. Although the people expressed a familiar intimacy with the fox, joking and teasing about getting possessed, they did observe the taboo not to look back.

As we walked home along the rice fields, we were on the border between two worlds. On the left was the pitch dark mountain, foreboding and holy in deep winter silence, home of *kami* and foxes. On the right, the Bullet Train sped past every few minutes with an earth-shaking roar, bright light streaming from the windows, blue electrical flashes snapping off the overhead lines. Beyond the tracks, in the distance, were the lights of high-rise apartment complexes, the garish multicolored neon of *pachinko* parlors and love hotels, forms of the ever-spreading highway culture. But between trains, the silence of the *kami*'s world in the mountains to our left reasserted itself.

Inari's foxes have been at home in both worlds: as messengers of the *kami,* concerned with production and growth in the cycles of nature, and as assistants to the *kami,* concerned with business and commerce in the cities. So long as Japanese people do not neglect to feed them, foxes will continue to inhabit the borders, guarding their jewels of spiritual and material treasure.

4
Symbolizing Inari: The Jewel

Last night in the fields I came to a big stone that looked like a Wishing Jewel, and I touched it. It was warm. North of the stone lay three foxes. I picked the white tuft off one's tail and saw it was a big white fox. "Wear red," the fox said, "when you bring me offerings."

At dawn I got twenty golden relics of the Buddha.

As I write down this marvelous sequence of dreams, I shiver again with joy and awe.

—Royall Tyler, trans., *Tamon'in nikki*

The jewel is a motif found in great profusion at Inari shrines and in association with the fox. One can find it gracing the top of stone lanterns, embossed on roof tiles, in the shrine or temple crest, and stamped on pamphlets and oracle papers from Inari shrines. In fact, representations of sacred foxes without a jewel are rare. One of the pair of foxes usually holds a jewel under its paw or in its mouth, or a jewel may sit atop its tail or head or decorate the base upon which it sits. Spirit foxes may effect their shape shifting by means of a magic jewel. The word "jewel" occurs with great frequency in the individualized names for Inari carved into worship stones on Inari Mountain: Jewel Princess Great Deity, Jewel Dragon Great Deity, Jewel Woman, Jewel Rock, Jewel Bay, Jewel Demon, Jewel Gathering, Jewel Sword, Jewel Harp, Jewel Forest, Jewel Woman,

Jewel Tail, Jewel Victory, Jewel Dew Princess—there are 802 names that begin with the character "jewel" and hundreds of others that contain the word (Fushimi 1965:124-136; 1966:175-189).

Several meanings are listed in Nelson's *Japanese-English Character Dictionary* (1962:607) for the character that can be read *"tama"* or *"gyoku"*: gem, jewel, precious stone, jade, ball, bowl, sphere, bulb, lens, bullet, shot, shell, billiards, tool, cat's paw, pretty girl, person, margin (in stock transactions), testicles, beautiful, round. The meanings cluster around the concepts of roundness, precious stone, and value. Written with a different character, *"tama"* or *"tamashii"* also means soul or spirit.[1] The meanings interpenetrate, and the soul is conceptualized as a ball of light or shining sphere. Mitama, or August Spirit, refers to the manifestation of a *kami*. The jewel may be a pearl or other precious stone, but its value usually derives from sacred and not material value. It may grant wishes, perform magic, and serve as a receptacle for a *kami* or for buddha nature. The jewel may be perfectly spherical or onion-shaped; comma-shaped jewels *(magatama)* and *hyōtan* gourds have some of the same qualities as the round jewel. Foxes are not the only possessors of these jewels: they are also the property of dragons, *tengu* (mountain goblins), snakes, and Buddhist figures such as Nyōi Kannon

Wish-fulfilling jewels carved in the base of a stone lantern in the precincts of Toyokawa Inari, Aichi prefecture.

and Jizō. No matter who holds it, the jewel signifies or grants great treasure, spiritual or material.

Early and Mythic Meanings

A folktale found in both the *Nihon shoki* and the *Kojiki* tells of two brothers who lived during the Age of the Gods. The elder, named Hono-susori no Mikoto, had the luck of the sea in the form of a fishhook; the younger, Hikohohodemi no Mikoto, had the luck of the mountains, contained in a bow. They exchanged these implements, but neither had any success at all. So the elder brother asked for his fishhook back, but the younger brother had lost it. The younger brother traveled to the palace under the waves and recovered the fishhook with the help of Toyotama Hime, who became his wife. When he returned to the upper world, his father-in-law gave him two magic jewels that controlled the tides and taught him to use them to control his difficult brother (Aston 1972, I:94).[2] An adaptation of this tale is found in the late-twelfth-century *Mizu kagami,* in which the female regent Jingū Kōgō uses these jewels to subdue the troops without bloodshed in her invasion of Korea in the year 200 (De Visser 1913:142–143).

Jewels are said to have been worshiped as *kami* and also served as the repository for the *kami (shintai)*. The *kami* of the Himekoso Shrine is said to be a red jewel; the jewels in Izanagi's necklace became the *kami* of the storehouse shelf, Mikuratana (Katō 1937:28). The repository of one of the five *kami* worshiped as Inari at Tamatsukuri Inari in Osaka was a large *magatama* curved jewel. As soul or spirit, jewels are connected both with fertility and birth and also with death. They contain the animating force that creates a new life and leaves the body when it dies. In a contest to determine sincerity, Amaterasu the sun goddess and her impetuous brother Susanoo chewed up and spat out the other's regalia, and five male *kami* were born in this way from Amaterasu's jewels (Philippi 1968:76–77). The ritual seems to have been designed to activate the spirit in the jewels (and sword) in three ways: "Shaking the articles with a jingling sound was . . . to induce the latent spiritual forces in them to awake and go into action. Rinsing them in a sacred well was to impart to them the generative powers latent in the waters, and blowing a misty spray reflected a belief in the life-giving powers of breath" (Matsumura in Philippi 1968:76, nn. 2–3). Spirit shaking to revive a flagging energy — of the sun, a *kami,* a dying person, or the emperor — continues to the present in a ritual called *tamafuri* (spirit shaking), *tama shizume,* or *chinkon* (spirit pacification) (see Blacker 1975:43f). The emperor and empress participate in the *chinkon* ritual during the enthronement ceremony; the rite is said to create good spiritual balance for the ceremony as well as to prolong their lives (Holtom 1928:85). In this ritual, a garment is shaken ten times and a cord is knotted (Ellwood 1973:126). Sometimes the power to restore the spirit of life was contained in a jewel—such as the *Makaru kaeshi no tama,* the "jewel endowed with a miraculous power of restoring the dead to life," mentioned in the Heian-period *Kujiki.* Among the Ten Sacred Auspicious Treasures were the "Life-Inspiring Jewel," the "Jewel of Perfect Health and Strength," and the "Jewel Warding Evil from Roads"—items used in the *chinkon* ceremony for the emperor and empress (Katō 1937:27 and 100). Other magic jewels increased life *(ikutama)* and increased abundance *(tarutama)* (Kokugakuin University 1985:64-65).

A type of *chinkon* ritual is held annually at the Fushimi Inari Shrine. This winter solstice ritual called Mikagura (honorable dance for the *kami*) was performed at the imperial palace and also at the Inari Shrine until 1544. It was revived at the shrine in 1862 (in a petition to the gods to repel the Western barbarians) and now is a yearly event on the same day as the Ohitaki Festival (November 8), when three huge bonfires are lit during the day to burn tens of thousands of prayer sticks *(hitaki-gushi)* of the faithful. That evening, in the darkened precincts of the shrine, a small fire is kindled in front of the main sanctuary and, two by two, priests come to the fire, sit opposite each other, and play an archaic melody on a series of traditional instruments. In the climax, a single male robed in white performs a dance characterized by slow, stately movements. In his arms he holds a large *sakaki* bough, to which is affixed a large circle of reed, said to symbolize the sun. This ritual was traditionally performed just when the powers of the sun were the weakest.[3] The fire, the archaic shamanic dance, and the sun circle were designed to reinvigorate the sun's power (Fushimi 1977:89-99) in a kind of sympathetic magic. At the Inari shrine the specific intent is to restore the energies of Inari, who has depleted her powers during the growing season in helping the rice mature and now faces the winter cold.[4]

The jewel has even stronger associations with new life when it functions as a kind of womb or egg.[5] Spiritual power develops inside sealed containers that are simultaneously empty and full—rocks, gourds, earthenware vessels, boxes from the undersea Dragon Palace, covered wooden boxes. (See Ouwehand 1964:121-125; Blacker 1975:98-99.) Divine children in Japanese fairy tales often are born from peaches, bamboo stalks, gourds, and melons. An example of a jewel serving this function is from a story in the classics about a Korean prince in Japan. In the Korean kingdom of Shiragi, a "woman of lowly station" took a nap by a swamp and "the rays of the sun shone upon her genitals like a rainbow." She became pregnant as a result and gave birth to a red jewel. A man who had observed the whole sequence asked her for the jewel, which she gave him, and he wore it tied about his waist. Some time later, he got into trouble with the prince of the land, Amenohiboko, over a misunderstanding about a cow but was able to buy his way out of jail by giving the jewel to the prince. The prince took the jewel home and placed it near his bed—whereupon it changed into a beautiful woman whom he married. Although she served him faithfully, he became increasingly arrogant and unkind to her. She told him she was too good for him and would return to her ancestral land. (Because Japan is the land of the sun, and the sun's rays caused her birth, she thought of her homeland as Japan.) She then left secretly by boat for Japan. He too went to Japan, though to a different location from his wife, married again, and had many children (Philippi 1968:291-293).[6] Here the red jewel is itself born of woman and then later delivers the Japanese princess. In the *Nihon ryōiki* (3.31) we find another story in which a virgin gives birth to containers of spirit. A virgin from Mino was pregnant for three years and finally gave birth in 782 to two stones about five inches in diameter. The stones increased in size every year and were enshrined after the *kami* Inaba possessed a diviner and said the rocks were his children (Nakamura 1973:265-266; *NKBT* 70:411).

Tales of this sort form the prototype for shamanic rituals in which the women were possessed by the *kami*, often a snake or water deity, and spoke oracles. The *miko* (spirit medium) was called Tamayori Hime, which literally means spirit-possessed female, and Blacker notes that the possession was both spiritual and sexual (1975:118). *"Tama"* occurs frequently in the names of courtesans and prostitutes and is related to earlier notions of the *miko* priestess as the divine "mistress" of the *kami* (Ouwehand 1964:156 and 165). The jewel that gestates divine spirit may therefore be a rock or round container, a womb, or a woman's body as sacred vessel. Similarly, women had a special relation to the *tama* of the emperor, which contained the imperial charisma. When the emperor died, his body was held in a mortuary hut where women, especially those with whom he had had sexual relations, were secluded with him and performed rituals *(tama shizume, tamafuri)* to try to entice the *tama* back into the body (Ebersole 1989:145 and 171). The mortuary space was "essentially a female preserve" (p. 171) where the unique imperial *tama* dwelled until it could be properly transferred into another body. Interestingly, the women often wore strings of jewels *(tama)* that could act as repositories for the unsettled spirit (pp. 175 and 213).

Rocks may also delay birth—such as those used by the Empress Jingū when she was pregnant on a military campaign. Accounts of the positioning of the stones vary: the *Kojiki* says she tied white rocks in a sash around her waist (Philippi 1968:264-265); the *Nihon shoki* says she "inserted [them] in her loins" (Aston 1972:229); the *Manyōshū* has one in each sleeve (Nippon Gakujutsu Shinkōkai 1965:202-203; *NKBT* 5:70-73). The idea may have been sympathetic magic to block the birth—or perhaps the sacred child's spirit was believed to move to the rock, where it grew more slowly.

At the time of death, the soul may visibly leave the body in the form of a round shining ball called *hitodama* (human spirit). It is reported to be blue and white with red spots, or bluish-red, with a flat, round head and a tail; when it rests on the ground it loses its light and becomes many small black insects or bits of charcoal (De Visser 1914:81-82). Meteors were thought to be *hitodama*—such as the one that fell to earth with great noise in 899, mentioned in the *Nihon kiryaku* of the eleventh century (De Visser 1914:81). The round head and curved tail also suggest the shape of the *magatama* jewels, and this may have been part of their power. In time the manifestation of a *hitodama* came to be associated with unhappy souls, and by the seventeenth century there were many stories of this sort. People who had been murdered or unfairly accused would rise from their graves as fireballs that might effect revenge or would resume their human shape and settle their unfinished business. In a 1686 tale, a Buddhist priest was wrongly accused and killed by a man who thought the priest had seduced his wife. From the priest's grave, a fireball arose and killed the man along with his family (De Visser 1914:84). The appearance of the *hitodama* may be benign, however, and simply indicate that someone has died or deliver a message of gratitude to someone still living (Joya 1963: 437). Embree (1939:263) reports the distinction his informants in rural Japan made in 1935 between *hidama* and *hitodama*. The former were fireballs—formed, it seems, of the souls of rice or barley that was wasted or burned. This fireball had a tail, and its whizzing out of the house was an extremely bad omen for that household. *Hitodama,* on the other hand, were balls of light without tails, about the size of a light bulb, and appeared to the relatives, no matter how far-flung, of a person who was about to die. After the person's death, this ball of light could be seen hovering about the roof. If the person was not good and did not go to paradise, his soul might lurk around the living in this form.[7] A contemporary shamaness told me that she sees the *kami* as balls of bright steady light; she sees the souls of dead people in similar form but with a sparkling, flickering light.

Early Japanese notions of the soul, elaborated by later Shinto scholars, held there are several souls, which are fairly autonomous. The most developed system has four souls:

nigimitama: gentle spirit; tranquil and mature, mild, quiet, refined; makes adjustments to maintain harmony

aramitama: rough spirit; violent, wild, raging, raw; power of nature, ability to battle

sakimitama: lucky spirit; happy, flourishing; gives love, blessings, creates

kushimitama: wondrous spirit; mysterious, awesome, invention, discovery; causes transformations, heals[8]

The four spirits seem to be of unequal importance, and different thinkers have described the relations in different ways. *Nigimitama* and *aramitama* are usually thought of as opposites, and Motoori held that *sakimitama* and *kushimitama* were two aspects of *nigimitama* (Herbert 1967:61). The main point is that they are not aspects of one soul so much as autonomous parts. This is symbolized by the separate enshrinement of the different souls of a single *kami*—as at Ise, where Amaterasu's *aramitama* has its own name and shrine. In divination, Empress Jingū learns that Amaterasu's *aramitama* "may not approach the imperial residence"; during the same ritual three *kami* ask that their gentle spirits be enshrined in a place where "they may look upon the ships passing backward and forward" (Aston 1972, I:237-238). One *kami* in the *Nihon shoki* actually met his *kushimitama* and *sakimitama* (in the form of one being) and did not at first recognize them (Aston 1972, I:61). His *nigimitama* and *sakimitama* wished to live on Mount Miwa, so Ōnamochi built a shrine and they dwelt there as the *kami* of that mountain. In another example, when the Empress Jingū attacked Korea, the *nigimitama* of a *kami* protected her august person and its *aramitama* guided the troops (Aston 1972, I:229). It is significant that since the rationalization of Shinto in the Meiji period, no separate *mitama* of a *kami* have been enshrined (Herbert 1967:64).

A number of Shinto terms include the word *"tama"* or *"mitama"* to indicate the presence of the august spirit of the *kami*. The fence surrounding a shrine building is called a *tamagaki*, or "jewel fence"; the symbolic offering presented to the *kami* during a service is called a *tamagushi*, or "jewel stick." The Shinto equivalent of the Buddhist ancestral altar is called a *tamaya*, "jewel/spirit house," where the deified dead of the household are worshiped. A synonym for *shintai* (literally "deity body") is *mitamashiro* (literally "divine spirit representative"). Both terms refer to the object in which the *kami* resides while in the shrine or during a ritual.

At Tamatsukuri Inari Shrine, where the curved jewel is the dominant motif, the head priest has developed a kind of *magatama* philosophy. In addition to describing the four souls possessed by all people, which must be kept in balance, he elaborates a theory of social and marital harmony. If there is a good fit between two *magatama* in a yin-yang pattern, they form a circle and can roll smoothly. In similar fashion, when two people's souls fit in this way they can work well together to progress in the world. A special comma-shaped amulet helps keep these spirits in balance.[9]

Buddhist Jewels

The jewel in Buddhist iconography is onion-shaped, often with flames burning at the top. The generic term in Sanskrit for jewel is *maṇi* (Jap. *hōju*); it has magic powers to purify muddy water, drive away unhappiness and misfortune, and grant one's desires. Buddhist texts describe various origins of this jewel: it is found inside the brain of a dragon, inside a gigantic mythical fish called *makara* (Jap. *makatsugyo*), or inside a *nāga* (Furuta 1988:894; Saunders 1985:154–155). A *nāga* is a mythological water spirit, part human and part snake, that often occurs in Buddhist mythology. The jewel that grants wishes is called in Sanskrit *cintā maṇi* (Jap. *nyoi hōju, nyoihō, nyoiju*). This jewel symbolizes the original enlightened state of humankind in Kūkai's *Hizōki* (Furuta 1988:768), but its treasure is often interpreted not as enlightenment but rather as worldly benefits. In Buddhist thinking, this is not necessarily contradictory, as material forms may function as expedient means *(upāya, hōben)* on the path to enlightenment (Matsunaga 1969:127). The Buddhist figure most closely associated with the wish-fulfilling jewel is Cintā-maṇi-cakra Avalokitesvara

(Nyoirin Kannon in Japan). This bodhisattva takes thirty-three different forms to help sentient beings. The wish-granting form entered Japan as early as 605 and developed into a real cult about a century later (Matsunaga 1969:126). Three jewels represent the Three Treasures of Buddhism: the Buddha, the Teaching (Dharma), and the Community (Sangha). In one system of esoteric Buddhism this notion becomes abstracted into the following idea: the Buddha as masculine principle in the form of expedient means unites with the feminine knowledge of the law to produce the community of followers (Saunders 1985:154). The various symbolisms of three may appear as three jewels, as three flames on one jewel, or as a single jewel divided by lines into three sections. Kūkai reported in the *Hizōki* that when he undertook the *Ajikan* meditation on the Sanskrit letter *"a,"* which is designed to overcome dualistic views, the letter *"a"* turned into the *nyoi hōju,* symbolizing the "complete fullness in the jewel-dharma realm" (Furuta 1988:768; Inagaki 1985:4).

The *mani* jewel signifies Buddhism because of its meaning as a pure object, "which is said to keep always clean and bright and to shed a brilliant light on all surrounding objects" (Williams 1989:238). Even after it became a Buddhist emblem, the jewel picked up associations from indigenous ideas about magic jewels in the cultures into which Buddhism spread. In China, the jewel is a kind of pearl, associated with the moon and yin energy, and works as a protection against fire, which consists of yang energy (Williams 1989:319). In Taoism, it is a symbol of wealth and prosperity (Saunders 1985:154). Meanings cross over from the wish-fulfilling jewel of the *nāga* maidens (De Visser 1913:9–10) and the precious pearl of the Dragon King (De Visser 1913:189). *Tengu* goblins sometimes had a red jewel that enabled them to "see or hear all that happens in the three thousand worlds" (De Visser 1908b:37)—and here the magic jewel has absorbed notions from Buddhist cosmography. In fact, the Buddhist jewel turns up anachronistically in the *Nihon shoki* in a story purportedly about the year 193, when the Empress Jingū, associated with magic jewels, scoops a *nyoi* pearl out of the sea (Aston 1972, I:219). (Buddhism did not reach Japan until the sixth century.)

At Toyokawa Inari, there are a number of large fox statues in the precincts, and hundreds of smaller ones in a special area at the back. The jewel, however, is the more prevalent motif. Almost no object lacks it: it decorates prayer flags, stone lanterns, roof tiles; candleholders are jewel-shaped; the temple stamp is a jewel encompassing the mystical formula of Dakiniten; a flaming jewel heads the top of all oracle papers *(omikuji);* in

Fox hole in the shape of a wish-fulfilling jewel at the back of an *otsuka* rock altar. Fried tofu, rice, or coins are often found in front of, or just inside, the holes—offerings for the spirit foxes from devotees. Fushimi Inari Mountain, Kyoto.

special processions, the priests carry an ornate incense holder in the shape of a dragon clutching a large jewel; in the very center of the room in which the prayer services are held, a two-foot-high silver jewel rests upon five cushions of different colors. The priests never described the doctrinal meanings of the jewel when I inquired. They spoke instead at the level of popular understanding, saying it grants infinite desires *(musū no ganbō o kanaete kureru)*. Even so, there was one dramatic ritual that gave tangible, if unarticulated, form to the deeper Buddhist meaning of the jewel.

Every year, from December 6 to December 10, the temple holds a *shari kuyō,* a memorial service for a relic of the Buddha.[10] During the time of the service, the altar was covered in a red brocade with gold flowers and laden with red lacquered trays of offerings. Displayed only at this time were sixteen scrolls showing the disciples *(rakan)* of the Buddha. At the center of the altar rested the gold reliquary in the shape of a one-story pagoda. The priests began an elaborate ceremony of bowing to the floor, chanting sutras, and chanting while walking in a zigzag formation in front of the altar. They purified the altar area with water, incense, and flower petals, then brought offerings of tea, incense, and rice to the altar. The chanting sounded like a mournful Gregorian chant: slow, minor key, time beat incessantly on a wooden drum, crashes of cymbals, ringing of bells. A single male voice sang a line, the group of walking priests repeated it. All the while, hundreds of devotees filed into the back and sides of the altar room, many in a less than reverential mode. Contrapuntal to the chanting were the thuds and clinks of coins hitting and missing the offering box, the rasping of plastic bags, the laughs and voices of old ladies. Finally one of the priests went over and asked the chatterers to please put their hands together and act respectful. At the end of the service, the priests cleared away the tables and cushion at the center of the room and set out a chair facing the worshipers. A priest in a deep purple robe came out and delivered an informal, occasionally humorous sermon *(seppō)* telling us how this relic of the Buddha came to be in this temple. Then the acolytes played a tape of sutra chanting and used hand-held microphones and ropes to control the number of people making obeisance to the reliquary, lifting the rope to let a set number through at one time. The worshipers walked up a ramp onto the altar, made a small monetary offering, and bowed reverently to the pagoda.

I was watching all of this from down below, but one of the priests said I should go up too. So I got in line and shuffled along with the group. When I got directly in front of the reliquary, I had only a moment to look in but was struck by what I saw. Inside the open doors, on a lotus pedestal, was a silver jewel with gold flames on the top—this jewel housed the relic. Until that point, in my study of Inari, I had seen the jewel used to signify material wealth and realizing one's desires. It was not until this glimpse inside the golden pagoda that I finally saw the jewel representing spiritual wealth in the cessation of desire. Turner and Turner (1978:28) remind us that

> any religious system which commits itself to the large-scale employment of nonverbal symbolic vehicles for conveying its message to the masses runs the risk that these vehicles will become endowed by believers with magical efficacy. . . . Indeed, much catechizing and homiletic is directed against the popular tendency to take symbols literally rather than metaphorically. . . . For their worshipers [the symbol-vehicles] become instruments by which to obtain material goals: they cease to be aids to salvation *from* the material order.

The only way I ever heard the jewel described in the Inari context was in material terms: it grants wishes, makes one rich, and so on. It surprised me that the priests did not try to teach people about the doctrinal Buddhist meanings of the jewel. The temple magazines published by Saijō Inari and Toyokawa Inari in Tokyo did contain articles on Buddhist teachings and sutras, but these were separate from writings about Inari and little effort was made to integrate or even relate the two.

The Toyokawa Inari Temple transmits another tradition that depicts the mystery and potency of the jewel in a powerful, although hidden, icon. This is one of seven separate papers folded together inside the talisman *(ofuda)* that the temple provides to devotees. The papers are wrapped in a covering sheet printed with the name of the temple and tied with decorative string; the more expensive ones are then enclosed by a wooden box. Few people open the outer wrapper and look at the contents, which would be considered disrespectful and possibly even inviting retribution.[11] The jewel paper shows nine jewels arranged in three rows of three. A larger circle surrounds the central jewel and characters reading, "Buddha, Dharma, Sangha." The four characters surrounding the central stamp say *"chinpō goō"*. The first word means "treasure"; the second means "ox-king," referring to the *goō hōin*, a kind of picture talisman in which the characters are formed by tiny pictures—symbols or animals related to the deity or shrine. The term "ox-king" refers to an item of the highest excellence (*Ōzuka minzoku gakkai* 1978:251-252). The term is sometimes written with the characters for "ox" and "jewel" rather than "king," and this is particularly apt in the Toyokawa example. For by adding a single dot to the second character they have turned the king into a jewel—visually punning on the motif of which the talisman is constructed.

Not one of the priests had any idea what the nine jewels represented. One of the older priests sadly shook his head. When he was a young monk at this temple, he said, he asked the oldest priest the same question and he did not know either.[12] Each of the nine jewels contains smaller jewels in varying numbers, as well as lines and dots that seem to represent rice and water. The priest thought that perhaps each jewel signified the particular workings of Dakiniten. Another possibility is that they actually spell out some characters—as is the case at the three Kumano shrines, where tiny black crows form the characters for *goō hōin*, "most excellent treasure symbol," or at Hikosan in Kyushu where the same is spelled out by hawks (*Ōzuka minzoku gakkai* 1978:252).

Three other traditions at Toyokawa Inari are not specifically Buddhist but reflect folk ideas mentioned earlier of jewels or jewellike stones that slowly gestate spiritual power and the treasure that comes from inside vessels. The first tradition concerns a famous rock at this temple called the

Luck and Long Life Rock (Fukuju Seki). Because of this rock, the temple was also called Child-Giving Inari (Ko-sazuke Inari) in the early decades of the twentieth century. Tradition has it that around 1870, an old man dressed like a farmer came to the temple carrying this rock, wrapped in a rope holder, in one hand. Strange to tell, it took three or four men to carry it about fifty years later, because it grows a little each year. One year a smaller rock of the same variety appeared next to it, and people believed it was born of the larger rock. Women who had trouble conceiving a child came and prayed to this rock, and one of the most famous prewar souvenirs of this temple town was a cake in the shape of the smaller rock (Matsuyama 1990). According to the second tradition, the fragments of the Buddha's bones housed in the reliquary owned by Toyokawa Inari were also believed to grow. There are supposed to be about three hundred fragments of bone, of which about 70 percent are larger pieces. Every year another two or three pieces grow larger (Matsuyama 1990).[13] The third tradition is the pot owned by the old man named Heihachirō who arrived suddenly when this temple was built in the fifteenth century. No matter how many people there were, the small, round, almost jewel-shaped pot always contained enough rice, vegetables, or tea to feed them all. When someone asked how this was possible, Heihachirō said: "Nothing is impossible because I have three hundred and one assistants *(kenzoku)*." After the head priest died, the old man never returned, but his pot is still venerated in the inner sanctuary of Toyokawa Inari. Heihachirō is held to have been a manifestation of Dakiniten, the hundreds of assistants to be spirit foxes (Matsuyama 1990).[14] Although worshipers sometimes knew the story of the magic pot, I never heard them recount traditions of the growing rocks or bones. One priest did mention he had vaguely heard something about the rocks twenty years earlier, but it did not seem to be a well-known tradition at present.

Material wealth has long associations with the jewel: the dragon and its jewel decorated Japanese paper and metal money in the Meiji period (Griffis 1876:381); the jewel itself may be made of some precious stone or pearl; having a magic jewel grants wishes; and the treasure ship of the Seven Lucky Gods is always piled with jewels and other symbols of wealth. Inari was sometimes included as one of the Seven Lucky Gods in the early days of this concept. A woodblock print given by Toyokawa Inari priests to devotees depicts the Seven Lucky Gods on their treasure ship with Dakiniten flying above the ship astride a white fox. The stone used in the folk divination called heavy/light rock *(omokaru ishi)* at many Inari shrines takes the shape of the wish-fulfilling jewel in most cases. At Fushimi Inari Shrine, the onion-shaped tops of two stone lanterns serve this purpose. The stone used in a Fushimi-affiliated lay worship center has been deliberately cut and polished into this shape. I have also seen a round rock used, housed within a square box into which a jewel-shaped opening had been cut.

Recently the branch temple of Toyokawa Inari in Tokyo has created a new form of Inari called Yūzū Inari (mentioned briefly in Chapter 2). *"Yūzū"* means financing, adaptability, flexibility; *yūzū shihon* is circulating capital. This form of Inari is the deification of the jewel held in the left hand of Dakiniten, and its other name is Nyoi Hōshō Sonten. ("Sonten" is a title of respect.) In a fascinating move, the priests have substituted the final character of *"nyoi hōjū"* (wish-fulfilling jewel) with "birth" instead of "jewel," so that the nuance now includes the birth or production of wealth: "wish-fulfilling birth of treasure." Whether they consciously mean to invoke the generative power of sacred jewels or not, this aspect of Inari/Dakiniten gives birth to treasure. And they are not the least bit ambiguous about whether this treasure is spiritual or material: they write in the quarterly publication for worshipers that the reason for the enshrinement of this form of the deity was the "worsening economic state of affairs in the world and the beginning of Japan's own economic dark clouds," which could be improved "through the boundless compassion of the buddhas in the granting of the continued circulation of money" (Toyokawa 1991:7–9).

The small worship hall dedicated to this form of Inari was completed in December 1990. When I first saw it two months later, I asked the ladies worshiping there what deity this was. They replied that this was a deity of money *(okane no kami sama)* and said that if one prayed here money would circulate around and return to the petitioner. Above the difficult characters for *"yūzū"* was written phonetically the simpler term *"tane-sen,"* or "seed money." A stack of small white envelopes had been left for devotees. Each contained a shiny 10-yen coin, and this coin, placed in a wallet, was supposed to generate more money. In just a few months the priests had distributed over thirty-thousand of these envelopes (Toyokawa 1991:8). Again the metaphor of growth, seeds, and fertility crops up, but here the jewel's transformative, generative, numinous power has taken a numismatic form.

Fox Jewels

In China, the fox's jewel, the source of its power, is sometimes thought to lodge as a bright white pearl or small pill within its heart (Watters 1874: 49). This idea did not seem to take root in Japan, however, where the jewel is an external object. The only example of a similar sort seems to be the story in the *Nihon shoki* of the *magatama* curved jewel found in the stomach of a badger *(mujina)* killed by a dog in the year 58. It was offered to the emperor and is now said to be in the Isonokami Shrine (Aston 1972, I:184–185). The fox's jewel described in the *Konjaku monogatari* (27.40) is round, white, and about the size of a mandarin orange (*NKBT* 25:533.11). The *Unkon shi* describes it as a stone the size of a bird's egg, beautiful, and emitting a light at night (Komatsu 1990:55), while the *Shokoku kibun* describes it as a white, egg-shaped fireball that can fly through the air and glows at night as bright as a candle (Nozaki 1961:186). This jewel has special properties, including the power of transformation and the bestowal of wealth or wisdom. Stories differ concerning whether the jewel works for any owner or, rather, requires special knowledge without which it is simply a white rock. The magic jewel enables the fox to shift shape in one tradition. The other methods are by putting weeds or leaves on its head (Komatsu 1990:49, 53, 56) and by circling a tree three times (Mayer 1984:140). In China, the powers of the jewel were broadly transformative, for it was related to the elixir of life, which bestowed powers to see and communicate with spirits and revive unconscious people. The Chinese fox's jewel could also transform base metal into silver (Krappe 1944:125).

The fox's jewel may grant wealth: a folk tradition from Fukui prefecture states that one becomes rich if one picks up the object that sits on the tip of the fox's tail, called *hota* (Suzuki 1982:198). As we shall see, the jewel used to steal the life essence of ninety-nine boys in a Korean story also had the power to bestow the wisdom of heaven and earth if swallowed. And as we saw earlier, the jewel the fox mother gives to her child grants knowledge of the natural world. In a story from the *Konjaku monogatari* (27.40), possession of the jewel itself brings no benefit, but returning it to the fox incurs the fox's protection in life-threatening situations. A woman possessed by a fox played with a white ball as she announced that the fox had no ill intentions but merely needed food. When a samurai grabbed the ball, the fox persuaded him to return it, saying that because the man had no idea how to use it, it could not help him, but if he returned it, the fox would always protect him. When the possession ended, the ball disappeared (*NKBT* 25:533–535; Tyler 1987: 299–300). The fox did help the man when he was threatened by robbers in a dark wood. The treasure from the jewel in this case is the fox's gratitude and protection.

Sexual Meanings

In Japan, sexuality is one of the fox's most powerful associations. This notion, unlike others that are culture-specific, is also found to some degree in the West. In American slang, a sexy woman is "foxy" or a "vixen"; in a slightly older usage, one may "get foxed up" by women (Casal 1959:6). In Japan, however, although used as a derogatory term for a prostitute, *"kitsune"* has no adjectival forms meaning "sexy." Jewels, especially golden ones *(kintama),* probably suggest the slang meaning of testicles more often than spirits. And when jewels take the form of fox holes *(kitsune ana),* female genitalia are powerfully evoked.

The idea that the fox is a sexy animal is based on reasons other than its actual sexual or reproductive behavior. Unlike cats and rabbits, sometimes associated with prolific sexuality and fertility, the fox mates and produces a litter of cubs just once a year. The parents are usually a monogamous pair for at least the breeding season, and there is almost no visual differentiation between the male and female fox (Henry 1986:37). The only reproductive behavior that might give rise to ideas about intense sexuality is that when the pair finally mates, they remain united for at least thirty minutes to ensure fertilization (Macdonald 1987:105). It is not the fox's sexual behavior per se, but its body language and overall demeanor, that probably earned it its sexual reputation. The combination of "grace and elegance," plus its skill as "a lethal hunter" (Henry 1986:27), may be at the root of the attribution of powerful sexuality, usually powerful *female* sexuality, to the fox. The combination of a number of qualities—adaptive behavior that seems very intelligent, even cunning; the seemingly cruel way that foxes, catlike, play with their prey; the lithe sensuality with which they move; their solitary integrity—invites humans to see foxes as sexy. But the idea that foxes "possess lecherous . . . propensities" (Casal 1959:29) is a cultural projection and not biological observation—a point that may illuminate certain elements in a culture's construction of sexuality.

Chinese fox lore constitutes the raw material of the Japanese adaptations. And sexuality is the key concept here, for most Chinese fox stories are erotic (Johnson 1974:40). The central dynamic is that foxes transform themselves into women, have sex with men, and thereby become immortal by stealing away the man's life essence. But why should this be the case? According to the Chinese metaphysical system based on the concepts yin and yang, the fox has a preponderance of yin energy because it is nocturnal and stays hidden in its den during the day. Because this yin energy is protected from the debilitating effect of the sun, the fox can live for a very long time (Watters 1874:48). The reason foxes, regardless of gender, transform into women and sleep with men is because they need yang energy to balance their yin in order to advance spiritually (De Visser 1908a:10). In this explanation, the yang is believed to be contained in the male's semen (Johnson 1974:41). A more generalized explanation that does not limit the fox to the female role says: "This method is based on an important tenet in Chinese erotology, namely that in sexual intercourse the person who experiences the orgasm first loses a unit of life essence and if the partner can restrain orgasm this unit is absorbed," (Voegelin 1972:413). Chinese fox-women are well versed in "all the breaths and rhythms" and have restorative medicines for sexually exhausted men (Jameson 1951:278). A fourth-century Chinese man admits that his experience with a fox was "incomparably delightful" (Krappe 1944:124). Fox saliva was "given as a love potion to cold wives" (Watters 1874:49). Chinese foxes, then, are not necessarily evil, but they may damage their human lovers through their "extraordinary sexual desire" (Johnson 1974:40).

In Japan, in a diary entry dated 1144, Fujiwara no Yorinaga reported that a fox in the form of a woman seduced a sixteen-year-old boy within the imperial palace and gave him a sexually transmitted disease. He knew it was a fox because one had peered at him from under the eaves a few days before (De Visser 1908a:36). In another purportedly true story some centuries later, Matsuura Seizan, the lord of the Hirado domain, described the experience of one of his retainers in 1821. A man named Kumazawa, in spite of having a very jealous wife, managed to conduct an affair with their lusty maid. They met in an outbuilding, observed only by a fox. One day the maid met the master for sex, but it was really the fox in the master's shape. Even after the maid was fully satisfied, the fox would not stop, and she shouted for the master's wife in desperation. Kumazawa and his wife ran to the outbuilding, where only the maid was visible, but the situation required him to confess the affair. Before the fox left, however, it told them what medicine would relieve the woman's pain and advised that buckwheat noodles were a good cure for male impotence.[15]

This kind of tale abounds at the local level, and the details may be fairly risqué. But the fox-woman of incomparable beauty and skills known to all is Tamamonomae, for she tarried with the emperor himself. Her story is told in both No and Kabuki plays, *Sesshōseki* and *Tamamonomae (Asahi no tamoto)*, respectively.[16] The basic story is that an evil fox delighted in destroying governments by becoming the ruler's consort and bending him to her will. She did this to the king of India and to the emperor of China before flying to Japan during the reign of Emperor Konoe (1141-1155).[17] Tamamonomae was a flawless beauty, learned in the philosophies and literatures of distant lands, but she delighted in the deaths of others—and particularly cruel deaths were the only thing that would make her smile. When the emperor fell ill, a diviner realized that she was the source of the problem.[18] Upon discovery, she changed into a white fox (some versions say a golden, nine-tailed fox) and fled. Finally, as the warriors began to sharpen their skills for fox hunting by shooting dogs, she was forced into a rock in Nasuno. From that time forth, any living thing that passed too close to the rock died, and the area was strewn with bones.[19] In some later versions, she was freed from her horrible karmic bondage by the prayers of Priest Gennō and finally attained buddhahood. At the climax of the No play, the Life-Killing Rock splits apart and the fox maiden is revealed and then redeemed.[20] Even though Tamamonomae's sexuality is not directly stressed in the story, it is implicit because of her nine tails. The earlier textual versions of this story only say she changed into a white fox, but in later plays and in popular parlance Tamamonomae is known as the fox with nine tails.

In China, the nine-tailed fox was at first a very lucky omen (De Visser 1908a:9 and 151) and was even depicted as a symbol of immortality in Han (206 B.C.E.-220 C.E.) tombs (Lim 1987; Zhang and Zhou 1988: 143).[21] This is the Celestial Fox, one thousand years of age, of a golden color with nine tails (Mayers 1924, I:65). In Japan too, as we noted earlier, the *Engi shiki* mentioned the nine-tailed fox as being very auspicious. But there were negative Chinese traditions, as well, that the nine-tailed fox devoured men and caused the downfall of dynasties (De Visser 1908a:7-8). In a Korean story, the nine-tailed fox, the jewel, and devouring sexuality all come together in a haunting way. One hundred boys were sleeping at a country school one night. The youngest boy awoke to see a beautiful girl who kissed the boys one by one and left them dead. He hid—so that she only kissed ninety-nine—and then followed her to the graveyard when the rooster crowed. Suddenly she was in front of him, smiling and taking his hand, and trying to kiss him. He realized she was some kind of demon, perhaps a fox, and fought her kisses, realizing they had killed his companions. But then she succeeded in kissing him, pushing a jewel into his mouth, and sucking it back into hers, and as she repeated this action, his face began to get pale. She was sucking out his very life essence. He remembered that if one can swallow a fox's jewel and look at the sky, he will gain the wisdom of heaven. So when the jewel next passed into his mouth, he swallowed it, but in the succeeding struggle with the girl, he looked down instead of up, so he only acquired the wisdom of earth. He began to shout, and she disappeared. Later, when he arrived home, he knew exactly what had happened, for he now had the wisdom of earth, but no one believed him. The adults followed him to the graveyard, though, and suddenly a fox with nine tails in a woman's dress ran out from the large rock concealing a cave. When the villagers killed it, they discovered it had made tunnels into all the graves and eaten all the buried bodies (Zong 1982:18-20). Perhaps this boy, only seven years old, was so clear-headed because he was less susceptible to the woman's sexual charms than the older boys.

The stories about the depraved nine-tailed fox, in which the sex partner becomes a victim, represent one extreme of sex-related fox lore. At the other extreme, found in a fairly early Buddhist story in Japan, the fox willingly substitutes herself as the victim who dies for the sake of the man's sexual appetites, perhaps even for his religious development. In this scenario, a man sees a strikingly beautiful girl standing on the side of the road and tries to persuade her to yield to him. She tells him that if he achieves his objective he will die, but he does not believe her and thinks she is merely being coy. Finally, she agrees to die in his place and they end up spending the night together. She asks only that he copy the *Lotus Sutra* for the repose of her soul after she dies and, thinking it an unlikely prospect, he agrees. She takes his fan, and the next day when he looks where she told him to, he finds a dead fox with its head covered by the very fan he had given the woman. Finally realizing he had slept with a fox, he begins to copy the *Lotus Sutra* for her. He works at it during the forty-nine-day mourning period, and even before he finishes, he sees her in a dream in which she tells him she has achieved enlightenment due to the power of the *Lotus Sutra* (Ury 1979:96-98).[22] The fox mother Kuzunoha in the later version of the "come and sleep" story called the Fox of Shinoda Woods represents the heights of conjugal and maternal love. After her true form has been revealed, she writes a farewell poem to her husband on the paper door, using a brush held in her mouth as she cradles her young son in arms that will soon revert to paws:

If you miss me come and search
Shinoda Forest in Izumi among the wistful arrowroot leaves[23]

(Koishikuba tazunete miyo Izumi naru Shinoda no mori no urami kuzunoha)

Stories about foxes and sexuality may emphasize depravity or selfless-ness, the pleasures of satisfaction or the pain of surfeit, the positive as-pects of sex or its less wholesome aspects. Regardless of the polemical uses of the stories, the constant elements are the associations of the fox, usually in female form, with sexuality, usually extremely pleasurable sexuality. Sexual associations of the fox and the jewel also found their way into Inari beliefs. And although I separate notions concerning fertility and sexuality in this discussion, of course they often occur together.

Foxes, Jewels, and Fertility

From the beginning Inari has been associated with rice growing and the agricultural cycle. A central part of the early tradition, continued at some shrines today, is the prayers to the *kami* at the critical junctures of the rice growing season. At Fushimi Inari—even today when only a small percent-age of Japanese people is still involved in rice production—sacred rice is planted, grown, harvested, and presented to Inari in a series of ritual events at a sacred field within the precincts.[24] The first *kami* from the classics to be worshiped as Inari were food goddesses such as Ōgetsu Hime and Uganomitama. Until prewar times, seeds were sold at the Hatsuuma Festi-val at Fushimi Inari, and these seeds were popularly believed to be blessed by the *kami* for good growth (Fushimi 1969:43-44). Although human reproduction is often related to agricultural production, at least at the popular level, and ribald sexual rituals often accompany spring agricultural practices, these activities seem to have been limited at the Fushimi Inari Shrine. The journal of Fujiwara Akihira (d. 1066) indicates that some popular actors in the Inari Festival procession were dressed as husband and wife and engaged in some sort of sexual antics, which were greeted with a great roar of laughter from the crowd (Fushimi 1977:43). Probably the main reason this kind of activity was not more predominant is that Inari, although originating in religious practices relating to agriculture, quickly rose to the highest imperial rank and took on a broader and more urbane religious significance as well.

As Inari beliefs began to permeate preexisting fox lore, ideas from this earthy level seemed to find their way back to the original sacred center. At the foot of Inari Mountain is a shrine to Sanba Inari (Midwife Inari), popularly known as O-Sanba-san. Here the rock altar sits on a platform in which there are twelve "fox holes," now crafted out of stone and cement.[25] Buchanan says that this is where "divine foxes gave birth to their young" (1935:121), but the site may have originated in a real fox den at an even earlier time, as there were said to be many such dens on the mountain. A tradition still followed in this subshrine is known as one of the Seven Mysterious Traditions of Inari Mountain *(Inari yama no nana(tsu) fushigi)*. When a woman is expecting a baby, she should go to the Midwife Inari shrine to pray. The procedure is to buy a candle from the shrine office, light it, and pray to this form of Inari until the candle has burned to just a short stub. The woman should carefully take the stub home, and if she lights this candle again, when she goes into labor, the baby will be born during the time it takes for the stub to burn down and go out.

Some fox statues with a fox cub under the female's paw, rather than a jewel, are thought to have special powers in granting children to women who have trouble conceiving. One of the teahouse owners introduced me to this tradition at the Toyokawa Inari Temple in Tokyo. A stately stone fox couple flanks one of the paths: the husband fox is named Jūgorō; the wife, holding the cub, is Jūrokurō.[26] The wife of the teahouse owner, in talking with petitioners, has told many women of the powers of this fox, and their prayers are often granted—sometimes they even get twins. A believer's testimonial *(taiken)* in a Fushimi Inari Shrine publication describes a similar ascription of powers of fertility to a fox statue. A restaurant owner from Tokyo consulted with the head priest because she wanted to set up a stone fox—she called it a "Myōbu Sama"—at the rock altar on Inari Mountain where she worshiped. He recommended a rock carving shop in Tokyo, and the fox was ordered and then set onto the altar. From time to time she was seen praying there fervently, and one day, many months later, she returned to tell the head priest her story, which she could barely articulate for tears of joy. She had been very troubled, for she had no son through whom the family would continue, so her daughter married an adopted bridegroom *(yōshi)*. But after nine years of marriage they still had no child. She prayed and prayed at her rock altar to Inari, and finally got a grandchild. What she found mysterious was that of all the tens of thousands of fox statues on Inari Mountain, only hers had a tiny baby fox held securely under the mother's paw, and it was her prayers at this statue that were finally answered (Fushimi 1962b:5-6). It is probably because this fox statue was carved in Tokyo that the mother and baby form is represented here at all, for this style is far more prevalent in Tokyo than in Kyoto. Of the hundreds of fox statues on Inari Mountain in Kyoto, only two have baby foxes, whereas Tokyo Inari shrines are full of mother and cub forms.[27]

Some priests at Toyokawa Inari told me that about twenty years ago the temple had to remove a phallic-shaped rock which stood in front of the Daikoku Hall. This was necessary, they said, because women who came to pray for children were straddling the rock in an unseemly manner. A further elaboration of this tradition was that the rock was believed to be getting bigger. The priests suspected that some of the tour guides in town invented this tradition, which they thought was awkward. (This seems to be the same rock, described earlier, that gave birth to the baby rock.) This fertility tradition was by no means limited to Inari shrines, but it certainly constituted one facet of Inari beliefs. In a summer festival called Onma Matsuri at the Hikuma Shrine in Mito-cho (Hoi-gun, Aichi prefecture), a young man dressed in white and wearing a fox mask carries a large phallic symbol, which he uses to prod young women. Apart from the obvious significance of fertility, summer phallic rituals were believed to ward off the terrible diseases that spread easily during the humid weather. This fox marches in procession with the Seven Lucky Gods *(shichifukujin)*, melding notions of fertility in Inari beliefs into the broader meanings of luck and plenty, for which Inari, as a luck deity *(fukugami)*, is well known. This expansion of meaning occurred as Inari faith took root among people involved with commerce and trade in the latter half of the Heian period (Ueda 1983:284). In the Tokugawa period, money gradually replaced rice as the measure of wealth, and Inari devotees at the Ginza mint in the beginning of the eighteenth century created special offering "coins" imprinted with the characters for long life or luck or the picture of two foxes and a jewel. They had a particular connection to the Buddhist temple Aizenji at Fushimi Inari, which worshiped Shōten (Kangiten)—a deity consisting of male and female forms in sexual embrace *(Nihon rekishi daijiten* 1970:405). Here ideas of sexual and financial plenty seem to intertwine.

Foxes, Jewels, and Sexuality

While there is no denying the phallic nature of many of the tails of the sculpted representations of Inari's foxes, I believe that Western writers have overemphasized the presence of phallicism within the Inari cult and have missed the significance of the jewel. Buchanan devotes an entire chapter to phallicism and Inari in his 1935 monograph; this notion has been picked up and elaborated by subsequent writers (Casal 1949:53–57; Casal 1959: 47–49; Huggins 1925:2–3; Johnson 1974:63–64; Czaja 1974:251–264). Surely, earlier sojourners in Japan saw more evidence of such practices than remains today, for after 1868 the government issued orders to suppress such "indecencies" (Buchanan 1935:29). Buchanan lived in Japan in the 1920s and 1930s, just at the turning point of these beliefs from natural to unnatural:

> At many of the small Inari shrines scattered throughout the country, phallic emblems as objects of worship or as votive offerings may still be seen. The police have, in recent years, removed a great many of the most gross and obvious of the phallic symbols, nevertheless enough remain to convince the investigator of the strong hold that this cult had on the people. [1935:24]

Two criticisms of Buchanan's description of phallicism in Inari worship must be made.[28] First, he uses the term "phallic" when he sometimes means sexual, genital, or even vaginal, for he describes the lusty female *kami*, Ame-no-uzume no Mikoto, as a "phallic goddess" (1935:22). Second, he goes overboard in describing all the phallic objects used in religious ways in Japan. In addition to the fox tails and keys held in the foxes' mouths, which may reasonably be seen as phallic, he describes boulders on the mountain, stone lanterns, the Shinto fire drill, and Ainu *inao* worship sticks as phallic. Sometimes a cylindrical object is just a cylindrical object.

Just as important as the fox's phallic tail is the jewel atop the tail, in the fox's mouth, or under a paw. Buchanan sees this as merely the top part of the phallus (1935:21); Casal adds that in some legends jewels penetrate and impregnate virgins (1949:55). But I would argue that in addition to its possible meanings as phallus, the jewel resonates even more with meanings of womb. Fertility requires the equal participation of the feminine with the masculine, and paired fox statues often hold a key in one mouth and a jewel in the other, symbolizing the need for both. Another feature of many Inari shrines is the fox hole: a womblike cavern in the earth or under the shrine. Beliefs focused on this symbol seem to be dying out, but the holes themselves often remain, testimony to religious concerns of a former age. Originally they seem to have been real fox dens (Hartshorne 1902, II:203; Buchanan 1935:30), and in the same way that the fox was taken as Inari, actual fox holes were treated as Inari shrines during the Edo period (Hiraiwa 1989:4). Later the fox hole was constructed as part of a stone altar or shrine; a round or jewel-shaped opening was left near the bottom for the spirit fox. Lafcadio Hearn describes some elaborate fox holes in shrine buildings he saw in the 1880s (Hearn 1974:316–317), and these can be seen at the back of many Inari shrines today.

At one level, fox holes represent the locus of concentrated spirit power (Fushimi 1969:27) in much the same way as the jewel or gourd contains a developing spiritual power (Blacker 1975:98–99; Ouwehand 1964). But they also had a definite sexual meaning at the popular level. Making the circuit of the mountain, now known as "doing the mountain" *(oyama o suru),* was previously known as *hora meguri* (Casal 1949:37) or *ana meguri,* the "cave/hole circuit," and it is the last name that was taken in its slang sense as sexual.[29] When I mentioned this to some of the younger priests at Fushimi today, they seemed shocked and either denied it or said they had never heard of it. I still found offerings in front of and even inside the fox holes on Inari Mountain in the base of some of the *otsuka* altars, but I never heard any talk of the sexual meanings of fox holes from my informants (except the priest who described this custom from the 1930s).

Inari became the protector of prostitutes, and this is probably because of the association of such women with foxes.[30] Earlier we noted that a derogatory word for prostitute is *kitsune;* a geisha or prostitute who was enchanting to men was known as a "fox without a tail" *(o no nai kitsune)* (Koizuka 1982:190).[31] A satirical poem condenses both meanings: "Even now we are apt to be bewitched / By white-faced foxes" (Nozaki 1961: 131). "White-faced foxes" can refer to the *byakko* spirit foxes or to the thick white powder used on the faces of female entertainers. The term *"kitsune ochi"* refers not only to the separation of the fox from the body of the possessed person but also to the separation of the prostitute's body from her customer's the next morning (Koizuka 1982:192).

But apart from the fox association, these women were often fervent devotees of Inari, who became their protective deity. In China, too, prostitutes were said to pray to a "fox-elf" (Watters 1874:54). The Inari shrine in the Yoshiwara pleasure quarters in Yokohama was a very elaborate one, that was visited by "more than one handsome girl, with brightly painted lips and the beautiful antique attire that no maiden or wife may wear" (Hearn 1974:315). On New Year's Eve at the establishments of the Tokyo Yoshiwara district, in place of the auspicious lion dances, they had fox dances *(kitsune mai; kitsune odori)*. The fox-masked dancer held a sacred wand *(gohei)* in one hand, sacred bells in the other, and danced to thank the *kami* for the good luck the house had received during the past year (Koizuka 1982:200–201). Because Inari shrines were often located near the pleasure quarters, humorous poems in the Edo period used "worshiping at Massaki Inari" as a euphemism for spending the night in Yoshiwara (Asō 1976:25). Another poem elides the Inari shrine, foxes, fox possession, and prostitutes: it says that if an old man worships at the shrine, the distance is short and he returns home soon, but if a young man goes, he will be welcomed and "possessed by a fox" and will be gone for two days (Asō 1976:26). Foxes, Inari, sexuality, tricking, and rice all come together in this humorous haiku *(senryū)*: *"Massaki no shippo o teishu mitsukerare."* The densely packed meaning is something like: the husband who says he is going to Massaki Inari but really goes to Yoshiwara will be revealed by his fox tail sticking out of his otherwise plausible disguise (Asō 1976:25). Instead of the usual two characters for *"shippo,"* tail, here the second is substituted with the *"ho"* of *"inaho,"* ear of grain. Somehow the tail is not just any fox tail but also a ripe ear of rice—resonating even more with Inari, and perhaps suggesting something phallic as well. Although not all geisha worship Inari, the association of Inari with *geisha* continues today to some extent. Images of Inari shrines recur throughout Itami Juzō's movie *Ageman* about a geisha who brings luck to her patrons. Abandoned as a baby at an Inari shrine, she prays fervently to the Inari shrines in her home and yard several times during the story.

We get a closer look into some of the tensions that underlay this glamorous world of the geisha in the descriptions of worship at a rural Inari shrine in Suye (Kumamoto prefecture) in 1935 by anthropologists John Embree and his wife Ella (Wiswell). Embree describes the contrast between the pretty geisha and the farm women from the man's point of view:

> Inari is a god of crops, more especially of rice, and, as such, many farmers have him in their houses. He is also the god of prostitutes and *geisha*, and, as such, he is enshrined in every *geisha* house and brothel. Thus by a curious combination the main Inari shrine of Suye, besides being patronized by farmers and sick people, is regu-

larly visited by *geisha* from the Menda restaurants. They come, dressed in gay *kimono,* the first and fifteenth of every month (new calendar) to pay their respects. After praying, they sit about on the platform smoking and talking before walking the two or three miles back to Menda. They form a sharp contrast to the farm women and doubtless serve as a strong inducement to their husbands to visit Menda restaurants. [Embree 1939:254]

Ella Wiswell's notes on the contradictory feelings of the local women about the geisha give us some insights into the plight of both groups of women:

The big Inari shrine drew the largest crowd. The restaurant girls from Menda gave a strange touch to the festival. One group, which stayed for a while, got very drunk and reeled all over the road on their way home, followed by a group of village children who thought it was a circus. . . . The local girls watched them as if they were some kind of strange animal, and looked and listened with surprised expressions to the girls' raucous voices telling men what to do, smoking all the while. They did some singing and dancing at the party. . . .

In the afternoon as another group of Menda restaurant girls was returning from the Inari shrine, Mrs. Tanimoto and Mrs. Hayashi came out to look at them. They criticized the bright kimono, made remarks about their always going by the village office [where they know many of the men, who are regular customers of the establishments where they work], although, in fact they did so to avoid the horses that had been brought in for inspection that were blocking the path, referred to the girls as horses, and in general showed much resentment of them. I am always struck by the injustice of this attitude, since no girl here is a prostitute of her own accord, but is sold by her parents. The couple who tend the Inari shrine are much more friendly toward them, but of course they depend on the donations the girls leave there. [Smith and Wiswell 1982:142-143; brackets in original].

Some of the complexities of this situation are summed up in the following humorous poem (Asō 1976:27):

Wearing a very sour look
The wife goes to pray
At the syphilis-curing Inari

(Kasamori e nyōbō butchōzura de iki)

Kasamori Inari in Tokyo became famous for miraculous cures of this disease. At the Kasamori Inari subshrine in Kuzumi Jinja in Izu, a custom developed that incorporated notions of tricking the fox into syphilis-curing prayers. Syphilis-curing *kami* were ususally petitioned with red dumplings, but here the *kami* was offered mud dumplings *(tsuchi no dango)*— to be replaced by red dumplings *(akai dango)* if the cure was effective (Kimura 1986:222–223). A humorous poem (Asō 1976:27) shows that Inari has been elided with the fox and that humans try to trick the fox in this custom:

> With mudpies
> Inari is also
> Tricked by humans
>
> *(Tsuchi dango Inari mo hito ni bakasareru)*

Foxes, Jewels, and Fire

The fox's jewel may be more than luminous—it may be fiery. In China it is described as a "fiery ball" (Krappe 1944:125) or a small red firelike ball surrounded by light-blue flames moving up and down in the air (Li 1948:6). In an 1811 Japanese text it is a "fiery ball flying though a window" (De Visser 1914:93). Foxes were also associated with unusual meteorological lights, as well, and as early as 637 a meteor accompanied by loud thunder was explained as being the howlings of the Celestial Fox *(ama-gitsune)* (Matsunaga 1969:257; Aston 1972, II:167).[32] The fox was connected with meteors in China, probably because both have long tails (Matsunaga 1969: 257). Sometimes elided with the fox's jewel is fox fire, or *kitsune-bi*. This appellation is given to will-o'-the-wisp fires or lights that mysteriously appear at night, often in a line. Rain does not extinguish *kitsune-bi*; in fact, sightings often occur in the rain (Nozaki 1961:129 and 190f). A Shizuoka writer actually saw such a ghostly procession of lights in his youth. He describes a line of reddish lights moving faster than a walking pace along Mikan Mountain. There was no road there, and the lights had to pass between the trunks and leaves of the orange trees, but strangely the trees did not seem to block the lights, for they never flickered at all. He lived in a small village, and says he surely would have known if a group of people were out walking at night (Suzuki 1982:199). A row of lights is sometimes called a foxes' wedding *(kitsune no yomeiri)* or a lantern parade.[33]

Just how the fox produces this fire is a matter of varied opinion. As we have seen, it may come from the fiery pearl. Some traditions say the light is a torch made of horse or cow bones, or horse hoofs (De Visser 1908a:104; Suzuki 1982:198). A Chinese idea sugests that fire comes from the tip of the fox's tail, either by stroking it or striking it on the ground (De Visser 1914:74; Watters 1874:49). This method is graphically illustrated in the twelfth-century *Chōjū giga* animal scroll by Priest Toba of the Kōzanji Temple. In this humorous parody of court life, all manner of animals walk on two legs and wear Japanese dress, and the fox uses his fire-producing skill to make a signal for an archery contest.[34] Examples of this belief at the popular level do not seem to exist (Suzuki 1982:198), however, so perhaps it was a Chinese idea that was known to the educated but never gained popular currency. Alternatively, fox fire was thought to come from the mouth of the fox, another notion with Chinese antecedents (Watters 1874:49). A 1756 tradition describing the lights as a foxes' wedding at night attributed the light to the expelled breath of the foxes (Suzuki 1982:198). A variation on fiery breath is the idea in Wakayama that fox fire is actually the shining drool *(yodare)* of the fox (Suzuki 1982:198).[35] De Visser wonders if the notion of fox-emitted light originally derived from the "glare of their eyes in the darkness" (1914:93). This is one of the striking features of real foxes that can have a startling effect. Macdonald caught his first fox for a radio-tracking experiment at about 8 P.M. and describes the "burning yellow eyes that stopped me in my tracks—eyes, the like of which I've seldom seen since." After he attached the collar, the fox ran off but turned and looked back from forty yards away, "his remarkable eyes burning back along the torchbeam" (1987:22). In the photograph on the facing page in Macdonald's text, the fox's eyes reflecting the camera flash look like two shiny gold coins.[36]

Foxes are not the only creatures in Japan that produce ghostly fire. Other varieties include light produced by spiders, sea bream, and octopuses, fireballs that are the vital spirit of large old trees, fire of weasels *(itachi)* and night herons *(goisagi)*—and the souls of dead people described earlier (De Visser 1914:75–78). After fox fire, the most culturally embellished varieties were the fires of badgers, *tengu,* and sea dragons. Ghostly fire exists in Korea, but it is not associated with foxes at all.[37]

A number of traditions in both China and Japan elaborate the connection between foxes and fire. The Ōji Inari Shrine in Tokyo is famous for the fox fire visible there on the last day of the year when all the foxes in that area gather together, and it is also well known as a fire-prevention shrine (Koizuka 1982:126). Hiroshige's famous woodblock of this shrine shows dozens of ghostly foxes and their flames under a large tree (Fukuda 1975:34). The fox fire visible here had another benefit too: the lights foretold the productivity of the following year's rice season—the more lights, the better the crop (De Visser 1908a:153; Nozaki 1961:207). Certain fox barks warn people of fire throughout Japan (Suzuki 1982:196); a fox named Ohana saved Daitsūji Temple in Nagahama from a major conflagration and people still offer her spirit fried tofu in gratitude.[38] In a seance before the Hayama Ritual in 1957, a number of different deities possessed the medium; when Byakko Inari (White Fox Inari) came, he was asked about fires, and told the villagers where two would break out (Blacker 1975:259). And in an 1144 diary, the remarkable protection against fire enjoyed by a certain house, even though fires occurred in the surrounding houses, was attributed to the spirit foxes living there because of the presence of a shrine (De Visser 1908a:36-37).

When foxes effect revenge, it may be in the form of fire. We noted earlier that after a samurai wounded a fox, it dragged itself to his house and set it on fire in retaliation in the *Uji shūi monogatari* (3.20) (Mills 1970:218; *NKBT* 27:152). Part of the bureaucratization of Shinto in the Meiji period involved the centralization and merger of all the small shrines in the same area. In 1906, Tōkame Inari in Tanashi (Tokyo) was forced to relocate within the Tanashi Shrine. Around 1937, after an old woman in the area began having dreams in which Inari appeared, there was a fire late at night at a factory near the shrine. As the firemen ran toward the factory carrying their lanterns on long poles, they saw a number of small lights going in the other direction without a sound. People said these were the foxes fleeing the fire and returning to the site of their original shrine. Even though it was three decades later, the local people decided that the fire was retribution for having moved the shrine, and so they rebuilt it in its original location (Miyata 1988:134-135).

Foxes are said to hate smoke and sulfur. The first is used to drive out real and spirit foxes, while carrying matches is said to protect one against the tricks of a fox (Suzuki 1982:193). Fire, foxes, and blacksmithing all come together in the Heian-period story *Kokaji,* a Nō play written in the fourteenth century. Cloistered Emperor Ichijō (r. 986-1011) commanded Munechika, the blacksmith of Sanjō Street, to forge him a sword. Worried because he had no assistant, Munechika prayed at the Inari shrine, where a young male attendant *(dōji)* appeared and offered his assistance. When the sword was completed, he inscribed Munechika's name on the front and "The Little Fox" (Kogitsune-maru) on the back (Iwai 1983:293; Fushimi 1954:55–56; Kusano 1953:109–114)—for it was a divine fox attendant of Inari that took human shape and helped the blacksmith. All this resonates with the Chinese alchemical tradition, noted earlier, that the fox's jewel could transform base metal into silver (Krappe 1944:125).

The fox is associated with fire and light in other cultural traditions as well. "Eerie phosphorescent light (as of decaying wood)" is called "fox fire" in English (*Webster's Tenth New Collegiate Dictionary,* 1993); in Finnish mythology, the aurora borealis is called "fox light" (Ball 1927: 139); in the Bible, Samson ties torches to three hundred fox's tails; Ovid describes incendiary foxes in *Fasti,* iv.705 (Gubernatis 1872:138). There are several reasons why people in different cultures may have linked the fox with fire. Seen in the right light, the fox's eyes do seem to burn or glow. The red fox is described as "flame colored" by Henry (1986:57). And when I have watched films of foxes running through fields at dusk, the white tip of their tail is far more visible than their reddish fur, and it actually looks like flames or jewels bobbing along. Although fox zoologist David Macdonald told me that the events at his first fox sighting at age twelve were nothing more than coincidence, I remain unpersuaded:

A friend of my father's had lured a fox into taking scraps of food from his garden. So, when my parents went to a cocktail party at his house, I, too, was invited to see the fox. At length, the lights were dimmed and some food thrown out for the fox. Minutes passed and feet began to shuffle, clearly not all the gathered assembly felt the same enthusiasm for this vigil as I did. Then the fox came. For five or ten seconds a fleeting shadow moved eerily about the garden. Its sudden departure was heralded by a surprisingly loud hissing noise as a box of matches in my father's trouser pocket burst into spontaneous combustion. The ensuing dowsing of the flames with a soda-water siphon emblazoned the already momentous occasion all the more vividly in my memory. [Macdonald 1987:14–15].

The Jewels of Inari's Foxes

Another type of fox jewel is made of fox fur *(kitsune no kedama).* A white ball of fuzz was enshrined in a small wooden box as a fur jewel at Toyokawa Inari. It was said to have been sighted floating down a river by a woman in the Meiji period. When she realized what it was, she retrieved it and worshiped it in her home Inari shrine. One of the "Seven Mysteries" of Toyokawa Inari is a pure white fox fur ball. It is said to be a large, round ball, about six inches in diameter, of white fur collected by a priest from the area of the fox mound (Kitsune-zuka). Usually fur balls lie still, but this one is said to stir up twice a day (Matsuyama 1990).[39] One of the shrine carpenters at Fushimi told me the following story about a fur jewel in Shinshu. Someone painstakingly collected the bits of hair left by foxes on the shrubbery as they followed the same path. When it was the right size, this person gave it to the owner of an inn who was known as a devout follower of Inari. Somehow he lost the ball, but one day, mysteriously, it appeared sitting on top of a foot of snow. His carpenter friend urged him to take care of it properly, and he began to do so. The innkeeper also put out fried tofu for the foxes who lived in that area on the fifteenth of every month. Three years prior to telling me about it, the carpenter had the chance to hold the fur jewel in his hand. He reported that it was light and fluffy like goose down, but warm to the touch.

Representations of Inari's assistant foxes usually occur in pairs, a male and a female. The wish-fulfilling jewel is almost always included in the representation: sitting on the foxes' heads, under a paw, or, most commonly, held in the mouth of one of the foxes. The other fox frequently holds a symbolic object in its mouth—most often a key, but also a scroll or sheaf of rice. Of these, the jewel has had the longest association with the fox, and there are continental antecedents and resonances with the dragon's jewel (Komatsu 1990:53).[40] One priestly interpretation given to the jewel and key is that the jewel represents spiritual or material treasure and the key signifies the access to these treasures (Fushimi 1969:19). A woman who practiced fortune-telling from a small booth within the Fushimi Inari Shrine grounds on weekends described her understanding this way: "The jewel is the treasure, the gift from Inari for which you pray, but you yourself must unlock the place in which it is stored. The deity does not simply grant all prayers; the petitioner too must make efforts to bring about the desired result." The key and jewel are sometimes seen as fertility symbols: in this case the jewel is the "treasure of children" and the key "opens the storehouse of the treasure of children" (Iwai 1983:296; Casal 1959:47). These symbols may relate more broadly to the fertility of rice, especially when the "phallic" object is a rice sheaf *(inaho)*. In many Dakiniten depictions, the female figure riding the fox holds the key and jewel. (In place of the key may be a scroll or sword.) A colored scroll picture from the temple Kōseiji on White Fox Mountain shows a jewel and sword in the hands of the Dakiniten, a sheaf of rice in the mouth of her fox mount, and a jewel and key in the mouths of the two white foxes attending her. Jewels also decorate the tips of the three fox tails and Dakiniten's crown.[41]

The fox's scroll has an ancient Chinese association, for in the twelfth century B.C.E., during the Chou dynasty, a Celestial Fox appeared with a book of knowledge in its mouth. After this followed the submission of the eastern barbarians to the central government, so it was regarded as a very good sign (Ball 1927:135). At the Nichiren Saijō Inari, the scroll is interpreted as being the *Lotus Sutra,* their central text. It was otherwise said to be the teachings of the *kami* or the secrets for human happiness. Gorai gives a highly imaginative although rather gruesome suggestion for the scroll and jewel symbols held by Dakiniten's foxes: he thinks that the scroll describes the recipe for Dakiniten sorcery, and the jewel represents the heart which Dakiniten comes to devour six months before the victim's death. But he adds that the jewel symbol also resonates with the name of the Shinto version of Inari—Uganomi*tama*—and so Buddhist and Shinto meanings come together in the jewel of the Inari fox (Gorai 1985:103).

The Buddhist *nyoi hōju* almost certainly found its way into Fushimi Inari iconography through Shingon Buddhist influences.[42] There were similarities in the native ideas, however, which made for rich, multilayered symbolism. The three jewels refer not only to the Three Treasures of Buddhism, but also the three peaks of Inari Mountain, each of which housed a deity. Shinto *kami* are often called *"mitama,"* a homophone for "three jewels." A number of classical poems in *waka* form refer to the three lights of Inari and call to mind the other meanings of three treasures, *kami,* and mountains. For example:

> My shining on people's prayers to me
> Remains in this world
> In the three lights[43]

The most famous poem containing this image is probably the one written by the Emperor Godaigo, part of the *Yoshino shūi* anthology, in which he asks Inari to lend him the three lights because he is lost in the dark near the Inari shrine (Fushimi 1985:12). Lamps, jewels, *kami,* and even foxes converge in the "three lights" of Inari. For in the endless punning that occurs in Japanese, the name Sanko Inari can be written as "three lights" or "three foxes."[44]

Wooden fox statue with traveler's hat. Hole in belly contains mirror and tiny male and female human forms. (Author's collection.)

Balancing Oppositions

Although the fox symbol is not addressed or manipulated during an Inari ritual, it is almost always present on the altar, facing the priests and worshipers. It greets the devotee's every visit to an Inari shrine and looks down on him from the home shrine. Its importance was downplayed by most priests, however, some of whom were seriously concerned that I was getting a distorted picture of Inari practices and beliefs by focusing too much on the fox. I remain firmly convinced of the central importance of this very concrete but undogmatized symbol. Its meanings for people vary, and have varied over the years, and this is part of its strength:

> Religious symbols in general have to be perpetually re-interpreted, and in a living religion there are always dangers of petrification and reforms which rise up in an endeavour to rebuild the original conception and translate into something more modern and adapted to the needs of a new historical period. You have the same thing in an individual, for even if you have a very deep experience, this may wear out; the truth of yesterday is no longer the truth of today, and what was once a supporting ideal becomes a wornout system which

prevents further inner development. In such a case the truth of yes-
terday must be set aside for what is *now* the truth of one's own
psychic life. [Von Franz 1980:85]

Because there is no defining narrative about the fox in Inari worship—but,
instead, a multiplicity of local stories and varieties of meanings that change
emphasis over the years—and because the fox itself as shape-shifter embodies change and variation, the symbol has neither ossified nor lost any
"original" meaning of the fox. One reason the fox and jewel symbols have
had such power and longevity in Japanese culture is that they contain a
number of oppositions held in creative tension. They are specific in symbolizing certain basic oppositions but flexible enough to take on new concerns in different eras or for different people. For the majority of people,
these meanings are neither articulated nor even necessarily conscious. And
this is why they are still so powerful: they are alive and functioning. I
suggest that the fox and jewel function, at one level at least, as a symbol
of wholeness in Japan. This kind of symbol contains a number of opposing
qualities in equilibrium and functions as a model for maintaining healthy
balance and conscious awareness of elements one may have trouble accept-
ing as belonging to one's own personality or culture.

Spirit foxes can cross the boundary from their world to ours, but we
cannot join them in theirs.[45] Unlike tales of journeys to the dragon's undersea palace, I know of no story in which a human goes into a fox hole
and sees its treasures. Foxes may bring messages or gifts from the other
side, marry humans, even have children by them, but when they are discovered to be foxes, they always return to "the forest." Many stories
describe foxes imitating humans, but in an eighteenth-century text, when
a man imitates a fox by jumping over a row of torii, he falls into the hell
of animals (De Visser 1908a:62). This shows that the fox is not of our
world, although it visits us, and that it occupies a sacred space to which
we have no direct access. Depending on one's attitude toward one's own
foxlike parts, the manifestation of a fox within a human body (in "fox
possession") may be perceived as an oracular and beneficial arrival of the
sacred or a terrifying sacrifice of the personal ego: a fox gift or a fox trick.
Unlike most Western cultural interpretations of the fox which are pre-
dominately negative, the Japanese cultural elaborations, as we have seen,
are balanced between the positive and the negative.[46] No negative fox
image is without a corresponding positive one: they are canny and sly, but
also cautious and intelligent; they are uncanny and eerie, but also sacred

and beyond rational knowledge. This balance seems to have been present from the earliest records of foxes in Japan.

Like the fox, the jewel too contains a number of oppositions. The jewel represents both spiritual and material treasures: it is soul as well as wealth. It represents the gestating womb, but magic jewels may also delay birth. Jewels bring forth wonderful riches for the person pure of heart, but tales describe the avaricious neighbor who sees these blessings and, with a heart full of greed, plants the same seed or asks the same magic animal for the jewel, only to find toads, spiders, and centipedes inside his jewel. The pearl hidden in the depths of the earth or sea relates to the moon and tides; the flaming jewel flies through the skies and generates its own light. They symbolize the highest religious aspirations both in the cessation of desire and in the granting of desires. Jewels as soul bestow life and also can suck it away. They animate the body while it is alive, hover above it during serious illness, and fly away when it dies.

Related to the jewel is the fox hole. Fox holes were the actual dens in which foxes lived, sometimes the inner chambers of *kofun* tombs, which were often worshiped as Inari shrines. There was a belief in the Edo period that all fox holes in Japan lead via a subterranean passage to the sacred Inari Mountain in Kyoto. When *fukugami* (lucky *kami*) beliefs entered Inari worship, the holes were seen as treasure troves deep in the earth. So these holes were seen as paths to a sacred space, repositories of treasure, but impossible for humans to enter. The treasure could be obtained by a relation with the guardian foxes, but not directly retrieved. The fox hole has meanings relating to both womb and tomb. It was the place where foxes gave birth to their young and, when they lived in graves,[47] where people were buried. It is a jewellike space that encompasses the fox and its treasures. The fox hole symbolizes birth, death, and spiritual rebirth.

The round and cylindrical objects held in the mouths of the guardian fox statues represent the male and female generative organs but also, more abstractly, the qualities these symbols suggest. Necessary to psychological balance, regardless of one's gender, are what may be called "the phallic" and "the yonic." If the sexual terms are too gender-specific, these two may also be thought of as yin/yang, but I use phallic and yonic because these are the forms the symbols and their cultural stories suggest. The phallic is not limited to males and the yonic to females: these are two modes of being that are found, in some combination, in persons of all genders. That the phallic and yonic are to be taken metaphorically rather than literally is indicated by their symbolic rendering. Rather than simply depicting the genitals on fox statues, we see jewels and keys held ostenta-tiously in the foxes' mouths. In the hundreds, perhaps even thousands, of fox images I saw in Japan, only once did I ever find the genitals carved in the appropriate place on the fox pair. In some cases, sex was indicated genitally on the male fox but not on the female statue. The phallic in-volves such activities as springing into action, moving, crossing bound-aries; it is active, social, connecting; it may be aggressive.[48] The yonic is contained, nurturing, gestating energy; it is solitary and spontaneous. Phallic energy breaks out; yonic energy contains. Clearly both of these modes are necessary to a balanced human life. The fox and jewel symbols emphasize this balance by reiterating it in several ways. Fox statues occur in pairs of male and female. At the tip of the ithyphallic fox's tail rests the jewel, and in their mouths are the jewel and key. They may be en-closed within the jewellike space of a fox hole, guarding the developing treasure of more jewels.

This layer of meaning has deep cultural roots in Buddhist esotericism, influential in the early days of Inari's development. Shingon teachings use sexual symbols to configure nonduality, and the jewel and key (or scroll or rice sheaf) held by the attendant foxes most probably derived from Shingon doctrines. The two mandalas used by Shingon picture the Womb World (Taizōkai) and the *Vajra* World (Kongōkai). The womb and the *vajra* (thunderbolt) symbolize compassion and wisdom, respectively, and the two mandalas are said to signify the contrast between such concepts as centrip-etal and centrifugal force, nurturing and actively doing, and harmony and development (Yamasaki 1988:149). Ritual offerings to the Shingon deity Kangiten include Japanese radishes (daikon) and "bliss buns" *(kangi-dan)* (Sanford 1991a:312).[49] Japanese radishes are unmistakably phallic; the yonic bliss buns strikingly resemble a wish-fulfilling jewel in pastry form;[50] this is reiterated in the jewel and sword sometimes held in the figure's hands. Shingon rituals to Aizen Myōō were sometimes "highly eroticized" (Sanford 1997:8), and the temple within Fushimi Inari, Aizenji, enshrined this deity. Although the present-day Fushimi materials do not emphasize the Buddhist meanings, one publication does describe the jewel and key as "like yin and yang, heaven and earth. From the workings of these two come all things, all change" (Fushimi 1969:19).

This layer of meaning may not be consciously perceived by many worshipers of Inari, but it has a powerful impact on the senses when one undertakes a circumambulation of Inari Mountain at Fushimi. Following a stone-paved path and stairs up the mountain and around the three peaks near the top, with continual walking, takes about one hour, but with stops to pray at various subshrines and rock altars, the circuit takes at least two hours. The route alternates between portions that are covered by tunnels—formed of closely set up torii sacred gates—and areas open to the sky. The red womblike tunnels provide a warm comforting feeling and keep the dark forest at bay. Then suddenly the torii thin out or end completely for a distance—opening onto space containing dark, mysterious clusters of rock altars built onto the high, steep sides of the path. The tall cedar trees and rock altars seem to surge upward, pulling the pilgrim's attention up from the path; the stone foxes glare fiercely from their pedestals, their tails pointing skyward. Movement within the tunnels feels horizontal, even when one is climbing stairs, for the sky is not visible. On the open path, the verticals dominate and one feels free but simultaneously exposed and vulnerable. These two modes alternate on the path as the tunnel sections open into the altar clusters in the forest. Even if the meanings of this alternation are never conceptualized in so many words, the visceral impact of passing through blood red tunnels—then suddenly emerging into an exposed space full of upward-thrusting clusters of rocks and trees—is almost inexpressibly powerful. To me the symbolism of the mountain path echoes that of the fox and the jewel, reminding the pilgrim that on the path of life there is a need for both deliberate (foxlike) action as well as patience for the things that grow (jewellike) without direct conscious intervention. This is not simply action versus passivity, but two complementary kinds of activity. For example, the way an ascetic gains spiritual power in Japan is by quiet contemplation, usually within a cave, in addition to vigorous activity such as pilgrimage and the waterfall austerity.

One day during my second year of fieldwork, I was poking around the dusty shelves of a souvenir shop in Toyokawa and came upon a wooden fox statue in the mode of the turned wooden dolls *(kokeshi)*. I thought it quite peculiar, but bought it anyway for my collection of fox representations. The more I looked at it, however, the more I came to see that it contained an even greater elaboration of the symbolism I have been describing here than most fox statues. This fox consists of two joined parts: a phallic-shaped body and a jewel-shaped head, turned on its side. The erect tail and the round hat, painted with a flaming jewel design, form another pair of symbolic oppositions. Most curious of all, this statue contains its own fox hole: a round opening cut into the belly of the fox. The inside walls of the hole are painted red; at the back of the hole is a mirror; in front of that is a stand with a tiny male and tiny female figure on it. Standing of equal height, the tiny female is dressed in red, the male in blue. The mirror in Japan represents the soul, something one tries to keep bright and polished, without clouds or dust. This fox takes its form from phallic and yonic shapes, reiterated in the tail and hat. In its womb, it is generating an image of the soul, which consists of a balanced pair of opposites expressed as male and female. The broad hat indicates that this fox is on a journey, so it is actively moving in the world, but it is also pregnant with a spiritual treasure, which is constantly growing and changing within. In this figure of the fox and the jewel, I find the image of dynamic wholeness that I think has served as an "internally persuasive" (Bakhtin 1981) symbol, albeit unconsciously, for the countless numbers of people who have worshiped Inari over the centuries and continue to do so today.

5

A God of One's Own:
Individualizing Inari

Certain statements about human nature become, as it were, common property, and so are accepted as self-evident. In the same way painters for ages painted shadows black, and it was not till the impressionists looked at them with unprejudiced eyes and painted what they saw that we discovered that shadows were coloured.

—W. Somerset Maugham, "A Man with a
Conscience," *Collected Short Stories*, vol. 4

In the same way that artistic conventions shape how we see and speech genres determine how we talk, internal assumptions about the way societies and cultures function—I call them dominant cultural representations—compel us to construe cultural forms in certain ways.[1] These ways of seeing, speaking, and conceptualizing one's world vary, often greatly, between cultures and include a range of possibilities within a given culture. Social facts that do not fit these patterns are, in terms of the dominant cultural representations, unseen or invisible, unarticulated or silent, even deliberately hidden and denied. But this does not mean they do not exist.

The Hidden Diversity of Inari

Most studies on Japanese religion to date have emphasized shared forms—the level of meaning that everyone agrees on to some extent—and it has been important to document these forms. But perhaps because of strong

and pervasive rhetorics of cultural unity in Japan, the detailed diversity has
not been studied so industriously, and therefore the situation within Inari
worship may come as a surprise. In this chapter we will see that one of the
most important features of Inari worship is its high degree of diversification
and even individualization of the deity.[2] Devotees do not simply worship
"Inari," but a separate form of Inari with its own name. Inari shrines
worship entirely different *kami* as Inari; traditions and symbols have a
multiplicity of meanings.

This feature of Japanese religiosity is particularly well developed in Inari
worship, but it can also be found in the worship of other Japanese *kami*
and buddhas. Robert J. Smith (1974:50) analyzed "this kind of microvaria-
tion in belief and practice" in ancestor worship. In his study of the Shikoku
pilgrimage, Reader finds that pilgrims develop a personal relationship with
Kōbō Daishi, "one that makes the pilgrimage an intensely individual affair
even when the pilgrim is traveling in a large group" (1993a:111). The image
of Bodhidharma has been adapted in various ways; McFarland says, "the
people have seen him as their own" (1987:115). Nelson argues that this is
a characteristic of Shinto in general: "shrine Shinto's *lack* of centralized
dogma, charismatic leaders, and sacred texts serves to promote rather than
hinder a broad-based public participation as well as to foster ties to business
and government" (1993:5). I argue that Inari goes even further, however,
because devotees are not merely interpreting the traditions in subjective
ways but, are quite actively changing them. Because of the considerable
shamanic component within Inari worship, new traditions easily come into
being as direct commands of Inari. This fact alone undercuts much of the
authority the priests try to claim. Moreover, it allows Inari to develop in
almost infinitely diverse ways, as people worship their own individualized
or personalized version of the *kami*. In this chapter I show the astonishing
degree to which Inari is individualized in both name and function. After
indicating how these functions relate more to personal religious concerns
than to social or group issues, I suggest that the fox as the main symbol of
Inari reinforces this emphasis on the personal as a balance to communal
forms of religion in Japan.

Deities Worshiped as Inari

Inari was first venerated as three deities (perhaps because of the three peaks
of the sacred mountain), a number that increased to five during the Kamakura period (1185–1392). But traditional identification of those three or
five *kami* has varied enormously, even within Fushimi Inari Shrine itself,

Four representations of Inari. From top left, clockwise: (1) Nonanthro-
pomorphic representation of Inari showing bamboo curtain, the name
"Uganomitama no Kami" surrounded by the shrine stamp, cedar
boughs and sickles, three jewels in a bowl, two snakes in rice bales with
cedar and a key in mouths (sometimes seen as silkworms and cocoons),
white and black foxes. Probably dating from the Edo period, distributed
by the Fushimi Inari Shrine. (2) Inari as fox carrying rice and sickle,
from Inari subshrine within Miyajidake Shrine, Munakata-gun, Fukuoka
prefecture. (3) Dakiniten, the main Buddhist representation of Inari, a
bodhisattva astride a white flying fox, carrying rice sheaves and a jewel.
(Scroll from Toyokawa Inari.) (4) Inari as old man carrying rice and
sickle with two attendant foxes under the names of the *kami* enshrined
at Fushimi as Inari. (Scroll painting in author's collection.)

where the names were not standardized until the government intervention during the early Meiji period. Identifying Inari with the food goddess from the classical mythologies at once created a proliferation of names because this *kami* had different names in the myths. Common to all the names is the word for food: *uga* (or *uke*) or *ketsu* (or *getsu*): Miketsu Ōkami, Ōgetsu Hime no Kami, Ukemochi no Kami, Toyouke no Kami, Toyouke Hime no Kami, Ukanomitama no Kami (or Uganomitama). Most Inari shrines today in the Shinto lineage describe at least one of the enshrined *kami* as one of those just listed. The central *kami* of the five at Fushimi Inari is Uganomitama no Ōkami. Some scholars hold that these are different names for the same basic food deity; others insist that these names represent unique *kami*—otherwise they would not have separate names. The several names may also represent various local traditions that coexisted rather than blending into one figure.

In addition to these manifestations of the food goddess, Inari has been identified as other *kami* as well. Names that occurred in Fushimi Inari shrine records in the various priestly lineages over the centuries include Waka-ukanomitama no Mikoto, Wakumusubi no Kami, Shinatōbe no Mikoto, Ninigi no Mikoto, Izanagi no Mikoto, Izanami no Mikoto, and Ōnamuchi no Mikoto (Fushimi 1969:7). In other records Inari was identified as still different *kami*: Susanoo no Mikoto, Ōichi Hime, Ōyamatsume, Ōta no Mikoto, Amanomihiko, Ōmiya Hime, Sarutahiko no Ōkami, Dōsojin, Takakōmusubi no Mikoto, and Kaminomusubi no Mikoto (Fushimi 1969:7).

Buddhist deities thought to be the original forms *(honji butsu)* of Inari were also worshiped at the Inari shrine. Considering the many different *kami* that were worshipped as Inari, it is no surprise that there were also several systems of associated buddhas. The following system of correspondence was recorded in the Muromachi period (1392–1568):

> Lower Inari Shrine: Nyoirin Kannon
> Middle Inari Shrine: Thousand-Armed Kannon
> Upper Inari Shrine: Eleven-Headed Kannon
> Tanaka Shrine: Fudō Myōō
> Four Great *Kami (Shi no Ōkami)*: Bishamonten
> Myōbu Shrine
>> Akomachi (female fox): Monjū

Osusume (male fox): Fugen

Kuroo (male fox): Miroku (Maitreya)

An Edo-period (1600–1868) tradition is completely different (Fushimi 1958:105):

Lower Shrine: Shaka Nyorai

Middle Shrine: Amida Nyorai

Upper Shrine: Yakushi Nyorai

Other buddhas mentioned as original forms of Inari in different shrine traditions include Kyakujin Zenji, Jizō, Kokūzō (Fushimi 1969:60), and Fudō Myōō (Fushimi 1976:69–70). And the Shingon priests at Aizenji Temple (within the Inari shrine) viewed the original Buddhist forms as the following (Ueda and Tsubohara 1984:27):

Lower Shrine: Dakiniten

Middle Shrine: Benzaiten

Upper Shrine: Shōten (or Kangiten)

This tradition, referred to as *Santen* (three devas), is most likely very old and probably was a continuous transmission from at least the time of Kūkai's description of the assistant of Inari as a combination of Dakiniten, Kangiten, and Benzaiten. Currently the *kami* worshiped as Inari at Fushimi are: Uganomitama no Ōkami, Sadahiko no Ōkami, Omiyanome no Ōkami, Tanaka no Ōkami, and Shi no Ōkami.

Regional Variations

Even an ostensibly nationwide tradition such as the Three Great Inari Shrines of Japan (Nihon no sandai Inari) takes on local variations. This list usually includes Fushimi Inari and Toyokawa Inari, but the third shrine depends on who is speaking: usually it is the largest Inari shrine from that person's region. Thus people in Kyushu include Yūtoku Inari in Saga whereas those in the north say, on the contrary, that the third shrine is Takekoma Inari in Miyagi. Kanto people may include Kasama Inari (Ibaragi), while Kansai tradition often holds the third to be Saijō Inari (Okayama). A shaman who did austerities on Inari Mountain in Kyoto told me that the eastern tradition included Fushimi, Takekoma, and Kasama; people from western Japan usually list Fushimi, Saijō, and Toyokawa.

This tradition of the top three (or five: *godai Inari*) Inari shrines is a popular one that is sometimes denounced by the clergy. Some priests at Fushimi thought the notion was ridiculous. One said if anyone asked him which shrines were included in the *sandai Inari,* he would not answer. (The priests who disliked this tradition tended also not to approve of the high degree of individualization of the Inari deity itself.) Sometimes, lesser-known Inari shrines claim a place in the Big Three or Big Five to increase their stature. A Taikodani Inari pamphlet includes itself in the Big Five along with Fushimi, Kasama, Yūtoku, and Takekoma (Taikodani, n.d.). This tradition excludes the two large Buddhist Inari, one of which is located fairly close by. So in addition to regional variation, there is sometimes concern with sectarian consistency.

The tradition of having three *kami (Inari sanza)* or five *kami (Inari goza)* is found at many Inari shrines besides Fushimi Inari, but the sets of deities are not constant.[3] For example, the Inari of Five Happinesses (Inari Gokō Daimyōjin) enshrined at Tamatsukuri Inari Shrine in Osaka begins with Uganomitama no Ōkami (a food goddess; the *kami* most often worshiped as Inari today). But the next four are totally different from those of the Fushimi lineage: Shitateru Hime no Mikoto (daughter of Ōkuninushi), Wakahirume no Mikoto (said to be the younger sister of the sun goddess), Tsukiyomi no Mikoto (the moon *kami*), and Kagutsuchi no Mikoto (*kami* of fire) (Suzuki 1988:33–34).

At Takekoma Inari in Miyagi, the second-oldest Inari shrine in Japan, the three deities enshrined are Ugamitama no Kami, Ukemochi no Kami (two food *kami*), and Wakumusubi no Kami (Takekoma Inari Jinja, n.d.). Hanazono Jinja in Shinjuku enshrines the expected food deities Ukanomitama no Kami and Ukemochi no Kami, but the third deity is Yamato Takeru no Mikoto, a legendary hero (Hanazono Jinja Shamusho 1971:1).[4] A private shrine on Inari Mountain in Kyoto called Araki Ōkami worships three forms of the Inari deity, but three forms not found in shrine tradition. They are Araki Ōkami (Rough Tree Great Deity), Aratama Ōkami (Rough Jewel Great Deity), and Shirasuna Ōkami (White Sand Great Deity). As we shall see, these are individual forms of Inari in the *otsuka* tradition and have no connection to the official Shinto mythology contained in the classics. Thus the outward form of three or five *kami* enshrined together as Inari is fairly widespread, but the content varies considerably from shrine to shrine.

The Notion of "My Inari"

The concept of individual Inaris does not derive from my own observations only; it was mentioned by many informants involved with Inari worship and is thus a "native term." Priests at both the Shinto and Buddhist centers where I did my fieldwork described this feature of Inari worship to me and held varying opinions about whether it was a legitimate form of worship or not. Even the ones who disapproved of it did not deny it was a key fact of Inari worship. A Shinto priest thought the impulse to worship "my own Inari" *(watashi no Inari sama)* developed around the late Edo period and accounted for the great spread of Inari shrines at that time. He could not think of any other Shinto *kami* to whom people felt such an intimate connection—and that could be individualized to this degree.[5] Another priest at Fushimi said, "If there are one hundred worshipers, they will have one hundred different ideas about Inari" *(hyakunin hyakuyo)*. A Catholic woman at a lay worship group's Inari ritual in the countryside asked the priest who had come from Fushimi Inari Shrine to describe Inari in a sentence. He replied: "Inari gives blessings to each person in an appropriate and personalized way." Still another Fushimi Inari priest expressed the same idea: "Inari is a different *kami* to each devotee, shaped by what each person brings of his own character, how he understands the world." When I got to Toyokawa Inari, I found much the same sentiment expressed by the Zen priests there. There, too, people often worshiped Dakiniten as a form of Inari with a unique name. A priest at the branch temple in Tokyo told me: "Like the six Jizōs *(roku Jizō),*[6] different Inaris listen to different people's prayers."

The *Kanjō* System

Kanjō is the technical term for the reenshrinement of a *kami's* divided spirit *(wakemitama, bunrei).*[7] The original *kami* remains in place in his shrine, but a portion of his spirit is ritually separated and housed in a new location. Priests explain it as something akin to lighting a new candle from a burning one: the light of the first is in no way diminished as it becomes two. In contrast to an *ofuda*—a talisman with the name of the shrine or *kami* written on it that (the priests say) must be renewed every year—the *wakemitama* is a portion of the *kami* itself and thus permanently "alive" in its new location. Inari has been divided and reenshrined with far greater ease and frequency than other Shinto *kami*. In fact, Inari is cited as the example of a much-reenshrined *kami* in the *Dictionary of Shinto*'s definition of the term *"kanjō"* (Anzu and Umeda 1968:281).

The first recorded example of Inari *kanjō* is from 842, when the official Ono no Takamura had a divided spirit of Inari placed in his scepter of office *(shaku)* and carried the deity in this way to Mutsu no Kuni (Aomori), where he served as the lord for some years. When he returned to Kyoto a few years later, the people of that region asked him to leave Inari there, and this shrine later became Takekoma Inari (Fushimi 1969: 30). Another was reenshrined in 1057 in Iwate when Minamoto Yorichika defeated Abe no Yoritoki; this later became Shiwa Inari Shrine (Fushimi 1969:30). In 1194, on his imperial pilgrimage to the Inari shrine, Emperor Gotoba decreed that only the (Fushimi) Inari Shrine could perform this ritual of division and reenshrinement and, moreover, that only it had the right to transfer Inari with its imperial rank *shōichii*. Because there were abuses of this right—sometimes the *kami* was reenshrined directly from branch or reenshrined shrines to new ones—the Fushimi shrine provided a certificate of authenticity with every divided spirit (Fushimi 1969:32; 1977: 50). The practice of unofficial reenshrinement was so widespread by the Edo period that the government sent a letter to the Fushimi shrine asking for their policy on this matter. The case that had brought this matter to their attention was that of a farmer who, finding a fox hole in his thicket, had had an Inari called Shōichii Toyokatsu Inari Daimyōjin enshrined there.[8] The reenshrinement ritual was performed by a religious specialist named Imamura from the Tsuchimikado sect of Shinto.[9] The priests at Fushimi Inari Shrine replied that Emperor Gotoba had granted them this right in 1194, that the different priestly lineages associated with the Inari shrine had secret rituals for doing the transfer that were passed down from master to disciple, and that the performance of this rite by others was a great annoyance to the shrine (Fushimi 1977:50). It is not mentioned how this particular case was resolved, but it is unlikely that the practice of reenshrining Inari from shrines other than the Fushimi shrine was slowed.

When the Fushimi Inari Shrine was nationalized in the Meiji period, the practice of *kanjō* continued for a time. The difference now was that where previously a certificate of authenticity listed the name of the priestly lineage that had done the ritual,[10] it now listed the centralized shrine itself with the high government-assigned rank of Kampei Taisha (major imperial shrine). When the government stopped the practice of *kanjō* at all shrines in Japan, the Fushimi Inari Shrine petitioned the government: not only did its income depend on this practice, it argued, but this custom had existed "from long ago" and accounted for Inari's wide dispersion throughout the country. Worshipers were clamoring for the return of the practice, the shrine contended. Ultimately the government was persuaded to let the shrine reinstate the practice—but forced the shrine to change its terminology so it would not look like only this shrine was allowed to continue the *kanjō* practice, which was actually the case. Previously the divided spirit was called a *wakemitama;* now it was called a *shinpu,* "sacred talisman."[11]

It seems that when the Inari deity was reenshrined, a new name was often assigned to it in addition to the appellation "Inari." In the Edo example cited earlier, the non-Fushimi priest reenshrined a divided spirit of Inari as Toyokatsu Inari Daimyōjin, "Abundant Success Inari Great Bright Deity," and presumably it was he who chose the new name. It seems that the name could be chosen by the deity herself—revealed through a divine dream or shamanic oracle—or it could be assigned by a priest. In many cases today, people do not know how their Inari got its name. Examples of both methods still exist. An Osaka family worships three forms of Inari in a monthly service conducted by a shamaness who comes to their home, and these names were revealed many years ago by another shamaness to the mother of the present head of household. Here the three Inaris are White Jewel, Stone Shrine, and Plum-Pine. A ninety-two-year-old Shinto priest told me that he sometimes assigned names to the Inari divided spirits he reenshrined. In this case, the naming did not involve a revelation from the deity but the selection of an auspicious and appropriate name based on the function of the new Inari. For the Inari of a prosperous Osaka company he chose Toyomitsu Inari, "Abundant Light." The "toyo" he took from the name of an Inari deity, Toyouke no Kami, as he thought the name would be conducive to business prosperity. There were other personal ideas about the reenshrined Inari deity besides the name, which can be seen in old certificates of authenticity. In addition to the devotee's name and place of residence, his own idea of the deity's character and own hopes were sometimes recorded.

Today, most of the large Inari shrines will provide a divided spirit of the Inari enshrined there. Fushimi continues to do so. In fact, it has developed a yearly festival, Motomiya Sai, in which all those people who have received a divided spirit in recent years are invited back to the shrine on July 22 and 23. In 1990, the priests mailed out 80,000 invitations to all the people they have on record who have a reenshrined Inari. These divided spirits, available to anyone without regard to income or status, are themselves sorted into nine separate ranks. The brocade-covered boxes holding the *kami*'s spirit range in height from about six inches to fourteen inches and in price from $120 to $4,000.[12] Smaller Inari shrines such as Tamatsukuri Inari Jinja in Osaka, which has one resident priest, also reenshrine the Inari deity but do so only about twenty times per year. Here there are no ranks and the price is left up to the discretion of the devotees, who tend to pay $400 to $800. At Toyokawa Inari, worshipers may receive a kind of divided spirit of Dakiniten: here it is called *goshintai* (true body)[13] or *gobunrei* (divided spirit). Devotees buy a small carved statue of Dakiniten and then participate in a ceremony to animate it *(kaigen; shō o ireru)*. There is no ranking of divided spirits at Toyokawa as there is at Fushimi, but the worshiper can buy statues of different quality ranging from $600 to $1,000. The delicately carved statue sits in a three- to four-inch-high miniature shrine with double doors, and this fits into a wooden box with a jewel-shaped hole cut into the front. Regular devotees carry these statues with them when they come to the temple for monthly or yearly prayer services, and the statues are placed on the altar during the service for that person. At the Nichiren Saijō Inari divided spirits are also available, but here one cannot add a personal name to the deity (at least officially). I saw an old statue from this shrine that did have a personal name written on the box, evidence that this was an earlier practice (or was done without the priests' knowledge).

When people reenshrine a form of the Inari deity under a separate name, it may be worshiped for a specific function. Thus the individualization of the *kami* paradoxically widened Inari's appeal, for all the new functions were taken to be specialties of the original deity.[14] Aston describes Inari's diverse functions around the turn of the century: the patron of blacksmiths and prostitutes, he was prayed to for agricultural prosperity, a faithful husband, winning at sumo, return of stolen goods, to cure colds, to avert smallpox and measles, for wealthy and quickly bored patrons for geisha, and even for a son to divorce his wife (Aston 1905:162–163). These various functions change as society changes, as industries become obsolete, as illnesses are eliminated. The protection of silkworms and mulberry, although still cited by certain shrines as a function of Inari,[15] has almost totally dropped out; the assurance of business prosperity, however, continues to increase in importance.

There are cases in which Inari was reenshrined in a home or business for some specific reason, great success followed, and the new function was thereby added to the repertoire of Inari's specialties. An example of this is fishing—certainly not one of Inari's original functions on the landlocked mountain in Kyoto. Nevertheless Inari became the patron deity of the fishing industry in certain areas, and one now finds "fishing success" listed as an official virtue *(shintoku)* of Inari back at the original mountain. Worshipers can buy an amulet *(ofuda)* for fishing satisfaction and safety at sea *(tairyo manzoku; kaijō anzen)* as one of the four basic amulets available at this shrine.[16] The functions of some reenshrined Inaris, however, may be too specific to enter the larger picture—such as the tooth-ache-curing Genkurō Inari in Osaka on Genshojizaka and even the famous cough-curing O-Seki Inari on the mountain.[17]

Otsuka shinkō: Rock Altars to Individualized Inari

Another form of individualizing Inari occurred in the latter part of the nineteenth century, just before the start of the Meiji period. This was the setting up on Inari Mountain of rock altars called *otsuka* to specific forms of the Inari deity. This custom grew slowly at first and initially was opposed by the priests. Around the seven sacred spaces *(nana shinseki)* on Inari Mountain,[18] devotees were setting up rocks with what the priests termed "strange names" carved into them. The priests' first warning that this practice was forbidden was issued in 1869 (Meiji 2), at which time they set up three signboards denouncing the custom. Seven years later they issued another order to abolish the "stones with strange names carved into them" that people continued to haul up the mountain in the dead of night in spite of the prohibition. The practice did not abate, however, and the next year, 1877, in the second month, the shrine applied to the government for permission to set up the stones. This permission was given in the fourth month. Now the practice was seen as a legitimate form of worship by the priests, who began to regulate the custom. By the year 1897 (Meiji 30), the notion of "my own Inari" *(watashi no O-Inari sama)* was firmly entrenched at Inari Mountain (Toriiminami 1988:147–148).

Although one line of thought has it that the *otsuka* phenomenon was related to the suppression of syncretism in the shrine proper, which caused it to spring up again on the dark mountain paths (Ueda and Tsubohara 1984:27), another priest has argued that the *otsuka* would have developed whether or not Buddhism had been suppressed. Toriiminami Masatoshi thinks the roots of individualism in Inari practice were already deep during the Edo period, and this was the logical development of the "my Inari" phenomenon. In either case, people's desire to have religious forms

Cluster of *otsuka* rock altars to individualized forms of Inari on Inari Mountain, Kyoto. Stone foxes flank candle holder above three flaming jewels. Devotees have left the miniature torii and tied votive bibs onto the foxes as offerings.

tailored to their particular needs was expressed over the priestly prohibitions for almost a decade and, finally, prevailed.

At present, there are some ten thousand rock altars on Inari Mountain, both inside and outside the shrine's property. The rocks usually have from one to three (and sometimes more than ten) names carved into them, so that the number of names under which Inari is worshiped on this mountain alone is several tens of thousands. Unlike the reenshrined spirits of Inari during the Edo period (such as "Abundant Success Inari"), here the individualized names do not usually include the word "Inari." Rather, following the individualized appellation (referring to the form, specialties, or locale of the deity), one finds the generic title "Ōkami" (Great Deity) or the more syncretic "Daimyōjin" (Great Bright Deity). Some of the more popular names can be found on more than one stone; others occur only once. The following is a sampling of some of the individual names for Inari (Fushimi 1965; 1966):

> Aotama Ōkami: Blue Jewel Great Deity
>
> Akagitsune Ōkami: Red Fox Great Deity[19]
>
> Ise Shi Daimyōjin: City of Ise Great Bright Deity
>
> Kyōō Daibosatsu: Sutra King Great Bodhisattva[20]
>
> Toyotaki Myōjin: Abundant Waterfall Bright Deity
>
> Sokuba Ōkami: Fast Horse Great Deity
>
> Sanshu Ōkami: Three Protections Great Deity
>
> Senshoku Ōkami: Dyeing Great Deity
>
> Ōsugi Ōkami: Great Cedar Great Deity
>
> Inazō Ōkami: Rice Storehouse Great Deity
>
> Arakuma Ōkami: Rough Bear Great Deity
>
> Sentō Ōkami: One Thousand Beans Great Deity
>
> Kurotatsu Ōkami: Black Dragon Great Deity
>
> Utahime Daimyōjin: Song Princess Great Bright Deity
>
> Shirahige Ōkami: White Beard Great Deity

In addition to these individualized versions of Inari, the names of other Shinto *kami,* Buddhist deities, and Kōbō Daishi can also be found on the stones. First-timers on the sacred mountain often express amazement at the myriads of deities worshiped here, but old-timers are comfortable with the concept and even joke about it. A woman with whom I did the mountain pilgrimage called the mountain "the department store of shrines" because any of Japan's hundreds of *kami* could conveniently be found in one location. The head priest of Fushimi Inari Shrine joked that although the old name for October is Month Without Gods (Kannazuki) (because all the *kami* are said to gather at Izumo Shrine), all the eight hundred myriads of *kami (yaoyorozu no kami)* of Japan are in residence at Inari Mountain year round (Ueda and Tsubohara 1984:27).

There are two ways to get one's own rock altar devoted to a specific form of Inari. The first is to set up a new *otsuka;* the second is to worship at an existing altar. The first course is increasingly difficult—not only because costs are prohibitive but because space to set them up is limited. Fushimi Shrine does not permit any more *otsuka* to be erected within the shrine's precincts although there is plenty of land available.[21] One parcel of land called Miyukibe was made available in the 1970s for new *otsuka,* but that area is now full. It is, however, possible to take over an old altar that is no longer being cared for or one that has fallen over. One may not use private materials or simply bring a carved stone; the work must be contracted through the shrine. (The rough cost was given as about $16,000.) It is still possible in theory to set up an altar on some of the privately owned pieces of land on the sacred mountain, which are indistinguishable from those on shrine ground, but even here there are serious land limitations, so this course may not provide a solution.

The other method of acquiring a personal rock altar is to pick one of the ten thousand or so existing altars, and use it as one's own.[22] In the largest lay worship group *(kō)* associated with Fushimi Inari, the leader consults with the *kami* and assigns a particular altar and *kami* to each member (or family) in her group. That person then requests an official divided spirit of Inari from the shrine and worships it under the name on the altar in her home as well as on the mountain. Although I saw groups waiting for others to complete their prayers, I did not witness any antagonism over sharing an *otsuka.* There are so many altars on the mountain, it is probably rare for two individuals or groups using the same *otsuka* to encounter each other.

At Saijō Inari, there are also *otsuka*-like stones called *hōtō* (literally "treasure tower"). They are the same shape as the *otsuka* and have the six characters "Praise to the Wondrous Lotus Sutra" *(namu myōhō renge kyō)* at the top center and the names of the deities carved underneath. Here the name of the deity is followed not by "Ōkami" (Great Deity) but by "tennō" (Heavenly King). This deity is not supposed to refer to Inari (as Saijōi Kyōō Daibosatsu) herself but to one of her seventy-seven assistants *(shichijū shichi massha)*. Nevertheless there is a division by function, and people make a circuit of the numerous shrines and stones, praying for different needs to the different assistants of the deity.[23] Some of the individualized versions of this Inari are:

> Arakuma Tennō: Rough Bear Heavenly King
>
> Higuruma Tennō: Sun Wheel Heavenly King
>
> Enbiki Tennō: Pulling Karma Heavenly King
>
> Daisōjō Tennō: Big Priest of Truth Heavenly King
>
> Inari Tenjin: Heavenly Deity Inari
>
> Chisui Tennō: Earth and Water Heavenly King

Some of these forms have special functions: Arakuma is an ancestral deity to whom people pray for business prosperity and passing exams; Higuruma is related to literature, Enbiki to romantic connections; Daisōjō is invoked to avert fires, Chisui to avoid senility.

Although Toyokawa Inari does not have this practice, there is at least one *otsuka*-like stone at the branch temple in Tokyo. An exception is the establishment in recent years of the Spirit Fox Mound at which people dedicate fox statues with unique forms (each fox is a little different) and their own name prominently carved on the base. The more common pattern is for the lay worship groups to donate objects to this temple, and rather than personalized objects of worship these donations tend to be utilitarian items (dishes, tables, curtains, ashtrays) marked with the name of the *kō*. It is for this reason that worship at Toyokawa, especially at the main temple, has a different quality than at most other Inari sacred centers. Unlike Fushimi, Saijō, Yūtoku, and other large Inari shrines and temples that allow for personalized worship in the setting up of rock altars, torii, and the like, at Toyokawa people can only dedicate fox statues or prayer flags that are taken down and burned every three months. Therefore, the individualized forms of worship, which serve both as expressions of particular beliefs as well as incentive or instruction about belief, do not exist at Toyokawa Inari. There the worship remains more impersonal, which gives the institution far more control over the symbols than is the case at Inari sites where personalized and popular forms are prominent.

Examples of "My Inari"

The sentiment that unifies the various narratives of people who feel a personal connection to Inari is intimacy *(shitashisa)*. This is expressed, in a kind of backdoor familiarity,[24] by worshiping at the back of an Inari shrine as well as the front. People with bad coughs do not even have to leave their homes, but send a postcard to O-Seki-san, the Inari of coughs. The post office delivers the cards to the main shrine, and priests carry them up to this Inari's mailbox on the mountain. An early poem that now appears on Sacred Oracle 24 *(omikuji)* shows the rude lengths to which this feeling of intimacy could go:

> I pound on the three sacred fences of Inari Mountain
> Beseeching the *kami* to answer my prayer

Most worshipers use nicknames for the three forms of Inari on the three peaks of the mountain. The *kami* of the Upper Shrine is known as Suehiro-sama (Mr./Ms. Prosperity; literally "wide at the end"), the Middle Shrine's deity is called Aoki-sama (Mr./Ms. Green Tree), and the Inari of the Lower Shrine is familiarly known as Shiragiku-sama (Mr./Ms. White Chrysanthemum). Multiple banners with these nicknames decorate the altars of the three peaks, and it is by these names that the deity is addressed and referred to. It is doubtful that many worshipers other than priests know the official names of the *kami* enshrined.

A woman who fervently worships at Toyokawa Inari Temple in Tokyo says: "I have worshiped Dakiniten [Inari] for ten years. When I pray to my ancestors, I feel that I must not ask for anything, but only give thanks to them. But in front of Inari, I feel I can speak frankly. I feel very close and can discuss anything. When I had to hire a new person for my business, Inari helped me to know which applicant was the best. I have a very comfortable relationship with Inari." A Toyokawa priest explains the intimacy in terms of the Buddhist hierarchy: "Inari is the deity closest to humans—it is like your own mother, it grants your wishes. In times of illness when even a doctor cannot cure you, you have no alternative but to ask Inari. Buddhas have various ranks, and Dakiniten is in the *ten* (deva) rank, which is the closest one to humans. So Inari has a very intimate relation with people." An article on this-worldly benefits of Inari beliefs gives some hints about the psychological role this intimacy may play in a culture where keeping up appearances is exceedingly important. The author suggests that even people who seem very fortunate—politicians, actresses, company presidents—have certain problems and needs they can tell to no one, but they can always turn to Inari (Koike 1976:60). Japan is a society where reciprocity and paying one's debts are taken very seriously (Benedict 1946), sometimes to the degree of not asking for help because of the debt one will incur. And this too is part of the appeal of Inari. For no matter how big a request one makes of the deity, there is no worry that one will later have to repay someone in kind (Koike 1976:64). Inari seems to strike a balance between being famous enough to give people confidence that he can help them but not so identified with a mythic or historical personality that he cannot be individualized to fit their particular problems.

The other side of this feeling of familiarity, however, is terror at his retribution. For although Inari is approachable, he is not to be taken lightly. Inari's retribution *(tatari)* is renowned for its power, and even people who do not consider themselves "religious" or "superstitious" would be loath to destroy, desecrate, or even slight an Inari shrine. One of the priests told me a story from the mountain. A rich doctor added his own stone to a rock altar on which three stones were already standing, thereby insensitively blocking the other three with the new one. Shortly thereafter, he and his whole family perished when their house burned, and people interpreted this tragedy as Inari's anger at being treated improperly. Inari's retribution was in fact the reason it received court rank in the ninth century, for the emperor's illness was believed to have been caused by Inari, angry that trees had been cut on the sacred mountain. A proverb bluntly expresses the sentiment: If you slight Inari, retribution will strike you *(O Inari san o somatsu ni shitara, bachi ga ataru)* (Hiraiwa 1989:2). The notion is particularly strong about moving an Inari shrine or simply abandoning an Inari shrine when one moves (Miyata 1988).

Tamahime Inari

Tamahime Ōkami is a personal form of Inari worshiped by a group of devotees centered on a mother and daughter with shamanic gifts.[25] The mother's mother had these talents, as well, and it was she who first began worshiping this form of the deity. The mother, Mrs. Umeda, lives about a three-hour train ride to the west of Fushimi Inari. The daughter, Haruko, has the same length of commute from Tokyo on the Bullet Train, and they meet monthly to worship at their rock altar and do austerities on the sacred mountain together. Often some of the mother's local followers and friends accompany her, and Haruko almost always brings fellow workers and even customers from her shop. Mrs. Umeda can actually see the form of this deity; Haruko can occasionally visualize it; and although the others cannot see it directly, they sense its presence to various degrees. It appears in at least two forms: a human female and a dragon deity *(ryūjin)*.[26] Haruko's male colleagues, exceedingly devout, told me they perceive Tamahime Ōkami as heat, cold, wind, or the sudden stopping of the wind. One said, "Even though it is cold out today, when we worshiped Tamahime Ōkami at her rock altar, I felt suddenly warm and light, as if I were floating in the middle of the universe." When Mrs. Umeda is with them on their pilgrimage, they are able to get specific messages from the deity, and answers to their questions, mediated through the shamaness. But even when she is not present, they feel the presence of the *kami*.

Once I accompanied just the three men on their pilgrimage, because the women had to schedule their trip on a different date. After they had laid out elaborate food offerings at the rock altar to Tamahime and chanted a number of prayers, they sat and had a cup of tea with the family that ran the local teahouse. The elderly grandmother of the house came out to chat and told many stories about the powers of the ascetics of old. These people, she explained, learned spiritual power with their whole bodies, not just their minds, like people of today. They could freeze a chicken in its tracks just by looking at it, so great were their powers. The three men bowed low to this woman in gratitude after their chat. Later they told me they believed that Tamahime Ōkami had sent her to speak to them because Mrs. Umeda could not be with them. When I asked the youngest man how he felt about this *kami*, he simply replied: "Tamahime is our protecting deity" *(mamorigami)*.

When this *kami* arrives in dragon form, it is a tempestuous, exhilarating experience for those who can perceive it. On one pilgrimage—this time only of women (Mrs. Umeda, her daughter Haruko, a customer of Haruko's, and I)—the manifestation was particularly powerful. They laid out offerings, lit candles, and chanted a short Shinto prayer. Then Mrs. Umeda called to the deity to come, made the *kuji* shouts of purification, and raised her clasped hands above her head. With fingers interlocked and palms upraised, she twisted her palms upward in a rolling motion. Then with her left hand on her hip, she churned the air with her right arm extended, drawing circles with index and middle finger pointed outward.

She called to the *kami*-as-dragon, felt the wind rise, sensed the presence, then finally saw the deity approach in a kind of whirlwind. Later, when she performed the waterfall austerity, the dragon appeared to Haruko. Only Mrs. Umeda stood in the waterfall; the other women refrained because of pollution taboos.[27] But while Haruko was chanting along with her mother in the falls, she beheld, for the first time, a vision of a huge dragon holding a gold jewel in its mouth. And when we reached a certain rock altar on the mountaintop later in the pilgrimage, Tamahime made her third appearance to these followers. While they were praying, the dragon appeared to Mrs. Umeda and placed its golden jewel in her hand in gratitude to us for doing the pilgrimage that day. Mrs. Umeda held out her hand, palm upward, which she said held the golden jewel, and we all stroked the palm of her hand, a rare opportunity to touch a dragon's jewel. These three manifestations of the *kami*-as-dragon were considered quite auspicious, and Mrs. Umeda said that something very positive would happen to each of us in the near future.

Great Pine Great Deity

Another individualized form of Inari is worshiped as Ōmatsu Ōkami, "Great Pine," at a rock altar that takes the shape of a guitar-shaped gourd *(hyōtan)*.[28] The altar is flanked by two rocks shaped like *shōgi* tiles, the markers used in the chesslike game. For an alcoholic man in a lay worship group who has remained sober with the help of this deity, this form of Inari has critical importance. Because alcohol consumption is an expected part of many employment situations in Japan, Oda-san drank a great deal with his colleagues in the evenings, but his drinking got out of control and he started drinking from early morning and began missing work. His wife and mother, exceedingly worried about him, consulted with the shamanic leader of this Inari worship group. They persuaded him to come along on a monthly pilgrimage, and the leader assigned Ōmatsu Ōkami as his personal version of Inari. She said that the gourd was a traditional sake container and that *shōgi* was a type of gambling, so this form of Inari was particularly strong in dealing with such addictions.[29] The wife and mother often wept tears of gratitude when they prayed at their special rock altar, which embodied his problem in such concrete form. When I first did the pilgrimage with this group, Oda-san had been sober for four months. By the time I left Kyoto, he had had his one-year anniversary and was looking substantially healthier.

Chizuko Hime: The Living Goddess

I first heard about this woman when I asked Fushimi priests if they knew
of people who worshiped at both Fushimi and Toyokawa Inari. In general, they did not—with the exception of Chizuko-san, a geisha who lives
in a resort town on the ocean. Hers is the most extreme case of individualization of the deity, for she herself is a living deity *(ikigami)* named
Princess Chizuko Great Bright Deity (Chizuko Hime Daimyōjin). She is
not really a form of Inari but was commanded by Dakiniten to worship
her own divinity at both Toyokawa Inari and Fushimi Inari and also at
the sacred center of the new religion Konkokyō. I include this example
because, although she does not claim to be Inari, she and her followers
worship herself *as* deity at two main centers of Inari. The incarnation of
a deity in a living woman's body is a common pattern in the new religions,
but within Inari I knew of only one other group that considered its leader
a living *kami*. A few people thought they had a special conduit to the
kami: one priest felt that he became the deity during a ritual dance, and
various shamanic healers had direct communication with Inari (and sometimes other deities also). Most informants, however, made a distinction
between themselves and the deity.

Chizuko is radiant, beautiful, and self-assured. The day I met her she
was wearing a white linen suit with beaded panels down the front. Her
black hair was pulled back and held in a jeweled barrette. She wore large
pearl earrings and some impressively large diamond rings on her fingers—
one of the more elegant worshipers I had seen. She had trained as a geisha
and had made her living by helping her mother, also a geisha, manage
thirteen others in a profession that was becoming financially unstable for
them and emotionally exhausting. Chizuko was beginning to have health
problems, too, when suddenly, about fifteen years ago, she was possessed
and told she was Chizuko Hime and instructed to worship at the three
sacred centers mentioned earlier. After this revelation, her heart problems
disappeared. Told to stop managing other geisha, they shifted their business to property management.

In their home altar, Chizuko, her mother, and her daughter (a three-
generation female household—none of them has married) enshrine Chizuko Hime, Dakiniten, and the main deity of Konkokyō. Like the three
generations of women who worship Tamahime Ōkami, all three women
in this case have special spiritual powers. The grandmother, a fervent
devotee of the new religion, believes that her faith helped to bring this

incarnation to pass. Chizuko as the *kami* speaks oracles. Her daughter has profound dreams about divine snakes and rock altars to Inari.[30]

Alone or with her family, Chizuko makes a pilgrimage to Fushimi and Toyokawa five or six times a year; she takes a group of followers twice a year in the spring and fall. At Fushimi she set up a stone altar to Chizuko Hime; at Toyokawa she donated a stone fox and flower holder in the Spirit Fox Mound, as well as two large banners to Dakiniten inside the inner temple (Okunoin), all inscribed with the name of this living deity. When her group worships at these two sites, they recite a brief Shinto prayer, then a unique prayer she received while possessed by the deity. She also has a monthly ritual at her home altar *(tsukinamisai)* to which a variety of people come. The women are very proud of the sectarian diversity of people who attend—even high-ranking priests of various sorts who cannot discuss their real troubles with others where they work. The women say their worshipers include people formally associated with Zen and Nichiren Buddhism, Shinto, various new religions, even Christianity, and all are sure to be helped by this *kami.* Even a priest from Fushimi Inari Shrine, they say, who was involved in an accident and had leg problems for three years, was fully healed within a month after he prayed here.

These examples are only three among the many ways people define, reshape, and individualize Inari. Although Chizuko's case is a little different, worship nevertheless centers on two Inari institutions where she set up an *otsuka* stone altar and dedicated a fox statue. From her external behavior, therefore, it is impossible to tell that hers is such a radically personalized kind of belief.

Worship of Inari: Following One's Heart

A Shinto priest at Yoyogi Hachiman Shrine writes that in Inari worship there is no prescribed form to which one must adhere, because "a specialty of Inari is that the worshiper trusts and follows her own sincere heart" (Hiraiwa 1989:5). A priest at Fushimi Inari, when asked how to worship properly, responded: "There are no rules. Each person, *in his own way,* should make a small monetary offering and pray" (Koike 1976:59; italics mine). I have heard priests express this sentiment in various ways (although some were troubled by extremes of personal interpretation). One called Inari worship "free style": people do what they like. This approach is possible, in contrast to religions with prescribed forms for prayer and devotion, because Inari is flexible, adaptable, versatile *(yūzū).* The same priest explained to a group of American university students who came to learn about Inari that "for followers of Inari, forms of faith and worship take very different, very personal, forms." At the Zen temple, Toyokawa Inari, one of the priests explained, in response to a devotee's question of whether to enshrine Dakiniten in a Shinto *kamidana* or Buddhist *butsudan,* that either style would be fine: "You should use whichever style fits in better with your family's religious situation. If you have one kind of altar but not the other, it is fine to worship Dakiniten there. Whichever is more comfortable for you."

People tend to use Buddhist and Shinto worship styles fairly indiscriminately at the various Inari sacred centers (see Nelson 1996:136–139 and 148). The standard convention is that obeisance to a Shinto *kami* consists of two hand claps and Shinto prayers *(norito),* while for Buddhist figures one clasps one's hands (silently) with palms pressed together *(gasshō)* and chants sutras *(okyō).* But, as with much religious practice in Japan, personal styles vary enormously. Worshipers chant the Buddhist *Hannya shingyō, Nembutsu,* or *Daimoku* in front of Fushimi Inari's sanctuary and pray in Shinto fashion at the buddhist Toyokawa Inari. Incense, usually considered an offering appropriate to buddhas and Buddhist figures, is used in Inari worship, although almost always in private worship and not by priests.[31] Buddhist Inari *dō* often have torii standing in front; people may use Buddhist prayer beads *(ojuzu)* at Shinto Inari shrines. In general, people worship in ways they were taught by their parents or grandparents, and eclectic forms abound.[32]

New worship styles also come into being in the lay worship groups, especially those with a shaman or shamaness as leader. One religious leader I met in a teahouse on Inari Mountain explained that his form of worship was to clap, not twice, but sixteen times. He said when a Shinto priest claps twice, this represents heaven and earth, but when he claps sixteen times, this represents all sixteen directions of space. He chants both sutras and Shinto prayers and uses Buddhist prayer beads. A couple sitting in the teahouse, on their first visit to Inari Mountain, asked this man, seemingly an authority, many questions, for they were totally bewildered by the significance of the thousands of different names on rock altars, fox statues, and lack of a central figure on the main altar in the sanctuary *(honzon).*[33] Even though they had received a formal prayer service in the main sanctuary, there is no basic pamphlet about Inari or the mountain. Thus newcomers are forced to learn from other people, although it is not easy for Japanese people to ask questions of strangers.

The lack of a doctrinal pamphlet from the priests perpetuates the great variety of interpretations about Inari, for people learn from other people, and the great number of personal styles continues to grow. A Tokyo Inari group run by a shamaness has a number of practices unique to that *kō,* for the *kami* guides her in almost every detail of running the household and the worship group. She collected thirty-one inspirational sayings told to her by the deity and made them into a calendar she distributed to her followers. When they drink a tiny cup of sake after a service—a tradition found only there—they save the last drop, reverently pour it into the palm of their left hand, rub their right thumb in it, rub their thumb and forefinger together, then touch these two fingers to the problem spot on their bodies. People touched their faces to become more attractive, their throat to get rid of a cough; stiff shoulders and lower backs were probably the most often rubbed spots. Moreover, there is some cross-cultural borrowing. When an Inari shamaness went to Korea to conduct a ritual to cure one of her clients, a Korean-descended Japanese, she was impressed by the mountains of food offerings used in Korean ritual—a custom that influenced how she herself used food offerings from then on. She also began using paper money more symbolically in rituals by tying it with rubberbands around prayer sticks, then planting them upright in uncooked rice.[34] After the ritual, the money was carefully unfolded and deposited in the bank, where it was believed to help more money accumulate.

Inari Mountain: Multiple Interpretive Worlds

Some of the multiplicity in Inari derives from the changes we would expect given its long history and wide geographical range in Japan. After an Inari was reenshrined far from the parent shrine, it could develop in new ways, and some of these ideas might find their way back to the original shrine in time. But as we have seen regarding the *otsuka* tradition, diversity is a feature of the center, as well, even at the shrine itself, but especially on the sacred mountain, which is the setting for a vast range of practices, religious establishments, and hermeneutical traditions.

Most people assume that the entire sacred mountain is the property of the Fushimi Inari Shrine and that all the sacred establishments on the mountain are related to the main shrine. This is not the case. The shrine owns only a fraction of the mountain acreage; the rest is owned privately. The main torii-covered paths and the back road are owned by the shrine, but the land flanking some of the paths is privately owned.[35] It is almost impossible to tell this merely from looking, however, as the *sacra* are for the most part the same as those used on shrine land to signify Inari: red torii, fox statues, jewel-shaped ornaments, *otsuka* rock altars, red and white banners with the *kami*'s name.

The private establishments on the mountain have a variety of relationships with the Fushimi shrine. The teahouses bordering the main pilgrimage route are privately owned by families who have been there for the last century or so. The land on which the building sits is owned by the shrine, but the house is owned and maintained by the family. The relationship here is symbiotic and usually cordial: the teahouse makes its living selling food, drinks, and offerings to the pilgrims on the mountain and agrees to keep its section of the path clear of snow and leaves. It derives its income from its location on Inari Mountain by performing a service to the pilgrims and to the shrine. The teahouse family keeps the *otsuka* rock altars in that area clean and may even make offerings at the altars that have no patrons at present. Teahouses on private land flanking the path perform the same function—selling food and offerings and maintaining rock altars—but they have no official connection with the Inari shrine. The shrine regulates the setting up of altars on its own lands but has no jurisdiction on private land, so prices and policies are different there.

In addition to teahouses, there are also private religious establishments *(kyōkai)* or private shrines *(jinja)*.[36] They may be registered as religious corporations *(shūkyō hōjin),* have a resident priest, usually Shinto rather than Buddhist, and rather eclectic traditions and teachings. They have no connection to the shrine but a strong connection to Inari. People working in the private religious establishments claim they provide a more personalized service to their followers than does the shrine proper, where they feel rituals are fairly mechanical and impersonal. The shrine priests, on the other hand, tended to see the private religious establishments as heterodox or opportunistic without proper ties to the "true" tradition. Pilgrims seemed not to be aware of this tension, and most thought that the whole mountain complex was part of the Fushimi shrine. Even when they did realize there was a distinction, they often ignored it, especially when their own rock altar was not part of the shrine proper. Most people I accompanied on their circuit of the mountain participated to some degree in both shrine and nonshrine traditions (although most did not think of it in those terms).

One of the more interesting of these private religious establishments

is called Fushimi Inari Honkyō Kanriki Kyōkai (Religious Establishment
of the Original Teaching of the Power of Relationship of Fushimi Inari).
Located at the foot of Inari Mountain on the back road, it consists of a
small plot of land crammed full of a wonderful collection of rock altars
and stone statuary on the left and a small building to the right containing
the home of the priest in the back and a large altar room with glass doors
facing the road. The basic teaching of this establishment is explained on
a paper that accompanies talismans sold here. In the center of the paper
is a flaming red wish-fulfilling jewel with the characters for *"kanriki"* in
the center. *"Kan"* means interval, between, space, relationship; *"riki"* is
power; *"kanriki"* refers to the power of betweenness that relates oppositions. The paper states: "Heaven and earth, water and fire, yin and yang,
male and female, plus and minus—in this way in the world the workings
of the energy born from the union of all oppositions is called *kanriki.*
Through the harmony of *kanriki* everything continues in eternal rhythm."

This religious establishment got its start forty years ago when the
founder had a dream in which the characters for two names of Inari
appeared: Yaoki (Springing Back Eight Times) and Kanriki (The Power of
"Between").[37] He went to Inari Mountain, searched for these names on
stone altars, and spoke with many people. Finally an old woman at one
of the teahouses told him these names could be found on an altar on the
far side of the mountain to the east. When at last he located the worship
stone, which had toppled over, he found it contained the names of eight
kami. Suddenly he realized the importance of the name Kanriki: it is the
relation *between* oppositions that is important, not the extremes themselves. The connection between god and people, sun and moon, light and
dark, is where we stand, and we must strive for the proper balance. He
worked very hard, attracted a number of people who found solace in his
insights, and was gradually able to create the small but impressive religious establishment that exists today.

In this tiny space is an array of religious *sacra* that has grown in
number in response to the needs of his followers. There is a place to retire
old signature stamps *(hanko),* an altar for the souls of animals that have
been killed to feed people (butchers and chefs worship there), various rock
altars (oriented to the most auspicious direction, for geomancy is one of
their specialties), an underground cavernlike room containing a miniature
pilgrimage route of the eighty-eight temples of Shikoku—and in the middle of it all, a large granite statue of Inari in human form, holding a sheaf
of rice and flanked by two white foxes that seem to be soaring through

the sky. The atmosphere at this small center is warm and friendly, and the head priest, his wife, and his son (also a priest) have a close connection to the devotees. There is time for long discussions of problems and personal advice—impossible, for the most part, at the main Fushimi shrine, which has become too big and the number of worshipers too great. In fact, this was exactly why one devotee at Kanriki told me he came here rather than to the more famous Fushimi Inari: "Shrines have become 'one way,' unilateral *(ippō tsūhō)*, and priests have no time for consultation with the people who come there. Services are like a mechanical assembly line, with no feelings of human connectedness at all."

Another religious establishment is a private shrine with a teahouse. This is called "Toyokawa Inari." In contrast to the Buddhist temple with the same name, here worship of the Buddhist deity Dakiniten is conducted in a Shinto mode by a male Shinto priest. Although he does not know the origin of this site on the mountain, he thinks that probably a devotee of the original Toyokawa Inari in Aichi prefecture set it up. Today there is no formal relationship with the Toyokawa temple, although the priest and his aunt do go there to worship once a year. This establishment also worships Saijō Inari, and a bright red banner proclaims the name of the Nichiren version of Inari at the very front of the altar cluster, facing the path.[38] Regular rituals are scheduled here in the spring and fall, at New Year's Day and the summer purification, and monthly on the twenty-second, which is the festival day *(ennichi)* at the Toyokawa temple also. This establishment does not have a shamanic tradition but follows standard Shinto practices within a richly syncretic field of symbols and deities. The land comprising this shrine is filled with four hundred rock altars, five statues of Fudō Myōō, a statue of Kōbō Daishi, three Jizōs, a Kannon, and a set of the twelve bodhisattvas who protect each of the twelve houses of the zodiac (and hence one's birth year). In addition to the teahouse's standard fare of offerings for the *kami*, they sell books of magic formulas *(majinai)* and certain kinds of health food.

Most of the teahouses and religious establishments are characterized by syncretism, a respect for the diversity of personal religious experience, and long-standing and close relationships with devotees. The master of the Yakuriki teahouse told me that his family had lived there for about a hundred years and said that the same worshipers and their descendants had been coming there to pray and chat over a cup of tea. The difference that people spoke about was not between Fushimi priests and other priests and religious specialists on the mountain but, rather, between the main Fushimi shrine as a rather impersonal and bureaucratic institution and the warmth that characterized the associations of devotees and priests, religious specialists, and others on the mountain. The Fushimi shrine has two branch offices on the mountain—at the Okusha and Gozendani—and there too relations between worshipers and priests were warm and affectionate. One priest at the latter office, high on the mountain by the main waterfall where people did austerities, said that although he was employed by Fushimi, his job felt more like that of a village priest, conferring with people at length, giving advice, presenting petitions to the *kami*. He said that people who make it this far up the mountain usually have serious problems, and he feels it is important to give them as much personal attention as he can. Thus, it is the ethos of the mountain itself, and the smaller size of the establishments, that afford the time and space for dialogue to occur and relationships to form.

Pilgrimage to centers of Inari worship and circumambulation of the sacred space may be done by individuals, even in secret, but usually takes place in groups.[39] An important activity of Inari *kō* is pilgrimage to the sacred center on some regular basis, monthly, seasonally, or yearly. Once the group reaches the center, the content of the pilgrimage varies enormously: some pay the priests to conduct a formal *gokitō* prayer service; others ignore the priests and conduct their own service. Even in large groups, there is always much attention paid to each individual—the group often splits up mid-pilgrimage so that each devotee can literally follow her own path on the mountain. And when the pilgrimage is to a sacred center without a mountain, it usually has what I call the "mountain complex"—a concentration of *sacra* similar to those found at the Inari shrines with mountains: *otsuka* rock altars, subshrines, torii, sacred springs or waterfalls, traditions of folk divination, fox statues, fox holes, statues of religious figures, and so on. Even at tiny Inari shrines these symbols are used and interpreted in different ways, and this gives much individual flavor to Inari worship and pilgrimage.

The Fox as Metaphor for Individuality

Inari worship contains a great deal of individualization, and the symbol most often equated with Inari is the fox. Foxes in the wild are solitary animals, and the cultural associations with foxes in Japan involve behavior that is individual, not communal. Fox possession, being tricked by a fox, being seduced by a fox, receiving healing or a gift from a fox—such events never happen to groups, only to individuals. Real foxes are liminal creatures, living on the boundaries, and in Japan, where conformity is stressed to such a high degree, strongly individual behavior is also liminal. Such behavior may occur in the sacred space of Inari's mountains during the special time of pilgrimage, or it may break into regular time and space through fox possession or being tricked by a fox. In this case one's outrageous behavior is tolerated because it is not the person but the "fox" who is in control.

In an unusual survey conducted by the National Personnel Authority, new members of the government ministries were asked to "compare government officials to animals." In the opinion of recruits who had just joined their ranks, the most prevalent animal image of the Japanese public servant, was the dog with its associations of loyalty and reliability. Interestingly, the dog is a domesticated canine, an animal that runs in packs, an enemy of the fox. The second-ranked animal was the ant, because officials "work hard and in groups." The other eight animals in the top ten were elephants, cows, horses, turtles, mice, monkeys, bees, and bears. An article in the *Japan Times* (October 30, 1990) explains that the elephant was chosen because of slowness and size and the monkey "because the recruits cannot disobey their bosses." How different from these animals is the cunning unpredictability and independent behavior of the Japanese fox. In the stone images of foxes that are sometimes found in profusion at Inari shrines, great diversity is expressed in the wide range of their styles and moods. Of the images he saw around the turn of the century, Lafcadio Hearn tells us that "there is an amusing individuality about them all" (Hearn 1974:311). I often came upon people inspecting the fox statues at some Inari shrine or temple and, marveling how very different they all were, even though the basic form was stylized.

Two other symbols found with Inari's foxes help to reinforce cultural associations of individuality. Inari has come to be identified with the bright red color that distinguishes most Inari shrines and Inari torii, and bright red bibs are often tied around the necks of fox statues.[40] The foxes that hijacked the carriage of Minamoto no Takayasu in 1101 outside the Kamo Shrine wore red robes that "seemed to glow: one could see their colour, even though it was night" (Smits 1996:87). Red is traditionally the color worn by small children and old people who have completed their obligations to society. Only these two age groups are permitted to act willfully and selfishly without reprisal (Embree 1939:214). The expression for a complete stranger is *"aka no tanin"* (literally, a "red other person"). Strangers too are exempt from the tight social rules that bind social groups, and one does not have to observe social rules of politeness with strangers. The other symbol of Inari is the wish-fulfilling jewel, red or gold, which grants not generic wishes but a person's specific desire. As shown in Chapter 4, the other meaning of *tama* besides "jewel" is "soul," and this too is not a group but an individual spirit.

The fox symbolizes not just the selfish side of individuality but the psychological separation from the protection of the group—a necessary step in the development of independence and adulthood. In the first scene of Kurosawa's film *Dreams (Yume),* the little boy's mother warns him not to go into the woods during a "foxes' wedding"—that is, when rain is falling from a sunny sky. He disobeys her and sees the forbidden sight of foxes processing through the trees. When he returns home, he finds that as a consequence of seeing the foxes he is no longer permitted within the walled compound of his mother's home. Before shutting the gate, she hands him a sword from the fox and tells him he must either kill himself or find the fox and ask for forgiveness. No longer able to hide behind strong walls of maternal protection, he clutches the sword and makes his way alone into the world, toward the rainbow, looking for the fox. Only if he finds and negotiates successfully with the fox will he live—otherwise he must die by his own hand. Seeing the foxes forces him to take his first step away from the family group; seeking the foxes forces him to begin his personal quest.[41]

Behavior that was traditionally diagnosed as "fox possession" included unusual eating habits, inappropriate use of language, inability to follow social norms, and, most interesting, newfound abilities in literacy (Hearn 1974:324–325). Other fox-possessed behavior included using abusive language, wanting to be always outside, dispensing money and goods like a millionaire, crawling on all fours, naked, and barking like a fox, destructive violence, and spitting (Nozaki 1961:218, 224, 235). De Visser mentions that people possessed by a certain kind of fox blurted out secrets and annoyed sick people (1908a:126). The only positive symptoms are the ones involving literacy. Perhaps the possessed person could write because some foxes were reputed to write. In the early nineteenth century, a fox living as a Buddhist priest named Kōan gave away many samples of his calligraphy (Manabe and Vidaeus 1975:15).[42] Naoe (1950) relates claims that fox-possessed people could speak classical Chinese. An illiterate girl in 1820, possessed supposedly by the spirit of a dead priest, began writing

"Praise to Amida Buddha" followed by this priest's signature. People came from afar to receive such a miraculous talisman—until someone noticed that two of the characters were incorrect and concluded it was not the priest's spirit at all but a fox or badger (De Visser 1908a:88–89). Nozaki gives an illustration of the name of Inari written on a tablet by a mid-eighteenth-century illiterate man while he was possessed by a fox (1961:216). Thus fox possession was not simply a transgression of social norms through obnoxious behavior: sometimes it empowered people to step out of their structural limitations through newfound skills in foreign languages, reading, and writing.

Today odd behavior is increasingly dealt with in a psychological or medical idiom rather than a religious one. During my fieldwork a young girl was brought to Fushimi Inari for a prayer service because she refused to go to school and neighbors suggested to her family that this might be fox possession. Ordinarily, though, refusal to attend school (tōkō kyohi) is seen as a phobia and treated accordingly. Apparently women are possessed by foxes more often than men in Japan. The cultural explanations for this, reported by Buchanan half a century ago, were that women "are more subject to hysteria than men," their willpower is weaker, they have more vivid imaginations, and they are more suggestible (1935:52). I heard much the same explanations during my fieldwork. Informants told me that women are more emotional than men, hysterical by nature, and more sensitive. These explanations were offered by women as well as men. No one suggested that perhaps women had less personal freedom than men or might be reacting against structural discriminations in the society.

When people get tricked by a fox, it is often the case that they have been drinking. And drinking is an activity in Japan that temporarily suspends the usual norms of behavior. It is a time when people are allowed to act exceedingly willfully and are even encouraged in this. The drinker is excused from outrageous behavior—"it is not him, it is the sake that is acting"—just as the person tricked or possessed by a fox was not thought to be personally responsible for her actions.

Shape Shifting as a Cultural Fantasy

Although changes are occurring, Japanese people are bound by familial, social, and employment obligations that require them to associate with the same basic group of people for a very long time. In most cases, they do not have the option of picking up and moving to a new location and

job when a situation becomes difficult. One result of this is a fantasy
called "desire for metamorphosis" *(henshin ganbō)*—one of the basic elements in the plots of a number of popular television shows.[43] Those
which are samurai period pieces *(jidai geki)* involve an average drifter,
traveler, crowd member, or newspaperman who is *really* the magistrate,
judge, or shogun in disguise. In mingling with the common folk, he always uncovers someone plotting evil, whom he brings to justice by the
end of the show. The actor Takahashi Hideki, who played Tōyama no
Kinsan in the original show, thinks the desire for change explains the
popularity of this kind of show: "The man who goes into town and seems
a bit of a bungler and not so bright, but is in fact clever, and a great and
righteous man—this is exactly the kind of theme Japanese people like.
Japanese people want to be able to turn into someone else like that"
(Wilson 1990:9).

Another shape-shifter emphasized this desire in her new role as professional clown. When school opened in Tokyo in 1990 to train clowns, it
received four times as many applications as the twenty-five spaces it had
available. Part of the job's appeal was expressed by a twenty-three-year-old
woman who said: "Once I put on the clown makeup, I can become different from what I usually am." Another woman explained: "The me, who
lived as an office lady, was not the real me" *(Mainichi,* May 24, 1990).

But again there is ambivalence here. For in Japanese the word for
monster is *"obake"* (changed thing). It is both desirable and monstrous to
become something different. The moral lessons of changed things are various: beings may change shape to do good or evil; to become something
they are not or to escape a bad situation. Although the literal meaning of
"henshin" is "to change the body," the samurai heroes are really only
changing clothes and manners—which is merely an exaggeration of a tendency already quite prevalent in Japanese society: the continual changing
of costume and even persona to fit the social context. Perhaps the cultural
message here is that to change shape skillfully, within limits, is to be a
well-adapted human being, but to go too far is to become a monster.

Ambivalence toward the Individual

At least one reason why the fox is both deified and demonized may be its
associations with behavior considered individual rather than cooperative
by Japanese culture. Such behavior is often attributed to the influence of
a fox: breaking social norms (because of fox possession or being tricked

by a fox), wanton sexuality, solitariness, or unusual eccentricity. I argue that the fox, among its many cultural meanings in Japan, symbolizes the positive and negative sides of individual behavior, which is not part of the dominant ideology in Japan. The norms of group conformity, harmony, and homogeneity do not make much provision for individual behavior, which is seen on the one hand as desirable, fascinating, and liberating but on the other as scary, unpredictable, and selfish.

Perhaps clusters of fox statues characterized by difference suggest individual expression—which may account for the fact that fox possession often took place at an Inari shrine (or after the person had visited one). But by the same token, a possessed person was often taken to an Inari shrine to be cured. The fox images, wish-fulfilling jewel, even the color red, may powerfully affect people, but the symbols have two sides. The goal is not to be a mere cog in the machine; but neither is it to behave selfishly. Rather, there is a subtle kind of maturity in Japan that involves learning to fulfill one's personhood within the bounds of society and social expectations (Plath 1980; Rohlen 1976).

I witnessed a very illustrative example of strengthening the individual to fit into the group. This example did not involve fox possession, but it did involve austerities on Inari Mountain amid hundreds of fox images. Tatematsu-san, a shamaness, was consulted about the behavior of a thirteen-year-old girl in junior high school who was in a great deal of trouble. Yuriko was tall, pretty, and very bright but had gotten involved with a bad group of kids at school and not just passively—she had become a kind of leader. She extorted money from people, shoplifted, stole bikes, skipped school, and never studied. Tatematsu-san said that because she was not attending school anyway, the two of them would live on Inari's mountain and conduct austerities until the problem was solved. The two of them lived in the fairly primitive building by the Seimei waterfall for well over two weeks,[44] following a rigorous course of waterfall austerity twice a day, circumambulation of the mountain, prayer *(norito)* study, and cooking and cleaning for themselves. There was no television or radio in the building, and the lifestyle was fairly rough. It was late November and chilly at night on the mountain. On the two Sundays, Yuriko's relatives came and did the pilgrimage and waterfall austerity with her, both as moral support and a kind of pressure. And before I realized what was happening, I myself was part of the "cure" as well—held up as an example of someone who was really working hard *(gambatte iru)*—and was encouraged to come up the mountain daily to assist Yuriko with her study of English.

The shamaness told Yuriko they would stay there as long as it took to purify her of all her negative habits and develop the desire to return to school in a positive way. She added, at some length, that she was worried about her son who lived with her, for he had to cook for himself while she was here on this job—again, support and pressure applied simultaneously. One morning while they were on the mountain, the shamaness was possessed by the *kami*, who praised them both for the austerities they were doing. He said the time had not been sufficient to persuade Yuriko to return to school, however, and if she were not ready in three days they should stay for a further week of extremely strict austerities. They ended up leaving after two more days. Later reports indicated that despite the time she had missed, Yuriko was doing well at school.

What had happened was rather complex. Yuriko was the center of not just the shamaness's attention for over two weeks, but that of her family and everyone else they encountered on the sacred mountain. The austerities were hard, but they were for her benefit, and she learned the prayers and various routines quickly and well. The irony of the situation was that she was being strengthened as an individual so that she would go back to school, avoid the bad kids, and conform to the school's expectations of behavior.[45] If we think of the much-quoted proverb, "The nail that sticks out gets hammered in" *(Deru kugi wa utareru),* this treatment was a kind of compassionate tempering of the nail before hammering it in. This rather extreme example shows that making a personal version of Inari does not promote wanton individualism. In fact it is a way of acknowledging individual concerns, dealing with them, and thereby being able to continue functioning in a society that does not give them much formal attention. Yuriko's grandmother, who participated in the waterfall austerity, said a very wise thing to Yuriko before they began: "Doing austerities will not change other people at all. You cannot make your parents and friends behave the way you want them to. Your parents will be the same as they always were. But *you* will change, and that will make a great difference in everything."

This is the key, I think, to understanding the fanciful pictures that depict foxes in groups, either family groups or work groups. I have argued that the fox is a solitary animal linked with certain kinds of individual behavior in Japan. But in Edo-period woodblock prints, we find fox families, fox weddings, fox parties, foxes in daimyo processions. The pictures show foxes standing on two legs, dressed in Japanese clothing, engaged in Japanese social and cultural activities. That they are *foxes* dressed like

Japanese suggests the association of certain qualities of the fox with these groups of people. Clearly the fox groups are a mirror of Japanese society. But because they are represented as *foxes,* the images perhaps signify the great diversity of people who constitute Japanese social groups. Like the clusters of stone foxes at Inari shrines, all different; like the thousands of altars to Inari with individual names; like groups of people who cooperate but also have personal parts to their lives—these depictions of Japanese people in fox shape make the point that it is separate people who constitute a group, no matter how homogeneous its outward behavior.

6
Shared Semantics and Private Persuasions

As you well know, the secret of community lies in suppression of the incompatible.

—Frank Herbert, *God Emperor of Dune*

Ideas about Inari, although unified by certain practices and symbols, are highly personalized, multiple, and even contradictory. People hold contending positions on key concepts pertaining to Inari—whether it is a Shinto or Buddhist deity, whether it takes male or female form, what relation the deity Inari bears to the fox. A great deal of Inari worship is individual and not group-oriented, and in many cases the devotee worships a unique form of the deity as his or her own Inari. Even within a single sacred center of Inari worship, there are numerous factions divided over attitudes and behavior toward the deity. Clearly this is not a homogeneous, unified, or primarily group-oriented tradition. The multiplicity that we now see as a defining characteristic of Inari beliefs is not, however, readily apparent. In fact, it is unknown to most Japanese, even those involved with the tradition: uniformity is assumed; diversity is unsuspected.

This chapter shows some of the ways the image of unity perseveres despite the great diversity in the Inari tradition. The question has two sides: why is the diversity not apparent; and if the diversity is real, why do the various factions not split off into schisms?[1] After examining some of Japan's dominant cultural representations about homogeneity and group harmony,

we will look at communicative styles that sustain these dominant representations by leaving personal understandings unarticulated or expressed only
as generalities or stereotypes. The silent centers of Inari are effective in a
nonauthoritarian way in countering the centrifugal forces within Inari worship, I argue here, and the assumption of shared meanings masks a vast
amount of private variation (and probably characterizes a number of other
institutions and traditions in Japan in addition to Inari). The chapter concludes by suggesting preliminary answers to two fundamental questions
about the Inari phenomenon: the reasons for its long history and continued
success and whether it parallels other Japanese institutions or is atypical and
marginal.

Harmony, Homogeneity, and the Group in Japan

Although the "group spirit" that characterizes Japanese society is popularly said to derive from age-old patterns of village cooperation necessary
for irrigation and rice growing, in recent years it has taken on ideological
overtones and at times has been strongly enforced by pressures from the
government. During the Meiji period, government leaders tried a number
of strategies to "modernize" Japan after the country was forced to open
its ports to the West. Throughout Japanese history it has been difficult for
large groupings to form, for factions have abounded; Meiji thinkers, knowing this, deliberately constructed or elaborated symbols and institutions
that would channel local, factionalized consciousness into a national unity
(Shively 1971:119). During World War II, this ideology was rigorously
enforced, and even today the notion of group harmony represents a dominant cultural representation (Miyoshi 1991:226).

Because these values are the ones Japanese emphasize when speaking
publicly, they are the ones that tend to get picked up in the studies of
Japanese society carried out by foreign scholars (as well as Japanese studies about themselves). For a time, foreign scholars produced studies on the
"group model of Japanese society," which investigated the cultural production of cooperation, harmony, and group behavior and downplayed
conflict, discord, and individual behavior. The group model describes Japanese social organization as based on the family, hierarchically organized,
a benevolent paternal figure at the top, with relations throughout characterized by selflessness, cooperation, harmony, loyalty to group, and *amae*
(being nurtured) in vertical groupings of mutual dependence (Befu 1980a:
29-31). Originating in the "classic" anthropological works published just

before and after the war (such as Embree 1939 and Benedict 1946), this emphasis pervaded the social science scholarship until the late 1970s (Befu 1980a:31). In Japan itself, another genre of writings that underscores homogeneity is the less scholarly and more pervasive *Nihonjinron* (theory of the Japanese people).[2] It argues for the uniqueness of the Japanese people and culture and emphasizes the qualities of group cooperation, harmony between people and with nature, and nonverbal communication—characteristics that are held to separate the Japanese people from all others. Literally hundreds of books have been published in Japan on the topic, making reflexive interest in Japanese "uniqueness" almost a national sport (Befu 1984:68).

There is another side to the story, however, and documenting it has been the norm in Western anthropological studies about Japan from the mid-1970s until the present. These studies concentrate on what previous studies on group harmony had left out: conflict, heterogeneity, and individuality. Befu tells us that the group model cannot account for lack of harmony, paternalistic neglect, labor strikes, disloyal employees, the brutal enforcement of ideology during the war, egalitarian organizations, or the relationships between groups (1980a:31–35). He points out glaring holes in the model including the absence of women and women's work, historical change, motivation, and individual choice (p. 37). A number of recent ethnographies have attempted to present the full picture of life in Japan. Moeran notes the extremely individualistic (in the worst sense of the word) behavior of his informants in a small village of the type where cooperation and group spirit are usually said to be the norm (1985:102). Robertson's (1987) study of a suburban Tokyo festival shows that the ritual played out rather than resolved conflict in this neighborhood. The complex ways a person steers a course between group responsibility and personal desires are explored in studies that use the dynamic model of "engagement" (Rohlen 1976; Plath 1980) and in investigations of the paradoxes of personhood (Kondo 1990).[3]

It is perfectly clear to anyone who has spent time in Japan that there is cooperation as well as selfishness, harmony as well as conflict, group as well as individual behavior. What, then, accounts for the popularity of the "current collective representation among the Japanese" (van Bremen 1986:16) of a model that presents only part of the picture? And why have social scientific studies tended to focus on one side or the other? Some anthropologists explain the emphasis as ideological and not behavioral (Befu 1980a:36); others call it "shared vocabulary, not shared values" (Kelly 1991:422). I see the situation as one in which both sides are often present, equally true, but not usually equally expressed. That is: a situation may appear perfectly harmonious on the surface but actually mask or indirectly express a great deal of discord. Later in the chapter we will look at five categories of nonconfrontational communicative styles: screening, refraining, wrestling, othering, and layering. These strategies allow a surface layer of group convergence to prevail while simultaneously preserving, protecting, or even advocating a more divergent, private position.

Boundary Crossing as Methodology

Before describing these communicative styles, I must point out that the methods used in this fieldwork involved a great deal of boundary crossing (from the point of view of a single informant) which provided information that studying one sacred site or family of worshipers probably would not have discovered. This was rather colorfully expressed by some of my informants who identified me as "a fox." After thinking about what it meant to "be a fox" in Japan, I realized that the identification had to do, at least in part, with boundaries: being marginal, being able to cross boundaries, not being part of the group, mediating between categories and groups. These characteristics define the real fox, the cultural fox, the foreigner, and even more the anthropologist. The fox, like many other animals that take on important cultural and religious meanings for people, is a liminal animal (Douglas 1957; Leach 1964). That is to say, it does not quite fit into clearly defined categories of classification but partakes of elements of two or more groups. It is anomalous, out of culturally defined place, and thus simultaneously taboo and sacred. The fox is classified in the canid family, but to anyone who has watched a fox, it clearly looks and behaves more like a cat than a dog. Unlike dogs, wolves, coyotes, and other canids, the fox, like the cat, has vertical-slit pupils and an eye construction that causes its eyes to emit a greenish glow in dim light. It has long catlike whiskers, long catlike teeth, and flexible, partially retractable claws (that enable it to climb trees). Even more feline is its hunting behavior: it hunts alone, not in packs like other canines; it stalks its prey crouching and slinking; and when it finally attacks, it pounces like a cat rather than lunging like a dog (Henry 1986:70–74).[4]

Although the cat, too, is a shape-shifter and may turn into the form of a woman, while the dog only rarely plays this role, I have never seen this

similarity between foxes and cats noted in Japanese folklore. But the Ainu
(the aboriginal people of Japan) did note the similarities, described in a
myth about the origin of foxes and cats. A powerful demon named
Moshiri-shinnaisam came one day and challenged Mole, a benevolent
deity, to a contest of strength. Mole agreed, knowing that he was stronger
than the demon, but Moshiri-shinnaisam suddenly grabbed him and hurled
him into the hearth, where he burned up. As the demon was leaving the
house, congratulating himself on an easy victory, he was shocked to see
Mole standing at the door. This time Mole knocked Moshiri-shinnaisam
into the hearth and burned him up. When he saw that the demon was
trying to escape as smoke through the roof, he blew him back down and
the demon's spirit was finally subdued. Only his ashes were left.

> But although his remains looked just ordinary ashes, some black,
> some red, and others whitish, yet being the remains of a demon, they
> could not have the life taken out of them. That was impossible. They
> therefore changed themselves into foxes and cats. Thus it is we know
> that foxes and cats are close relations, being of the same family.
>   Hence it is a fearful thing to be possessed by either of these
> creatures, for as they owe their origin to a demon they partake of his
> demoniacal nature. [Batchelor 1901:503]

This dual or in-between nature of foxes may account for some of their
fascination to humans. Along with being "the catlike canine" (Henry
1986), the fox seems to possess the qualities of other animals as well:
Henry describes its "yellow serpentine eyes," "gazellelike body," and running style, which is more like floating, "as if it were half bird" (p. 27).

Apart from being on the boundary between classifications, foxes actually live on boundaries as well. For reasons related to hunting and
escape strategies, "they spend a great portion of their time traveling along
an edge of countryside where two habitats meet," and often these edges
are along human-made clearings where the woods meet fields, orchards,
and residential areas (Henry 1986:35 and 41). Further reinforcing the
liminal image is their habit of being most active at dawn and dusk, the
boundaries between night and day (Henry 1986:33). Clearly, Japanese
people had observed this tendency of foxes, for in the religious custom of
feeding foxes at the coldest time of year, *kitsune segyō*, food was placed
not only at shrines, graves, and other religious sites, but also at borders
and boundaries, places where real foxes and spirit foxes were known to
appear (Miyata 1988:121).

Foxes are associated with anything that deviates from the expected. At the turn of the century, foxes were blamed for the theft of rice or silkworms, or if a stone suddenly fell, or when things moved strangely (De Visser 1908a:124). When people behaved totally out of character—such as a mother leaving her child in the middle of a deserted moor—it was often suspected to be the result of fox tricks, bewitchment, or possession.[5] The widely known "foxes' wedding," as noted earlier, is the meteorological situation of rain falling from a sunny sky—a situation so contrary to expectations that it is described as feeling like a light bewitchment or a joke (Suzuki 1982:198). The most extreme example of "matter out of place" (Douglas 1966) being credited to foxes may be the case of the old man who witnessed the eruption of Mount Bandai in 1888, which destroyed an area of twenty-seven square miles. He was not even troubled when boiling-hot rain fell upon him, for he had concluded that the whole spectacle was "wrought by the witchcraft of a fox" (Hearn 1974:323-324). Not just matter—but people—out of place may be immediately suspected of being a fox disguised as a human. In the latter part of the *Genji monogatari*, the bishop of Yokawa and his aged mother are forced to stay in a run-down villa in Uji. Out back, at the foot of a tree, they find "an expanse of white" that turns out to be a girl with "long, lustrous hair, . . . weeping bitterly" (Seidensticker 1976:1044; *NKBT* 18:339f). The cluster of clerics immediately assume she is a fox and watch her for hours, chanting mystical phrases to protect themselves, before deciding she is, in fact, human. The poor girl had tried to drown herself in the river and was quite ill, but her radical displacement from culturally approved female spheres dulled the priests' compassion.

Foxes not only live on the boundaries, they cross them. And by crossing, they challenge them. The cultural elaborations of the fox in Japan position it to mediate between the human and the animal and the human and the divine. To be fully human is to know where one stands in relation to both the animal world and the divine. This does not happen automatically but is a culturally conditioned process through which each person passes. One learns where the boundaries are not merely through their description, but by hearing stories of the consequences of daring to test them or cross them.[6] It should not surprise us to learn that when a Kyōgen actor in Japan makes the transition from apprentice to master, he does so in the role of the fox.[7] After spending many years learning by imitation the exact forms *(kata)* that his master teaches him, the actor finally has a chance to debut in a performance which determines whether he has come of age in the profession. The play is the humorous *Catching the Fox (Tsurigitsune)*, in which the actor breaks every rule and style he has learned up to that point. In the role of the fox, he muffles his voice instead of speaking out, hunches over rather than standing up straight, jumps around in contrast to the rooted stance of other Nō and Kyōgen roles, and wears a realistic fox costume although all other animals are signified abstractly. This performance takes an hour—much longer than other Kyōgen plays. If he executes this role of the fox well, he becomes a master, which gives him the right to make subtle changes in the strict forms he has been taught and to define his own trademarks as an actor. So, too, all Japanese people, in an unmarked, perhaps unconscious way, have to position themselves in their various roles. And the cultural symbol of the fox shows them where some of the social boundaries lie.

Apart from my classificatory status as some sort of liminal being— certainly not Japanese but having some cultural competence—I was, like the fox, able to cross boundaries in a way not usually possible for Japanese people. My solitariness evoked strong positive and negative feelings: people seemed to envy me my freedom, but pitied me for being alone. Because my goal was to try to understand the spectrum of Inari beliefs, I could not ally myself with any one group of priests or worshipers. But several months into my fieldwork I began to realize the degree to which the many groups within Inari worship were separate and exclusive and trying to ally me with their particular clique or faction. I stood at a sacred center of Inari practices, but it consisted of not one tradition but multiple interpretive worlds focused on the same mountain and same set of symbols. After I realized the extent of these divisions, I was forced to become more foxlike, although I did not describe it to myself that way until I returned from the field and pondered why I had so often been seen as "a fox." I needed to maintain good relations with groups that considered each other dreadfully or even dangerously mistaken about Inari—to stay on the boundaries of all groups and not be pulled into one faction in a permanent fashion. I learned how to pop up here and there, to travel the edges. It was also the time I spent *between* places and groups, especially on trains, that was most valuable for gaining perspective. The lay workers at Toyokawa Inari were surprised at the freedom with which I moved in and out of the different hierarchies. One woman said I had a "free pass" *(furii pasu)* at the temple. This referred to my being able to come and go freely in the different offices and worker groups, most especially the priests' rooms, which seemed inaccessible to most outsiders.

Also like a fox, I learned not just how to stay on the boundaries, but to cross them. Again, this was not always conscious. When some barrier seemed arbitrary I would question it, find ways to get around it, whereas an insider would probably have accepted it at once as a cultural given. Of course I did not try to circumvent religious taboos, only bureaucratic ones. I did not really notice I was doing this kind of maneuvering until near the end of my study, when I was at the Buddhist Inari temple. One day, one of the priests laughingly told me that he and his colleagues were amazed and impressed at my skill in crossing boundaries. They had noticed this early on in my stay, they said, and enjoyed watching me figure out ways to get around certain barriers. I began to apologize, but they said they were not offended, for I seemed to sense when something was nonnegotiable and did not push in those cases. Apparently my boundary crossing was notable enough to be commented upon by a number of my informants. And as a research style it allowed me to observe how different groups related to each other via different communicative strategies.

Communicative Styles in Japan

The first three communicative styles involve silence, lack of talk, and nonverbal communication; the fourth may be verbal or nonverbal; the fifth style consists of the deployment of certain stereotyped or culturally prescribed "layers" of speech. These styles of communication character-ized many of the encounters I witnessed between different groups of Inari worshipers and, more often than not, prevented rather than facilitated the exchange of substantive information. I was in a position to see this be-cause each of the two parties (such as priests and a worship group) would have stated their position very clearly to me; but when it came to speaking directly with each other, their comments were indirect, vague, and very polite. In fact, once groups knew I was a crosser of boundaries, they sometimes tried to learn about the opinions or activities of another group directly from me—and then in the interest of discretion I was sometimes forced to use some of the same communicative styles I was observing.

There is a spectrum of reasons why silence or indirect communication may be employed in Japan. Some of the Japanese propensity toward vague speech may be attributed to the way the language itself works, in which vague speech is more polite and elegant than direct statement. Speaking at all may be "a rude assertion of the self" (Miyoshi 1974:138). There is also a distrust of language—a feeling that words may express only surface levels of meaning and may even undermine or destroy the feelings they express. In *Fox Fires (Kitsune bi)*, Enchi Fumiko says: "Actions do not betray, but language is filled with the danger of betrayal at any instant. This quality is what makes language both infinitely beautiful and infinitely frightening" (Seham 1986:3).

An informant once told me that if one verbalizes a feeling about someone to that person, the feeling is over, its potential dried up, whereas if one says nothing, the silence resonates with the feeling and it lasts far longer. Actions are valued far more than words, which are seen as slippery and not to be trusted, as in the expression, "There is no responsibility in words" *(kotoba ni sekinin ga nai)*. And some words can be very danger-ous, as the mayor of Nagasaki learned when he dared to express his opinion about the emperor's responsibility during the war and was shot by a right-wing extremist.[8] As this last example shows, silence (and non-confrontational communication) is not merely the absence of speech but is closely tied to the power relations implicit in who speaks and how (Foucault 1988:27).

Screening

In Japan, decorative screens *(byōbu)* are often positioned to tastefully block the view of some offending area that must of necessity be located close to more formal areas. Hanging curtains *(noren)* may serve the same function, hiding from sight the inside of the kitchen or private family areas without sacrificing access, space, or air flow. In the same way, literal and verbal screens may prevent the clear view of certain matters that are unpleasant or controversial. The screen need not be physical: it may be a state of mind that does not register the negative portion of the scene.

"Screening" in the world of Inari takes place in the careful editing of devotees' testimonials before they are published by the sacred centers. I knew a fascinating shamaness who had a small but devoted following. She had had a number of visions of the Inari *kami* and once saw the white spirit fox of Inari, an experience that moved her greatly. But when her profile was included in the quarterly magazine for worshipers, it was so sanitized and formalized that I did not even recognize it as hers. Their visions of the deity are precisely what gives these religious specialists cred-ibility in the eyes of their followers, but it is exactly these elements that the institutions edit out when they publish them as examples to the faithful. A priest at another Inari institution described his editorial policy, a milder form of screening than simply ignoring the offending material: he changes the language of the original so that a vision or direct experience of the deity or the sacred fox becomes a dream. In the example of the shamness just cited, the published testimonial described in formal language how devoted she had been to her parents (also shamanic religious specialists) and how devout she was in her everyday life. No particularly memorable or unique events were related. The feeling is very different from my interview in which she describes her vision of the spirit fox:[9]

Shamaness: Well, I have been granted sight of the *kami* from time to time. Inari wears a white kimono and holds a staff, and has a beautiful white beard.

KS: So it takes the form of an old man?

Shamaness: Yes. I am given sight of him in a garden. Also, the divine assistants *(gokenzoku san),* the [fox] assistants which you like so much, Karen [both laugh]—I have also seen them. They are exceedingly beautiful assistants. I hope I will be granted another vision of them before I die. I was doing a circumambulation of the mountain, and in the middle of the path, I clasped my hands together in prayer. It was during the day, so other people were passing by. I clasped my hands and prayed, and when I opened my eyes, suddenly there it was! It was about this big [she extended her arms about two and a half feet], its body. And its tail was about this long, so together about like this. [She held her hands about two feet apart.] I can't tell you how beautiful that tail was!

KS: It was a white fox?

Shamaness: Pure white. A snow white fox. Its tail was fluffy—how can I describe it? It was pure white with the loveliest fur! As I thought, "My goodness," it whizzed through the air. The assistant [fox] flew away. As it flew by in front of me, I saw the side of its body as it went by, then it turned its head for just a moment and looked right at me. Right in my direction.

KS: What a wonderful experience.

Shamaness: I had never seen a [fox] assistant before that, and haven't seen one since—only that one time. At least up until now. It flew right toward Ichinomine [the main peak of the mountain]. So I have seen that too, not the *kami* only. That time, it was so lovely. After that, when I was in that area, I prayed to see it again—it was so beautiful. I prayed, "Please allow me to see it once again." But although I kept my eyes open and timidly looked around, I never saw it again.[10]

If I had relied solely on printed materials from Inari's sacred centers, the intriguing and vital aspects of Inari worship would have been screened from view and I would have gotten a much different impression of people's experiences.

I was screened twice—literally—during my fieldwork on Inari. Once when a kind priest at Fushimi was willing to answer my questions, there was no one to relieve him at the long open window where he sat to process worshipers who wanted a prayer service. As he insisted it would not look right for a foreigner to be sitting inside this official priestly domain, he positioned me behind a screen, from which I asked my questions, feeling like a Heian court lady. It was not the actual presence of a foreign female, but my visibility to others, that was improper. On another occasion, I thought that the shrine would allow me to audit the lectures at the weeklong training session for *kō* leaders so that I could hear the shrine's formal positions on a number of topics. For reasons still unclear to me, there was a great deal of resistance to my presence: I would "disrupt the students' concentration"; they were "unsure it was appropriate"; and so on. Finally the week came and the priests agreed to let me attend the "interesting" lectures, which they selected. A priest positioned me in an adjoining room, behind a thick accordion curtain, where I could hear absolutely nothing of the lecture. Completely frustrated at this point, I was about to burst into tears and got ready to leave. A priest came to check on me, realized it was impossible to hear, and led me to the back of the lecture hall where I was again positioned behind two screens. Through a crack between the screens I could see the adult students whose "concentration I would disrupt." They were busily talking, giggling, turning around in their seats to speak to friends behind them, and sleeping.[11]

Screening also takes place when a neutral term replaces a problematic word and gives the illusion that the matter has been dealt with. We have seen that the Fushimi Inari Shrine was allowed to continue distributing divided spirits of the *kami* after the practice was prohibited at other shrines, but Fushimi was required to use the word *"shinpu"* in place of the former *"wakemitama."* An old man told me that theoretically one should not drink sake while on pilgrimage. But if one called it *"hannya-tō"* (literally, "hot water of wisdom"), it was permitted.[12]

Screening may be used to positive effect when some unreasonable prohibition needs to be circumvented and a new term screens the fact of continuation. But it can be used to avoid dealing with issues by simply hiding them, out of sight, behind a euphemism or a wall or a silence.

Refraining

By "refraining" I mean holding back from speaking, although there is a secondary sense of speaking "in the same old refrain" that may have the same effect as keeping silent even though verbal communication does take place. The word *"enryo"* (reserve, deference, forethought, modesty) has a very positive meaning in Japanese. It refers to a polite holding back in both action and speech: a person who is exhibiting *enryo* does not grab the last piece of cake or speak her mind freely. But refraining from speech may have a negative power component, as well, as when someone "forgets" to pass on a message or when a whole subject is surrounded in silence because it is too unpleasant or threatening.

In my investigations of Inari I observed refraining in several ways, some of which I noted in Chapter 2. People refrained from asking direct questions about matters of belief; priests refrained from correcting a person unless they were asked directly for advice; devotees and priests both refrained from speaking about their own beliefs except in certain private contexts. Priests found it very difficult to query worshipers directly on certain matters. When the leader of a lay worship group dies, for example, often there are succession difficulties. Priests would like to discuss the matter beforehand with the group leaders, but they find it impossible to ask them how they want the group to proceed after they are dead. Priests do not ask if a worship group's leader becomes possessed by the deity, either, although they are very interested to know the answer. By the same token, group leaders want to know what the shrine priests think of them or how they feel about certain issues. It was this kind of question that I sometimes found myself trying to fend off once I realized I was being used as an information source about another group.

A traditional version of this reluctance to inquire into personal and religious matters involves "fox owning" *(kitsune mochi)*. This hereditary ascription of certain families meant that neighbors believed the family had seventy-five tiny foxes who would possess or harm anyone who treated the family badly. It was never spoken of directly to the host family:

> The fox-owners are avoided as if they were snakes or lizards. Nevertheless, no one ever asks another point blank whether or not his family be a fox-owning family; for to do so might offend him, and

the result to the inquirer might be a visitation in the form of possession by a fox. The subject is therefore never alluded to in the presence of a suspected party. All that is done is to politely avoid him.
[Chamberlain 1971:119][13]

Almost everybody, priest or devotee, refrained from speaking about their
most personal religious convictions. There were set phrases anyone could
use safely, and by and large people did not speak specifically about personal beliefs. Even priests at the same sacred center kept personal beliefs
in a separate category from institutional positions and focused mostly on
ritual forms, which were followed precisely.

The clearest example of refraining I encountered concerned the formal interviews I began conducting at my first fieldwork site. My notion
was that by asking the same set of questions of devotees, priests, members
of lay worship groups, and others involved in the world of Inari worship,
I would be able to see differing attitudes between the various groups.
Most devotees, workers, *kō* leaders, and members were open to being
interviewed and were even flattered to have their ideas the focus of my
research. The Fushimi priests were exceedingly resistant to the idea of
being interviewed, however, and over the course of more than a year I
was able to get formal interviews with only a handful of the fifty priests.
For the first three months of fieldwork, I observed and asked general
questions. After I had a sense of what questions would make sense in a
formal interview, I discussed the possibility of interviews with my contact
at the shrine. In fact he had been puzzled by mere participant observation
and often asked me why I was not using standard questionnaire and
survey methods. Thus I was quite unprepared for his sharp reaction to my
proposal to work up a formal questionnaire. He doubted the shrine would
comply, he said, as everyone was "too busy." When I said I had almost a
year left and each interview would only take thirty minutes, he said it was
not so much a matter of time but they would not know how to answer
my questions. He said he would speak with his superior but doubted I
would be permitted to carry out this part of my project. For although he
had been assigned to look after me, the other priests were under no
obligation to talk to me or further my research.

My reading tutor, a male college student, suggested that perhaps the
priests felt they might lose face if they were unable to answer my questions.
The priest who had discouraged me admitted a few days later that keeping
up appearances was important at the shrine. If I asked the same questions

of fifty priests, he said, I would get exactly the same answers from each priest, as he would be answering for reasons of formal unity and not from his own convictions. I persisted and, over the course of two months, refined the questions with the aid of my tutor and the priest. The priest finally suggested some convenient times to interview him and his colleagues— which indicated to me that my questions were not particularly threatening and he was no longer resisting the formal interview. He still insisted, however, that all the answers would be identical. Although he and four other priests agreed to answer my questions, I encountered strong resistance from the others in various forms. Some kept "forgetting" to get back to me or to hand my list of questions to the head priest in preparation for interviewing him. Others simply refused to return my greetings, which made it impossible to ask them to help me. Still others pleaded ignorance: they "didn't know much" about the shrine and its history.

Prepared for a similar reaction at my second fieldwork site, I was delighted to find that the priests (at least in the office where I spent the most time) were agreeable, even enthusiastic, about cooperating. I attribute the difference in reception to the more tolerant attitude of the Buddhist priests about the diversity in Inari beliefs. At the Shinto shrine, my first fieldwork site, my interview may have threatened the appearance of unity the priests had worked so hard to create. In fact, even among the priests who did cooperate, there were rather striking differences of interpretation or personal conviction about matters connected with Inari. For preists too, as was the case with *kō* leaders and worshipers in general, family teachings were more important in shaping religious attitudes than were formal teachings received later in life. This was not apparent in everyday behavior, though, where all priests followed the prescribed ritual forms and did not engage in debates that would have revealed these matters.

The use of refraining may frustrate the observer attempting to document diversity, but it provides great freedom and privacy for those employing it. By not revealing a contrary position, a person may fit in with the group and thereby experience the security it affords, maintaining harmony and group unity. By refraining from speech in general, a pilgrim on the sacred mountain is liberated from his usual fixed position in society, for accent, dialect, and speech patterns soon reveal his social class, educational background, and regional roots. But refraining may also create a social situation in which people with different ideas are afraid to stand out because it looks like everyone else subscribes to the dominant idea. Refraining may help to perpetuate the great diversity in Inari. Because the priests are not pushing doctrines or trying to standardize beliefs, newcomers arrive at their own understanding or learn from each other—and the situation of many truths continues.

Wrestling

By "wrestling" I refer to a kind of silent negotiation that is confrontational but nonverbal (or at least nonvocal) and nondiscursive. The image which embodies this notion is that of sumō wrestlers: two large, seemingly immovable forces who fight a battle that is as much psychological as physical, based on stamina and agility, not only brute strength and size.

Nonverbal wrestling occurred in the world of Inari—particularly in conflicts between priestly centers and popular energies. The best example is the ten-year silent negotiation during which the Fushimi priests tried to stop devotees from setting up rock altars to personal versions of Inari. Even today this kind of struggle continues. Along the path on Inari Mountain someone has set up a tiny rock altar flanked by a pair of stone foxes, and several people have tied votive bibs on the foxes. Someone from the shrine, however, has hammered a small wooden sign into the ground behind the miniature altar that reads:

> This object is not here with the shrine's permission, so
> please remove it.
>> Sixth Month, Heisei 2 [1990]
>> Fushimi Inari Taisha, Management Division

The tiny unofficial altar and the warning sign, facing each other in a silent standoff, remained in place for the two years I was in the field.

Both the sacred centers and the worshipers have certain strategies they can use in this silent wrestling match. The priests can ignore popular practices of which they do not approve. Or they can make it difficult for a tradition to be continued—as when the Toyokawa priests simply took the childbearing rock that women were straddling and moved it to an inaccessible location. Or they may try to substitute an approved practice for a questionable one—such as the change in distribution of the unglazed earthenware cups used in the Great Mountain Ritual in January. In previous years, people scrambled in a wild free-for-all to obtain one of the cups after the ritual. Now the priests package the cups in a small white box and sell them on the day of the ritual in a dignified manner.

But devotees too have power, as evidenced in the rock altar struggle. In another case, the shrine had decided to cut down a dead pine tree on the mountain path and the worker had completed about half the job. When he returned to finish it, someone had placed a small red torii in front of the tree, which rendered it sacred, and the shrine was forced to leave the rest of the tree intact. This is the famous Raised Root Pine (Neagari Matsu). Today it exists more as reinforced concrete than original pine tree but nevertheless retains an important meaning for worshipers—it is one of the most important sites on the mountain. And devotees, like priests, can simply ignore the elements they do not like by screening them out as a strategy of silent negotiation.

The obvious consequence of wrestling is that a difference may be solved without overt conflict and no one need lose face. But without the two parties actually stating their terms, the contest may be one of endless posturing and no mutually satisfactory resolution. Or one party may win, not on the merits of its position, but because it had a brief advantage that ended the struggle.[14]

Othering

Defining one's self or group in contrast to another is what I term "othering." Distinctions in language and life are necessarily constructed through systematic oppositions and may be value-neutral: the red team and the blue team, the east village and the west village. But often a group is defined in contrast to another that is perceived to be inferior, negative, and dangerous—but, paradoxically, sometimes also desirable (Stallybrass and White 1986).[15] Often the values or characteristics projected onto the other are necessary for social functioning but in opposition to dominant cultural norms (Perera 1986:13; Dower 1986:235). Othering seems to be a widespread if not universal phenomenon that intensifies in times of stress and insecurity. Although othering may be used to define large political, ethnic, national, or religious groups, it is also used as a mechanism to define smaller groupings within any of these larger categories (Nakane 1973:90–107). Within Japanese society, so often described as homogeneous, there is an amazing proliferation of groups, although they may be based on "differences . . . so minute that they are scarcely discernible to the eye of the foreigner" (Smith 1983:93). Examples of these smaller groups proliferate: different schools within the same religious sect; schools within the traditional arts; factions within political parties or neighborhood associations.

Rather than "group society," the term *"groups* society" describes an important characteristic of life in Japan. The terms "inside" and "outside" *(uchi, soto)* refer along a continuum to association with or exclusion from some group.[16]

Inari worship is an interesting setting within which to examine the construction of inside and outside, for it is a voluntary religious association that does not particularly involve political, ethnic, or national identity. Nevertheless, as we have seen, groups and factions abound. In defining one group against another, exaggeration and reification often take place, sometimes based on hearsay, stereotype, or even imagination rather than consideration of actual facts. For the purpose of analysis, let us consider two parts to the definition of one group against another: "outsiding," the definition and exclusion of the other, and "insiding," the selection and solidification of the chosen group.

Groups of priests and worshipers defined themselves against some other group, usually seen as less authentic, enthusiastic, or correct. Sometimes division occurred along institutional or sectarian lines: worship groups of a primarily Shinto orientation thought that Buddhist Inari worship was not real Inari worship; Buddhist groups said they had no need to visit the Fushimi shrine because they worshiped Dakiniten-sama and not whatever *kami* was worshiped at Fushimi. But differences were often minor and nonsectarian: "They worship a male *kami* but we worship a female one"; "Their foxes are black but ours are white." Priests at Toyokawa Inari stressed that their Dakiniten had a different lineage than the deity by the same name worshiped at esoteric Buddhist temples in Japan. When pressed, almost no one could tell me specific details about the other style of Inari worship against which they defined themselves—their information was based on assumptions or stereotypes—but they usually had some vague notion that the other was inferior or even bad. Shamans explained this disinterest in other forms of Inari worship in terms of the deity's jealousy: if one moved indiscriminately from one kind of Inari to another, this might well bring down Inari's wrath and result in sickness or misfortune.

Creation and solidification of the group required, in addition to definition against some other, an elaboration of its particular character, insiding. This took concrete form in the special jackets, hats, sashes, badges, bags, or surplices *(kesa)* worn by each group during its activities and pilgrimage. These sartorial accessories helped create a feeling of its unity and enabled members to identify each other among the crowds of other worshipers.

Members of each group could speak of the characteristic that set their group apart from others. People told me that their group was the largest, or the most generous in terms of donations to the sacred center, or the oldest, or the most careful in following the teachings of the priests. Devotees led by a shamaness thought it was her presence and abilities that gave the group its character. After the Spring Ritual in the tiny house of a shamaness who led a small group of devotees, the members emphasized that I was seeing an authentic working-class *(shomin)* ritual in a simple Japanese home. They expressed this with great pride: although they all worked very hard and were not rich, they told me, they were rich in spirit. Contrasting their style of boisterous openness against that of "the wealthy," they told me if I were at a similar ritual among rich people, the people would be snobbish and cold and would probably serve me tea in a formal, rigid way devoid of any human feeling.

Often features considered unique by a particular *kō* were not. Several groups at Toyokawa Inari thought they alone were privileged to worship in two semirestricted areas—behind the main altar and inside the fence of the inner sanctuary (Okunoin)—and that this was due to the amount of their financial contributions or high regard by the priests. In fact, the priests said anyone could worship in those areas; they had only to ask. Another *kō* considered itself one of the few that bothered to actually spend the night in the temple and not at a fancy hot spring resort hotel as part of the pilgrimage, but in fact many groups still do this.

A lack of substantive communication may be involved in both outsiding and insiding—with the result that communication about actual belief does not take place between or within groups. In the first case, the group does not speak with other groups because they are defined as wrong, bad, or other, and therefore communication is not desired. Within their own group, members do not necessarily speak substantively with each other because they assume they are all in agreement about matters pertaining to the group. Worship tended to be group-oriented. I seldom witnessed activities, such as giving personal religious testimonials, that might disclose individual convictions and experiences.

The definition of one's own group against another group that is imagined to be very, even dangerously, different—as well as the lack of sharing individual understandings within the group—minimize the acknowledgment of differences that may exist *within* the group itself. This kind of uninformed othering leads to a reification of characteristics of both the other and the group, neither of which is accurate.

Layering

The preceding four mechanisms are ways to preclude substantive dialogue between individuals or groups. "Layering," which comes into play when dialogue must take place, involves the use of alternative discursive modes appropriate to the situation. The two "layers" are called in Japanese *tatemae* and *honne,* by which I mean "shared meanings" and "private meanings," respectively.

Verbal layering works at both a personal and an institutional level. Descriptions of the personal level in the literature usually emphasize the psychological dimension of the terms as a kind of moral dilemma: people are obliged to keep up appearances *(tatemae)* no matter what their personal inclinations *(honne)* (Koschmann 1974; Hendry 1987). This means that, in effect, the surface level is articulated and the real feelings remain hidden and unspoken, or spoken only in certain contexts. *Kō* leaders often employed this type of *tatemae* when talking with priests who had different ideas about certain matters pertaining to Inari. A woman told me, "I smile and nod when the priests tell me their ideas, but when it comes to my own religious practice, I must follow my own heart and the ways my parents taught me." A male shamanic *kō* leader expressed similar sentiments: "I follow the teachings of the *kō* office as *tatemae,* but in my heart, I believe what my father taught me." Employing *tatemae* is not usually seen as hypocritical. It may even be admired. Some priests were discussing another priest they regarded as rather stiff and serious, but they understood this to be because he actually tried to live and work at the *tatemae* level—that is, he never showed any private resistance to shrine policies and practices—and they respected him for this. But the deployment of shared discourse in place of personal opinions and experiences also separates people and prevents them from truly knowing each other. One evening, I ate dinner with some priests who, perhaps because of my presence and the resulting divergence from usual topics, were surprised to hear each other express unexpected sentiments. One marveled, "I have worked with these guys for over twenty years, but in some ways still know very little about them." A great deal of verbal exchange in Japan takes place at the level of set phrases *(kimari monku),* which conceal much and reveal little. When people are in a group, usually only the senior members speak: the others refrain from expressing themselves, especially if their ideas contradict those of the speaker. In this way refraining supports layering, and the group will appear to have a unified opinion. I often received very different answers to the same question depending on whether my informant was with others or alone.

This usage of *tatemae* and *honne* parallels the tension between duty *(giri)* and personal inclinations *(ninjō)* (see Benedict 1946:133–144 and 207–208) and implies that there is only one socially acceptable outcome: conforming to surface appearances as one's duty. But my informants used this set of terms in another way as well, a way that was more flexible, deliberate, even playful, as a few examples will show. (This usage was perhaps closer to the paired terms *"omote"* and *"ura,"* front and back.) One of my best informants was a Shinto priest with strong convictions about the importance of historical tradition and a suspicion of extreme shamanic behavior. But even he, in answer to some inquiry from me, would ask if I wanted to hear the *tatemae* or *honne* explanation. In this case, he did not mean the shrine's ideas versus his own but, rather, the official story versus the actual situation. He never acted as if he were revealing institutional secrets but seemed to imply, rather, that both levels of explanation were true in different ways. One level was the public discourse about Inari and the shrine; the other was the much more complex, multiple, messy level of actual belief and practice. He was not embarrassed or duplicitous about the real state of affairs, but he did not want to give it too much weight. Without the centering effects of historical tradition, he thought Inari beliefs would become nothing but idiosyncratic individual interpretations. One example of this usage concerns the rock altars *(otsuka)* on Inari Mountain. The priest told me that although the *tatemae* explanation is that *all* the altars are to various manifestations of the deity Inari, actually *(honne)* some of the altars were set up to Buddhist deities and yet others to the spirit of deceased shamans by their followers. In this case, the *tatemae* explanation covers the majority of cases and the *honne* provides the "messier" but more complete situation.

Another priest whom I met at a Buddhist Inari temple near the end of my fieldwork began our conversation at a very basic and rather formal level. When he realized I had been studying Inari for several years, he led me from the formal guest room to his office upstairs, a cluttered, homey room, and introduced me to his coworkers in this way: "She really understands, so you don't need to bother with the *tatemae* level but can begin with *honne.*" Clearly, this did not mean that everyone began telling me his private notions about Inari. It meant that certain institutional appearances did not need to be kept up—that we could skip the level of simplified generalizations and speak of the complex and even contradictory situation of actual practice. Nor do I mean to imply that there are only two layers and I got the deepest or truest information. Surely there are many gradations and nuances. The point is that both modes can be deliberately articulated. It is not simply a matter of personal feelings opposed to public appearances. An intimate couple can employ *tatemae; honne* can be spoken at large public meetings.

The usefulness of this understanding of *tatemae* and *honne* as something like system and mess, or convergence and divergence, is that it includes the usage that describes an individual in opposition to the social system as well as the more institutional uses I have illustrated. Examining both may be necessary to an accurate understanding of a phenomenon — for without systematic boundaries, there are only individual interpretations or particular cases; and without the individual examples there is only system as an ideal construct. Japan's two oldest extant compilations of myth and history demonstrate these two tendencies toward system and mess. Although the works deal with roughly the same body of material, the *Kojiki,* completed in 712, is a highly edited single narrative, whereas the *Nihon shoki* from 720 contains multiple, contradictory variants of almost each episode. These two modes of discourse at either the personal or institutional level are not contradictory but complementary. Both the widely shared concept and the qualified, particularized statements are true in different ways. I had numerous conversations in which the Japanese person would first respond in broadly shared cultural generalizations but then make a 180-degree shift in position without any apparent feeling of inconsistency. A particularly poignant example concerned dying for the emperor during the war. An elderly Japanese man told me that, like his comrades, he was prepared to do this — but later in the conversation he said that everyone at that time was forced to mouth those sentiments, though of course no one really wanted to die. Mothers did not care if Japan lost the war, they just wanted their sons back, he grimly added.

Layering has a nonverbal form in addition to the verbal layering of *tatemae* and *honne*. This is the elaboration of surface forms and outward behavior that may be at odds with interior content or personal feelings.[17] People may participate in elaborate religious rites without necessarily believing in them (Ellwood and Pilgrim 1985:109–110). The term for paying homage to a deity out of respect, even though one is not a believer, is *"hyōkeihō"* (literally, "surface worship"). To an observer this kind of worship might not be distinguishable from worship by a fervent devotee.

The use of layering acknowledges many strata of meanings, ranging from the most general, shared level to an individual's personal feelings, all containing some measure of truth. Layering may be coercive when people feel they must talk or act at the public level and are not free to express their own ideas. But it may also be liberating because talking or acting at the level of cultural cliché preserves one's privacy. That people can talk about both levels of meaning concerning their group or institution shows an awareness of in-group and out-group and the appropriateness of certain types of explanations for each group. If someone is a total outsider, the general, simplified truth of *tatemae* preserves the integrity of the group while explaining the basics of the matter. For an insider already familiar with the situation, the *honne* mode of particularity and complexity is more appropriate.

All five of these communicative styles—screening, refraining, wrestling, othering, and layering—tend to emphasize shared cultural representations by articulating them while leaving the other side of the story silent, implicit, or expressed in a nonverbal manner. These five are not the only communicative styles that do this, but they were the ones I noticed most often. Nor do I mean to imply that they are restricted to Japan, for similar styles are found in many cultures, implicitly or explicitly.

Spirit Fox Mound (Reikozuka) at Toyokawa Inari. Stone shrine in center houses Dakiniten; about four hundred stone foxes have been donated by devotees.

A Society of Hidden Divergence

Why is it so important that dominant cultural representations are maintained in Japan? Why—particularly within the sphere of a religious practice without ties to national mythology, the emperor, or the state—do devotees maintain such careful distance from each other and from the priests concerning their innermost religious understandings? Why are there not debates between Buddhist and Shinto worshipers of Inari? Why are priests from the various sacred centers so reluctant to meet each other?

In contrast to cultures in which intimate personal experiences quickly become part of one's public self-definition, the personal in Japan is private and carefully protected. It most certainly exists, but it is not revealed casually to outsiders. In a society where people work closely and seldom change jobs or residences, preserving this inner core of personal conviction and experience is very important. People tend not to inquire too directly about private matters. And if they do, there are effective linguistic phrases that politely block further inquiry. Within Inari worship, almost every devotee had some kind of "believer's narrative" *(shinja taiken)*—an account of a strange happening, vision of the deity, important dream, and the like—that they attributed directly to the workings of Inari. In fact, the clearer and more numerous these were, the higher the person's spiritual status in some circles. But although important in establishing authority and legitimacy, the believer's narrative is a highly personal and therefore very private kind of talk. In contrast to some new religions, where testimonials are highlighted, in Inari worship I found that narratives might be shared within a small, familiar group—the worship group, the faction of priests sympathetic to this kind of experience, the family circle—or they might not be disclosed at all. Several of my informants told me they had never told anyone else about the experience they related to me.

Political historian Kamishima Jirō (1990) has a model of Japanese society that helps to explain why the surface levels might be maintained even within a noncontroversial cultural practice such as the worship of Inari. He argues that in a divergence society *(isei shakai)* such as the United States, diverse elements are acknowledged to exist and tend to cluster into ethnic groups or classes. Differences can be categorized in terms of groups large enough to be significant. In a convergence society *(junsei shakai)* such as Japan, there are many diverse elements that "coexist separately," but they are scattered and cannot coalesce because the different elements are divided into small, powerless groups. This state of affairs, coupled with what he terms the "phobia about potential isolation,"[18] compels people to think they must converge into homogeneous groups. He explains:

> The Japanese people, in fact, are extremely diverse and heterogeneous; so much so that there never was a majority. Every individual is a member of a minority; but this fact itself is hidden. Each group is careful not to reveal too clearly its uniqueness lest it be isolated from the others. Its best strategy is to pretend to sympathize with the others while concealing its uniqueness and the qualities that set it apart, and wait patiently until the opportunity arises for it to embrace a majority view. On the surface, therefore, all groups and individuals seem to be united, but at a deeper level their alignments are not strong, for each holds different views. [Kamishima 1990:6]

This fits in well with my observations within the world of Inari. People within a group conformed to the practices of that group. It was almost impossible to elicit personal narratives within a group setting, but people were usually eager to relate their unique experience or beliefs to me in a one-to-one setting.

This combination of significant divergence, fear of isolation, privatization of the personal, indirect communicative strategies, and the ability to speak in shared terms, even though they may be at odds with actual experience, results in the perpetuation of discourses of unity in the face of great diversity. This is not a matter of duplicity; to some extent notions of unity and diversity are both true. This may also explain why language has a reputation for being untrustworthy in Japan. Language is the vehicle for the dominant cultural representations—the shared, "official" part of cultural discourse—and people are aware that these sentiments are only partly true and may actually be at odds with much valued experience. Therefore, people's actions and other forms of nonverbal communication are more highly regarded than their words.

Shared and Private Meanings in the World of Inari

Considering *tatemae* and *honne* to be—rather than false front versus private position—something more akin to centripetal and centrifugal tendencies that center and decenter permits an analysis of both institutional and individual usages with the same terminology. By shared meanings, I mean those that are the most general, widely known, and tend to move toward a system or a symbolic center. I do not use the term "official" because there is no central authoritative body within Inari worship that decrees what is orthodox; the word "shared" implies the participation, willing or unwilling, of a group of people whereas "official" may be only words at the center. Private meanings are those that are particular, messy, idiosyncratic, and often contradict or decenter the elegant but simplistic shared meanings that describe the system. Private meanings may be those of one individual or a group.

In the world of Inari worship, these two tendencies, toward a shared system and a private particularity, can be found at every level of organization. A person may describe herself as a worshiper of Inari, and to some extent another person will understand what this means. But the devotee may worship an individualized version of Inari unique to her household in traditions invented by a shamaness and not shared by other Inari worshipers. A worship group centers and organizes beliefs and practices for its members by providing a meeting place in the home of the leader, periodic rituals and activities, and traditions that probably combine ideas from priests at the sacred centers as well as innovations by the leader. But individual members will have their own understandings, often not publicly articulated, based on personal experiences of Inari and religious notions learned as children. Even group worship at a sacred center includes time for private worship. Sacred centers in the form of Shinto shrines and Buddhist temples, sometimes located at the foot of a sacred mountain, provide the settings for large groups of Inari worshipers who follow the same tradition. Priests conduct a yearly round of rituals and transmit some teachings. The sacred space tends to be richly iconic: it is the setting at which historical traditions unfolded. But here too, although worshipers appear to be doing the same things in the same space, their understandings of what they are doing vary enormously. Even the priests have differing views about the meaning of the rituals they perform and the deity they serve. Finally, looking at Inari worship through the widest lens focuses on the key elements and simultaneously includes the greatest amount of diversity as well. The deity called Inari, its representative symbols, and its history center the phenomenon. But there is no single center for the whole world of Inari, no space sacred to all worshipers, not even one image of the deity that is common to the whole. There are multiple centers, and the centers themselves are multiple.

Although Inari is multiple, it is also unified, but in a decidedly nonsystematic way. This study has shown both the shared and the private dimensions of Inari worship. The shared centripetal features include certain outward elements such as the early historical situation of Inari's beginnings, its representative symbols of the fox and the jewel, and its ritual centers. The more divergent centrifugal aspects include the myriad understandings of individual devotees, the development and metamorphosis of rival traditions in the history of Inari's development, the many different readings of the fox and jewel symbol, the individualization of the deity into thousands of unique forms, and the popular energies that may rework older traditions. If I had focused on the centripetal in Inari, perhaps doing a detailed analysis of one sacred center, my study might have described a fairly homogeneous system of consistent meanings similar to other cultural systems in Japan. If I had looked only at the centrifugal tendencies, I might have described the conflict, discord, heterogeneity, and individuality in Inari and juxtaposed it against mainstream Japanese religiosity as some sort of marginal or antistructural phenomenon. But both dimensions are equally true of Inari, and studies that emphasize harmony or underscore conflict in Japanese society are isolating one or the other side of the phenomenon. The shared, centripetal values are the ones articulated in Japanese culture and as such are easier to study; centrifugal values are expressed in settings that tend to be private and sometimes less accessible to easy observation.

The Value of the Centripetal/Centrifugal Model

The relationship between dominant values and their oppositions has been conceptualized in a number of different ways in the literature: "cultural discontinuity" (Fernandez 1965), "a culture's negation held within it" (Geertz 1973:406), "purity and pollution" (Douglas 1966), "structure and anti-structure" (Turner 1967), "the reversible world" (Babcock 1978), and "divergent or nonnormative practices" (Ortner 1984). Such analyses tend to privilege the centers or structures and sometimes contain an essentialist tendency. Bakhtin's analyses start the other way around: he assumes it is the *order* in a system that needs to be explained, not the mess (Morson and Emerson 1990:30). This mistake is particularly difficult to avoid when describing Japanese culture, for dominant cultural representations are verbalized with remarkable consistency and the oppositional representations expressed, if at all, in ways that employ the indirect communicative styles described earlier. It is impossible to understand a phenomenon fully without seeing the constant tension between centrifugal and centripetal forces.

Every utterance of speech is a unique instantiation of a set of shared symbols of communication. And the center, or system, is not immutable—cultural, linguistic, and political fictions notwithstanding—but is constantly, if imperceptibly, being changed by centrifugal usages.

In the world of Inari worship, we have seen that notions of correct forms of worship are influenced by popular energies, but individual understandings of Inari are also influenced by ideas that come from the centers. Perhaps because of the several pairs of Japanese terms that describe these related ways of speaking and seeing—shared and personal *(tatemae/honne)*; front and back *(omote/ura)*; public and private *(kō/shi)*—Japanese culture contains an implicit understanding that centering and decentering tendencies are relative. At both sacred centers where I studied, priests described to me the lack of absolutes *(zettai)* in Japanese culture and quoted pairs of proverbs that expressed exactly opposite sentiments. But at the same time, we have seen that it is also common in Japanese culture to articulate statements which support the centering representations. Within Inari, the relativity may be more obvious than in other, ideologically central, cultural creations.

When central authority is too rigid, it may get overthrown. And when the center is a religious institution, this may result in the formation of new sects. But when there is no center, or the center is too weak, the group may lose its identity as a discrete phenomenon. I think the balance between these two extremes is at least a partial explanation for Inari's continued existence over thirteen centuries. Although Inari's institutions have had ties to the government at various times throughout their history, and the government has dictated certain policies the shrines or temples were obliged to follow, Inari worship has never been totally controlled by the state or by its own central institution. Inari is not a *kami* mentioned in the official mythologies of Japan; its control is not necessary in the maintenance of myths of the state and its rulers. Moreover, Inari institutions are not particularly articulate concerning their values, so there is no clash with dominant cultural meanings. Inari has by and large neither participated in nor challenged dominant political-religious meanings in Japan. Therefore the government has neither co-opted nor suppressed it.[19]

There has never been an institutional center to Inari that prevented natural change and development from occurring; on the other hand, Inari has had enough centering tendencies to preserve an identity distinct from other religious forms. The positive results of this balance between centrifugal and centripetal forces are Inari's long existence, flexibility, popularity, and worshipers' feeling of intimacy with the deity. Its freedom from dogmatic insistence on "truth" permits the simultaneous coexistence of many truths. Although these many voices are not in dialogue, the absence of one "monologizing" voice permits at least the potential for dialogue, growth, and change. But the same silence that has protected the multiplicity in Inari also hides it from its own members. Even devotees themselves are seldom aware of the richness and variety within the world of Inari.

Is the world of Inari, then, a characteristic phenomenon in Japan or a marginal exception? It is both. Inari's heterogeneity becomes apparent only upon investigation of a number of different centers—to the average worshiper, the diversity is not apparent. The lack of definitive central dogma and single controlling institution, coupled with the lack of communication between groups, make it possible for multiple forms to exist without people realizing that they are not in perfect conformity. This seems unusual if we believe, literally, the dominant cultural representation of homogeneity. But in fact, mainstream cultural phenomena are probably more heterogeneous than is often realized because we tend to focus on their consistently articulated shared meanings rather than on their privately articulated diversity. Inari is perhaps exceptional in Japanese society for having less clearly defined centralizing rhetoric than other cultural phenomena, but it is typical in the ways that shared and private meanings are strategically deployed.

The Silence of the Symbols

The lack of schism despite the numerous factions within the world of Inari is probably because neither the shared nor the private meanings are very clearly or deliberately articulated. Priests at the sacred centers do not proselytize or even provide information about basic beliefs in Inari beyond short historical descriptions of the shrine or temple. Because of the lack of dogma from the centers, people may not even realize that their personal position is at odds with priestly notions. The communicative styles through which different factions relate are vague and conceal more about private positions than they reveal, so that even though groups know themselves to be different from other groups, they are not engaged in dialogue.

The unifying symbols of Inari, particularly the fox and the jewel, are rich, multivocal, and flexible. The deity Inari has a number of forms, variable gender, and a variety of specialties that have changed as Japanese society has developed. The fox is associated with change (shape shifting), variety, and boundary crossing. But unlike folk foxes in Western cultures, or Hermes, with whom the Japanese fox has much in common (Brown 1947), the Japanese fox is not cunning of speech. He usually tricks people through appearances, not words. In fact, Meiji folk wisdom had it that foxes in human form could speak only in fragments of words (Hearn 1974:331). (The telephone salutation in Japanese is *"moshi moshi"*—so one immediately knows that the caller is a fox if only one *"moshi"* is forthcoming.) Thus Inari's main symbol stands in opposition to verbal expression, which in Japan tends to be used for conveying culturally shared meanings. Fox oracles are rarely spoken, usually symbolic, necessitating a specific interpretation for that situation. The jewel too grants not generic but specific wishes to the petitioner's prayers.

It is the silence of these symbols that has kept Inari continually popular and free of sectarian strife over the centuries in Japan. Because there is no central myth, dogma, or scripture that accompanies the symbols, there is no fixed orthodoxy governing them. Their significance is not tied to a set of verbal meanings that becomes reified as the "Truth" about Inari.

From Rice to Riches—
the Inclusiveness of Inari

Rigidity isn't the same as stability at all. True stability results when presumed order and presumed disorder are balanced. A truly stable system expects the unexpected, is prepared to be disrupted, waits to be transformed. As a psychiatrist, wouldn't you say that a stable individual accepts the inevitability of his death? Likewise, a stable culture, government or institution has built into it its own demise. It is open to change, open even to being overthrown. It is open, period. Gracefully open. That's stability. That's alive.

—Tom Robbins, *Even Cowgirls Get the Blues*

If this study is ever read by my informants, some may think that I have included too much in my description of the world of Inari. Priests would certainly prefer to see less attention paid to the fox. Devotees may wish that descriptions of groups with different institutional or spiritual orientations from theirs had been omitted. It was, however, my goal to look at the breadth of the Inari phenomenon rather than single out one aspect in greater depth. And by doing this, I hope I have demonstrated something about the workings of a religious phenomenon in Japan and not just its articulated, centered aspects.

Inari appeals to all classes, spans institutional boundaries, and is found throughout Japan. The deity's powers are not limited to a certain specialization but include a range from agriculture to business, from childbirth to fishing, from stopping coughs to passing exams. Inari is worshiped in many manifestations—as a *kami,* in Buddhist forms, and in countless individualized versions. Inari appears as a young woman and old man, as a bodhisattva, as a fox, snake, or dragon. There is no "pure" Inari in the center of all this from which these aspects derive or deviate. Individual worshipers and groups do have centers to their beliefs or activities and take their own center to be *the* center of Inari. But the polysemic meaning of Inari is the whole complex, not one systematized corner of it. The Shinto priests' preservation of historically transmitted ritual, the Buddhist priests complicated relationship to Inari in invented traditions, the shamanesses' revelations from the deity, businessmen constructing Inari shrines at their company to promote financial success, unhappy women praying to Inari for a divorce, people standing in Inari's waterfalls to cure cancer, children and their father setting out food for foxes at the coldest time of the year—all this is part of the Inari complex, although it may not appear so from the perspective of any single one of these positions.

The worship of Inari has taken on different emphases as the concerns of Japanese society change, but central at all times is the notion of fertility in its widest sense. Although the chief association with Inari seems to be rice and rice growing, and the main symbol the fox, the power of Inari extends far beyond the agricultural and natural into social realms as well. Rather than agriculture or nature per se, Inari is concerned with growth, change, and increase in all spheres, including the human, social, and financial. Its main symbols—the fox, jewel, cedar, rice, snakes, and red torii—may also symbolize fertility simultaneously in several spheres such as the agricultural, productive, reproductive, sexual, and financial. Although the overall development of the specialties of this *kami* began with rice, moved to sericulture, metalworking, protecting warriors, success of commerce and industry, and abundant fishing, and ended up today as one of the main *kami* of business prosperity, it is not always possible to read a simple linear evolution of the deity itself, or a certain shrine, along this path. In fact, rather than a road of progress or an archaeology of superseded notions, the metaphor would seem to be one of echoes and resonances. For earlier notions may still be apt, may take on new forms or meanings, may be extended.

Although today the rice rituals are not well attended compared with those relating directly to devotees' occupations and well-being, they are symbolically central for the shrine (as they are for many Japanese people not actively engaged in rice production) (Ohnuki-Tierney 1993). Among the hundreds of devotees I met at this shrine and sacred mountain, I met only one farmer—and he grew oranges, not rice. Yet many Japanese people feel strongly about rice, which takes on broad meanings beyond merely being the traditional staple grain of their culture. This explains why the priests at Fushimi Inari recently created a new *omamori* consisting of a few grains of rice, still on the stalk, in a plastic case with golden background. The talisman is called *minori no mamori,* protection of the harvest or bounty—intended in its broadest sense.

Because the people prosper if the rice does, and because Inari as the *yama no kami* in the winter months was associated with the ancestors, ideas of human fertility also became part of Inari beliefs (Iwai 1983:296). Certain Inaris became associated with human fertility and the power to grant babies. This specialty has been eclipsed, however, at some Inari shrines in recent years. At Eijūji (Shinshiro, Aichi prefecture), which has a flourishing Muei (Prosperous Dreams) Inari shrine within the precincts, the Buddhist priest said that most petitioners' requests until recently were for a good harvest and abundant offspring, but now they are mostly for business prosperity. Inari's shift from rice *kami* to money *kami* makes sense because rice was the medium of exchange in Japan before the change to a money economy. The transition was made even easier because Inari became a *kami* of luck *(fukugami)*. The broader meaning of rice as luck can be seen in the popular custom found among older people at Toyokawa Inari, where a vegetarian meal is served as part of the prayer service. To leave uneaten rice behind is to leave luck behind, they believe, so they take home any leftover rice they are unable to finish.

The main symbols of Inari (fox, jewel, rice) have been updated to work in a high-technology, mostly urban, money economy, but they still resonate with previous layers of meaning in the natural world. Apart from the power of tradition, these images are still relevant because they use natural images to signify cycles of growth and fertility. Rather than images of positive development only, they contain at least implications of the balancing element: the decay and death necessary to natural cycles. The term that signifies this natural fertility in Japanese and has particular significance in Shinto is *"musubi,"* usually written with the characters for "spirit of birth/production." Notwithstanding its shift from "natural" to "social" spheres, Inari's symbols continue to exemplify *musubi.* In her earliest role as *kami* of food production, Inari represents not just birth and growth but also death and decay. For the death of the food goddess produced new life in the form of grains and animals to feed the Japanese people, ritually marked every year when Inari is born as the field *kami* in the spring, produces the crop, and "dies" back into the mountain *kami* identity in the winter fire ritual. But no matter what the role or symbol of Inari—the circulation of money in cycles of growth and recession, the birth and growth of children, the shape shifting of his messenger foxes— the idea of change is included.[1]

In addition to symbolizing transformation, Inari's power comes from embracing, not rejecting, elements that might seem negative or undermining of its image. One author terms this tremendous "power to embrace" *(hōyō ryoku)* an "obstacle-free adaptability" *(yūzū muge)* (Kimura 1986: 223). There are numerous examples of the inclusion of the "negative" within Inari, usually balanced by its positive equivalent. The fox image worries priests who are afraid that people will sink into base animal worship; but for many it also symbolizes the mystery, power, and fundamental ineffability of the sacred. Fox possession has two sides: it was desired when possession by the fox-*kami* produced oracles concerning the next year's harvest; it was dreaded when a less spiritually evolved fox took over one's personality. Fox trickery has two sides, as well, one playful and evoking laughter, the other retributive and evoking terror. Another double image within Inari is fire. Inari was the patron *kami* of firemen, who put out destructive fires, and also of blacksmiths who used fire to transform metal into useful tools. Inari evades simple classifications because it not only includes too much but includes oppositions. It is Shinto *and* Buddhist *and* "folk"; it is urban *and* rural; it is priestly *and* shamanic. It is involved in agricultural *and* industrial *and* biological *and* financial spheres. Its ceremonies range from the elegant forms of high Shinto ceremony to shamanic possessions in front of cluttered altars in dirty little houses. Inari is incredibly successful at adapting to developments in Japanese society: it remains relevant without deliberate priestly revision or rationalization. This is because its primary meaning is change, growth, shape shifting—not the particular sphere of life in which the change happens. Inari seems particularly adept at spanning, moving, and adapting.

Although it has the greatest number of shrines of any Shinto deity and is one of the most widespread forms of traditional worship in Japan, Inari is not emphasized—sometimes not even mentioned—in many studies of Japanese religions. This may be due to a belief that it is less worthy of study than religious phenomena which developed clear philosophical or soteriological teachings. Inari worship has the reputation among certain nondevotees of being superstitious and followed by people who are primarily interested in acquiring money. Whatever its reputation, perhaps Inari is understudied because it is too familiar and therefore taken for granted by most Japanese. Wittgenstein tells us the consequence of this familiarity: "We fail to be struck by what, when seen, is the most striking and powerful" (1958:129).

The world of Inari is a "nonsystematic unity": it is ever-changing, open; its truths are culturally unreified. In addition to denying that any part of Inari worship represents its central truth, we must recognize that this book is only one view of the whole. A great deal more work remains to be done on this rich and complex phenomenon. Agreeing with Bakhtin that "all endings are merely new beginnings" (1984a:165), we wait, with great interest, to see what shapes the messenger fox of Inari and future scholarship will assume.

Notes

Chapter 1 Introducing Inari

1. Okada (1985:74) from a survey by the National Association of Shinto Shrines (Jinja Honchō). This survey gives the number of shrines as 32,000; the *Nihon rekishi daijiten* says there are 40,000 (1970:405). The term *"kami"* most broadly means "deity." It includes the deities named in the classical mythologies as well as local deities that protect areas, villages, and families. *"Kami"* also refers to the unnamed and often nonanthropomorphized spirits found in natural phenomena (trees, rivers, waterfalls) and, finally, to a general sense of sacred power.

2. I use the term "Shinto" as a shorthand for non-Buddhist, "indigenous" religious practices, both "authentic" and "invented." Recent scholarship has shown the term to be highly problematic—its current content is largely a political construction of the Meiji period (Kuroda 1981; Grapard 1992)—but I use it because this study concerns Inari in the modern period when the current usage came into being. The surprise of many of my informants regarding the existence of Buddhist Inari temples shows the success of the government's attempt to create separate conceptual categories regarding sites and certain identities, although practice remains multiple and nonexclusive.

3. About $14 at that time.

4. For a detailed presentation of this material see Smyers (1993:chap. 2).

5. The comprehensive history of Inari is yet to be written, as most studies tend to focus on one aspect of Inari from a folkloric or historical perspective. Important sources in Inari's history are seminal articles on the history of the Fushimi shrine by Higo Kazuo, Nishida Nagao, and Ueda Masaaki collected in Naoe (1983c). Also in this collection is the article by Sakamoto on the vicissitudes of a Nichiren Inari temple—an article that ought to become the prototype for future scholarship on Buddhist Inari, details of which were deliberately obscured during the separation of Buddhism and Shinto. Matsumae's edited volume (1988) also contains a mixture of folkloric and historical articles; especially important are the two essays by the Fushimi Inari priest

Toriiminami Masatoshi based on heretofore unavailable internal shrine records. De Visser's early work in English (1908a) on the Japanese fox provides
a handy reference to early records and texts relating to Inari; the only major
study of Inari in English (Buchanan 1935) gives important details about the
Fushimi shrine during prewar times. Folkloric sources are numerous, and
many provide important histories of Inari's development at sites other than
the parent shrine (Miyata 1983, 1988; Ōmori 1989, 1994; Naoe 1983a).
Buddhist forms of Inari are richly presented in Gorai (1985); although the
main argument is weakened by lack of historical grounding, the scholarship
of Gorai and his students does much to restore this important aspect of Inari.

Fushimi Inari Shrine deserves much credit for two extensive publishing
endeavors. Since 1967, the shrine has published a journal called *Ake* that
contains scholarly articles as well as testimonials of devotees and poetry
about Inari. Any article in the field of Inari studies, whether or not the shrine
agrees with its position, will be picked up and reprinted in *Ake*. From the
1950s to 1980s, moreover, the shrine published *Inari Taisha yuishoki shūsei*,
a series of volumes containing a variety of historical records including those
from the Shingon temple Aizenji (located within Fushimi Inari Shrine) relating
to the Buddhist traditions in the early years of Inari. To do justice to the
complex, eclectic, locally variable histories of Inari, much more archival research is necessary.

6. Some of the material in this section appeared in slightly different form
in Smyers (1991).

7. It is interesting that in similar traditions involving the flight of a white
bird, the area is forsaken by the *kami* and turns barren. The growth of rice
in this story is interpreted as evidence of Inari's benevolence even after the
sacrilegious act of shooting at the rice (Fushimi 1969:18; 1977:71).

8. The founding year of 711 (Wadō 4) comes from a Heian-period text,
the *Nenjū gyōji hisshō* (949). The tradition that the founding was on the first
horse day of the second month *(Niigatsu no hatsuuma),* however, probably
related to the agricultural calendar. This was the day in the lunar calendar
when the mountain *kami* descended to the fields as the rice *kami* and farmers
began planting (Higo 1983:5 and 13-14).

9. I use "cedar" as the translation for *sugi;* more exactly it signifies Japan
cedar (cryptomeria).

10. This is found in a document dated 814, the *Shinsen shōjiroku,* the
New Compilation of Surnames, which states in the section on the Hata clan
that they were descended from the thirteenth-generation descendant of the
Ch'in emperor (Fushimi 1977:24).

11. Several suggested etymologies are: cooked rice (Takahashi 1931:2),
rice cutting or rice gathering (Casal 1949:12), sound of lightning (Naitō and
Shimokawa 1979:190). See the glossary for characters.

12. Conversation with Kuroda Takehiro, November 1985. The suggestion

has intrigued several scholars, but we have not yet determined what the original word might have been.

13. The custom of assigning court rank to *kami* began in the Nara period after 729 and is based on the Japanese view that humans, *kami,* and buddhas exist on the same continuum (Ueda 1983:282).

14. There seems to be no clear answer in the Japanese scholarship on this point, and most scholars who deal with these texts do so with little regard for historical contextualization. The Shinto scholars tend not to cite these Buddhist texts, although they admit there was a strong connection between Tōji and Inari both historically and in terms of people's beliefs (Fushimi 1977:82). However, that these texts are available at all for study is to the credit of Fushimi Inari Shrine, which gathered and published them in the *Shinkō* volume of the *Inari Taisha yuishoki shūsei* (Fushimi 1957).

15. Literary references to Inari pilgrimage are found in *Kagerō nikki* (Seidensticker 1964:61), *Makura no sōshi* (NKBT 19:210-211; Morris 1991:172), *Ōkagami* (McCullough 1980:154-155 and 215), *Konjaku monogatari* (NKBT 5:52-54; Brower 1952:646-650 and 1009-1012), and *Heiji monogatari* (NKBT 31:2130; Reischauer and Yamagiwa 1972:322).

16. Although it gives no details, *The Poetic Memoirs of Lady Daibu (Kenreimon-in Ukyō no Daibu shū)* mentions a poetry competition held at the Inari shrine between 1170 and 1175 (Harries 1980:65 and 94-95; NKBT 80:423).

17. This is the present main sanctuary *(honden),* designated by the government as an important cultural asset *(jūyō bunkazai).*

18. The spirit of Kada Azumamaro is enshrined in a subshrine within Fushimi's precincts, although it is not legally part of the Fushimi Inari Shrine. It was built in 1883 (Shimonaka 1937, I:335) or 1890 (Fushimi 1985:7) by a Fushimi priest, but in 1913 it was turned over to the descendants of Azumamaro who continue to run it. Because he was a great scholar, the shrine attracts students with prayers for academic success.

19. This idea is found as early as stories in the *Konjaku monogatari* and *Uji shūi monogatari,* when a fox is used to deliver a message from Toshihito to his family to prepare for his arrival with a guest. The fox used a combination of supernatural speed and possession: he ran to the family home, then possessed Toshihito's wife to deliver the specifics of the instructions. See *Konjaku monogatari* (26.17) (NKBT 25:458-463); *Uji shūi monogatari* (1.18) (NKBT 27:78-85); translated in Mills (1970:155-161) and Tyler (1987:118-122).

20. See Hardacre (1989) for a detailed study of the process and its results.

21. An incident concerning this guild appears in the *Nihon shoki,* in the Ninken chapter, in the year 493 (Aston 1972, I:396-397).

22. The five *kami* enshrined then are not the same five enshrined now; lecture by head priest Suzuki Kazuo on November 3, 1990.

23. From a recent temple pamphlet, "A Brief History of Toyokawa Inari"

(Toyokawa Inari ryaku engi). I translated this pamphlet at the request of the priests so that they would have English-language material for foreign visitors. See Bodiford (1993:37-43) for the history and hagiography of Giin in the Zen tradition.

24. Almost none of my informants, including priests, were aware of this iconographic difference, and the images were worshiped interchangeably. Murai Ichirō, who has been studying this topic for over thirty years, kindly instructed me about the Buddhist forms worshiped as Inari.

Chapter 2 Priestly Traditions and Shamanic Influences

1. See Nelson (1993) for a detailed study of a Shinto shrine and the training and ranking of priests at Kamigamo Shrine.

2. It has been possible, since the war, for women to become Shinto priests, and today they make up almost 8 percent of the Shinto priesthood. Of the 20,363 priests registered in 1990, 1,564 were women (conversation with Shimada Tatsuhisa of the Kenshūjo, Jinja Honchō, January 19, 1990). But with the exception of a few shrines such as Yasaka Shrine in Kyoto, female priests tend to be found in family shrines in rural areas, where they work as a team with their husband or have taken over from their husband or father.

3. Not all Shinto priests have college degrees, although this is the norm at the larger urban shrines.

4. Smaller shrines in Japan are family run and the job of priest is passed down from father to son (and now, sometimes, daughter). The eldest son is expected to take the job, but this is flexible. When the shrine does not generate enough income for two families, the son may work at a larger shrine to gain experience until he takes over his father's job.

5. I could not get specific figures concerning the shrine's financial situation. Not only would the priests not tell me directly, but the information is not on file in any public office. As a "religious institution" *(shūkyō hōjin),* the shrine pays no taxes and does not have to report its income to the government. Employees must pay taxes based on their salary to the government, however, and the parts of the shrine that are incorporated as profit-making ventures (the pilgrims' inn) do pay taxes. Every summer the shrine sends five employees chosen by lottery on an expenses-paid trip abroad. (Europe and Hawai'i were two recent destinations.) Much income seems to come from small items sold in large quantities: from the sale of wooden offering sticks burned in the November fire ritual (Ohitaki Sai), the shrine derives about $640,000 (200 yen × 40,000 sticks). During the New Year season alone, the shrine sells about 2 million oracle papers *(omikuji),* which, at 100 yen per paper, generates over $1.5 million.

6. This was actually a rather small number of priests, and had to do with

complex institutional factors. Some priests were unwilling to speak with me at all. Others assumed I was the responsibility of a certain office and so they did not have to bother. Others later told me although they had wanted to get to know me, they were of a lower rank than the priests I mostly spoke to, and so felt unable to approach me. On top of all this was the general nervousness of dealing with a foreigner, even though I was there for a full year and returned periodically during a second year. The priests who did speak to me were wonderfully kind and tolerant and exceedingly generous with time and information.

7. The Betsuin (branch temple) in Tokyo employs 34 priests and 44 lay workers, and this number swells to 120 workers during big festivals and at the new year.

8. Usually Sōtō Zen students go to Komazawa University in Tokyo, but some go to Hanazono University in Kyoto, a college of the Rinzai sect of Zen. University training does not necessarily restrict where a priest may work; priests at Myōgonji had also studied at Kōyasan University (Shingon sect) and the Tendai university on Mount Hiei. I met a priest at the Nichiren temple Saijō Inari who had trained at the Sōtō Zen temples Toyokawa and Eiheiji. One of the most dedicated Sōtō priests I knew had attended a Christian university. Sectarian lines are not usually crossed like this, but neither are they totally restrictive.

9. Most of the *okozō san* were from temple families; a rare few were interested enough in Buddhism to enter this life without family obligations. Another motivation to enter this path is to atone for some serious karmic misfortune in one's family, such as the death of a number of the children or the death of the father's first and then subsequent wives.

10. A number of Shinto or "folk" elements had entered the ritual calendar, but these were always celebrated in a Buddhist manner. One example was the temporary altar *(ehō dana* or *toshidana)* set up to the deity Toshitokujin (also called Toshigami or Shōgatsu-sama) at the new year. This deity moves to a new location each year, and the altar, suspended from the ceiling, faces the direction of that year, which is thought to be auspicious. The priests chanted sutras there on New Year's Eve, then offered the seven herbs for good health on January 7, after which the altar was dismantled until the next year.

11. See Reader (1986) for the status of meditation within contemporary Sōtō Zen in Japan.

12. I found this to be odd in Japan, where most institutions have at least one person who is well versed in its history. There was no library of basic reference materials at Toyokawa and no old records of any sort. (At least none were shown to me.) Saijō Inari, which seems to have had a parallel history during the Meiji purges, had an impressive library of reference books on Buddhism and Inari studies, and one priest there was very interested in the question of invented traditions.

13. He is referring to the proverb, "Because even a sardine's head can become an object of faith" *(iwashi no atama mo shinjin kara)*.

14. My erroneous assumption was based more on how Zen has been presented in the West than the way it functions in Japan. See Sharf (1995) and Bodiford (1993).

15. *"Hōben"* in Japanese, *"upaya"* in Sanskrit, this term means using whatever means are necessary, even if they are not doctrinally pure, in the salvation of sentient beings.

16. Buddhist sutras in Japan are written not in Sanskrit but in Chinese and recited using Japanese pronunciation of the characters. Ritual formulas (mantras), however, are sometimes in sinified Sanskrit, written in kanji (or katakana).

17. This is the assumption of most Fushimi Inari priests, even though most have never visited or studied Toyokawa Inari.

18. See Bouchy (1985) for a detailed discussion of these two styles of shamanic initiation among the Inari shamans. Both practice austerities to develop or control spiritual powers.

19. The "waterfall austerity" *(takigyō)* is the religious practice of chanting prayers in a waterfall, usually in a sacred spot in the mountains. It derives from the practices of the *yamabushi* mountain ascetics and is done, wearing white ritual garb, as a purification, meditation, or method of garnering spiritual powers. See Blacker (1975).

20. The priests at Fushimi Inari Shrine thought that women constituted about two-thirds of the shamans they knew. Bouchy found an equal number of males and females in her survey of Inari shamans but notes that their way of becoming a shaman differs (1985:179).

21. We should note, however, the important deviation from Chinese prototype by which the imperial institution in Japan emphasizes an unbroken genealogy rather than the Mandate of Heaven legitimating the emperor's position (see Smith 1983:12).

22. It would require too much space to describe the variations this tension between institutional and shamanic forms has taken throughout Japanese history. In general the two have been in a creative tension rather than an antagonistic one. See Kitagawa (1966), Blacker (1975), and Sansom (1943) for detailed accounts.

23. The parish *(ujiko)* now stretches from Matsubara Street in the north to Kujō Dōri in the south and from Senbon Dōri in the west to Honmachi in the east. The parish is divided into three areas that have different responsibilities during the Inari Festival in April.

24. I am describing "ideal types" (Weber 1949:90ff) of priests and shamans; as we shall see, the actual situation is full of hybrids and contradictions. One unusual man had training and licenses to be a Shinto priest, an esoteric Buddhist priest, and was sometimes possessed by deities. Possession,

however, never occurred at his place of employment, but only at home, in front of his own altar.

25. This is a mystical formula from the esoteric tradition that involves hand gestures (mudra) and a loud guttural shout. It is used to dispel pollution and harmful spirits. See Waterhouse in Kornicki and McMullen (1996:1–38) for a rich history.

26. Raw seasonal vegetables are usually included in Shinto offerings, especially shiny colorful ones. There is nothing inherently wrong with this offering. It would tend not to be given by a devotee, however, but would be purchased by the priests directly.

27. I saw several other cases in which a religious specialist supplanted an older tradition with a new one—in one case worshiping an older statue of a male figure as a female goddess. Her clients did not question what she told them.

28. There were exceptions to this general situation, however, for a priest might be very fond of even an extreme shamaness because they shared other ideas in common.

29. *"Dantai"* means group; *"atsukaisho"* literally means place of service; *"shibu"* means branch (office) or local chapter.

30. The yearly donation is called *ohatsuhoryō*, literally "amount of offering of first fruits." This term, reflecting the custom of offering the first of the harvest to the *kami*, is used in place of the terms "price" and "cost" at Shinto shrines. Therefore, talismans and such are not sold: they are given in exchange for an offering to the *kami*, an offering that these days takes the form of money.

31. In 1989–1990, these sums were roughly $8, $16, and $40, respectively.

32. They try to distribute these return gifts during the Great Festival for Kō Members (Kōin Taisai) during October but must mail out the gifts to members who do not attend. Over 80,000 people are registered as *kō* members, making this an enormous task. The priests try to ensure that each member gets the appropriate gift, for this is the only time during the year that the shrine is in direct contact with all its members. In 1989, the gifts were a vinyl bag with a fox printed on it, a coin purse, and, for the biggest contributors, a pocket calculator. Each member also received a religious calendar.

33. There are a number of religious groups in Japan that use the names "Inari" and even "Fushimi Inari" without express permission from Fushimi Inari Shrine. The priests do not like this, but there is not much they can do to stop it. A few years ago, there was some publicity about a "bathhouse of ill repute" *(sōpurando)* that called itself Fushimi Inari, complete with attendant "shrine priestesses." Of course, it had no connection to the shrine. The priests just ignored the embarrassing press, which soon died down.

34. The Nichiren-related Saijō Inari was similar to Fushimi in having a training course to license religious specialists, but similar to Toyokawa in not regulating *kō* very closely. The training period, *Aragyō* (Rough Austerities),

takes place twice a year for twenty-one days; women and men train separately. The priests keep track of religious institutions that are directly connected with Saijō Inari (about thirty-nine), but they felt that Inari *kō* were too fluid for them to register or regulate.

35. It is not clear how old this position is. Kada Azumamaro notes in his "Oral Transmission of the Inner Secrets of the Inari Shrine" (1694) that the fox derives from Kūkai's Buddhist history of the shrine, but *kitsune* (written with different characters) designates the ordinary state of energy *(ki-tsune)*, which is the name of the collective divine virtue of this shrine (Fushimi 1953: 329). Hirata Atsutane (around 1809) strongly states that people mistakenly worship Inari as a fox but the fox, in fact, is Inari's messenger (Kirby 1910:49). So there is evidence that some Edo-period National Learning scholars were at least as concerned as their post-Meiji fellow priests about the "fox problem."

36. See O'Keefe (1982) and Tambiah (1990) for studies of the tensions between "magic" and "rationality" in the West and their historical and philosophical constructions.

37. See Smyers (1997) for a description of the Seven Mysterious Traditions.

38. Although the naive use of the term "family" implies warmth and closeness, the actual family enterprise may be a far cry from this ideal. See Kondo (1990) and Hamabata (1990) for rich studies of family businesses in Japan.

39. I must emphasize that the priests themselves were generally exceedingly kind and generous to the visitors and to me. What I am describing is the overall ethos of the shrine, which they themselves acknowledged. Head priest Tsubohara generously gave me many of the shrine's published volumes for my study, and several priests patiently answered what must have seemed an unending stream of questions about Inari. These were wonderful people. It was the shrine, not the priests, that had a reputation for coldness.

40. See Chapter 6. This factionalism is not unique to Inari worship: it characterizes a great deal of behavior and social organization in Japan. Even groups opposed to mainstream norms are fragmented and cannot form coalitions that might challenge the status quo. The student movement Zengakuren, for example, began in the 1950s and split into at least thirty-two factions. One of these, the New Left Kyōsandō, produced in turn fifty-four factions. Disputes between factions were often violent. Steinhoff notes that "even during the peak years of violence in student confrontations with university and civil authorities, more students were injured in internal disputes than in clashes with external enemies" (1984:182).

Chapter 3 Symbolizing Inari: The Fox

Parts of this chapter were published as "Encountering the Fox in Contemporary Japan: Thoughts of an American Anthropologist," *Études sur les Cultes Populaires de Japon: Recueil à la memorie du Professeur Gorai Shigeru*

(Kyoto: Publications de l'École Française d'Extreme-Orient). They are used here with the publisher's permission.

1. Found in the *Nihon ryōiki* (Nakamura 1973:104-105; *NKBT* 70:67-69), compiled by the priest Keikai in the eighth century. Other versions of the story are listed in De Visser (1908a:20) and Mayer (1986:31-32). A later version is the famous *Shinoda no Mori* about the fox wife Kuzunoha.

2. "Come and sleep," *kite neru*, rendered as *"ki-tsu-ne"* (Nakamura 1973:105). Koizuka notes that although the etymology is clearly false, it is frequently cited (1982:12). Yet another pun lurks within this folk etymology: written with different characters, *"ki-tsune"* may also mean "come always" (Nakamura 1973:105, n. 7).

3. The snake, here called Miisan, is also a messenger of Inari. Uganomitama is one of the *kami* most often associated with Inari, but another form of Inari is called Ugajin, represented as a coiled snake with the head of an old man (often housed inside a wish-fulfilling jewel). Farmers used to begin planting when the snakes came out of the earth in the spring—they were seen as messengers of the grain *kami* bringing this critical information about timing (Fushimi 1969:42). Inari's iconographic snakes were sometimes interpreted to be silkworms when sericulture was a predominant sphere of Inari's protection. The snake is a symbol in Japan for luck and money, and some people keep shed snakeskins in their wallet to increase their wealth.

4. Japanese sources often cite Frazer's observation that in Europe the last sheaf of grain to be harvested was called the Wolf or the Fox (in addition to a number of other animals). For fox references see Frazer (1912, I:268, 287, 296-297).

5. The listing of the nine-tailed fox as lucky is curious, as it later comes to represent a very unlucky, wanton, depraved creature. But in China, too, the nine-tailed fox was initially a positive symbol of immortality that later took on negative characteristics. Details follow in the discussion of foxes, jewels, and sexuality in Chapter 4.

6. Translation also found in Smits (1996:84).

7. Text in Fushimi (1957:41-42). I am indebted to Jacqueline Stone for assistance with Buddhist terminology in this passage.

8. Until the Meiji period, Akomachi was worshiped in a building called the White Fox Shrine *(byakkosha)*. Osusuki and Kuroo never had their own shrines, but they were worshiped at designated rocks.

9. Fushimi's *Commentary on Beliefs* (1969:40) says this happened in Enkyū 3 (1071), but the *Chronology (Nenpyō)* (Fushimi 1962a:58) places it in Enkyū 4 (1072). The latter text mentions the imperial pilgrimage but is silent about the Myōbu tradition.

10. Or Kangiten. See Sanford (1991a) for a fascinating discussion of this Japanese version of the Indian elephant-headed deity Ganesha.

11. Cited in numerous records of priests at Fushimi Inari Shrine including

Shirushi no sugi (Fushimi 1972:56) and *Inari jinja ko* (Fushimi 1972:172) and in the nonshrine records *Yoru no hijiri* (written by 1738; Fushimi 1983:271) and the 1873 *Jingi shiryōfukō* (Fushimi 1983:257).

12. One of the two cosmological diagrams and meditation aids used by esoteric Buddhism. The Taizōkai is the Womb World or Matrix Realm; its complement is the Kongōkai, or Diamond Realm. Together these mandalas represent the "reality principle aspect" and "wisdom aspect" of the Buddha Dainichi (Inagaki 1985:254–255).

13. This sutra is one of the three used by the Shingon sect; the commentary was written in China in the eighth century (Inagaki 1985:33).

14. See, for example, the so-called Dakiniten Mandala at Osaka Museum, said to be from the Muromachi period. A color photograph of this work appears in Osaka shiritsu bijutsukan (1986:84). A similar mandala is discussed in Murai (1990).

15. This image would have been in sharp contrast to earlier ones of a female food goddess. See the discussion of the gender change in images of Inari in Yamaori (1986).

16. This is the position advocated by Murai (conversation) and Sasama (1988a; 1988b) and noted by Sanford (1991b:16).

17. A parallel taxonomic confusion seems to have existed in Old Testament translations by Talmudic scholars, where the fox and jackal were sometimes confused. The famous episode of Samson tying torches to three hundred fox tails and burning the Philistine harvest (Judges 15:4) should have referred to jackals (Macdonald 1987:85).

18. I use "sorcery" in a value-neutral sense here. The *Dakiniten-hō* and *Izuna-hō* were esoteric rituals that soon lost their orthodox goals of the realization of wisdom and became magical practices for the achievement of practical ends. They seem to have had a positive and a negative side, both very powerful. These rites could be used, sometimes by employing helping foxes, to drive out possessing foxes and other evil spirits; but they could also be used to harm one's enemies and therefore were seen by some as dangerous and heretical. See Sanford (1991b), Gorai (1985:85), De Visser (1908a:118ff), and Blacker (1975:55).

19. Story in *Kokonchomonju* (265); *NKBT* 84:214–219; translated in Tyler (1987:63–64).

20. There are almost no foxes living in Shikoku, the large island below the Inland Sea. Tradition has it that Kūkai, legendary founder of Shikoku's pilgrimage route of eighty-eight temples, drove them out—a wonderful irony in view of the fact that he (or at least his sect) may be responsible for the association of the fox with Inari.

21. See Manabe and Vidaeus (1975:13–14 and 18) for lists of fox names throughout Japan.

22. Badgers *(tanuki)* traditionally are shape-shifting animals in Japan. Al-

though there are important differences between the cultural conceptions of foxes and badgers in Japan, there is sometimes a structural equivalency and a badger will be worshiped as Inari or his messenger. In general, badgers are regarded as more humorous and less dignified than foxes. The more accurate translation of *tanuki* is "raccoon dog," not "badger" (Macdonald, pers. comm.), but I have decided to follow tradition at the expense of proper zoological taxonomy. The raccoon dog is found in Asia, and it is unique among dogs for its quasi hibernation in winter. It stuffs itself with fruit and berries in the fall and spends the winter in communal dens in a "period of lethargy" (Macdonald 1992:83 and 173).

23. Versions in De Visser (1908a:71); Buchanan (1935:41-42); Hartshorne (1902:317).

24. Some scholars think it may have come to Japan in the early Meiji period with American sailors (*Ōzuka minzoku gakkai* 1978:259).

25. See Smyers (n.d.) for a more thorough presentation of this material.

26. See episodes in *Konjaku monogatari* 16.17 and 27.41 and examples in Chapter 4 relating to sexuality and foxes.

27. The propensity to take the fox itself as Inari has parallels with the tension in Catholicism between theological and supernatural levels of signification of a symbol (Turner and Turner 1978:143). In the case of Inari, however, the situation is complicated by the absence of a central scriptural or narrative tradition.

28. Sex is only rarely indicated by the presence of genitals on the statue. As one faces the shrine, the male is usually positioned on the right and the female on the left. A priest explained that from the *kami*'s point of view, the male is always on the left, which is the side of the heart, and hence the most important side.

29. Fox statues are usually well proportioned, but for some reason the skinniest ones I ever saw were both at Zen temples. The black metal foxes in Toyokawa Inari's main hall are quite thin and their ears are a little too large, which may make them look even thinner. An exceedingly emaciated set, colored white, can be found at a subtemple to Dakiniten within Gion's Kenninji Temple: their bones jut out in a way most painful to look at. The priest there had no idea why they were so thin. The polemical use of foxes in relation to Buddhism would make an interesting study. In some stories, virtuous priests exorcise or expose an evil fox; in others, priests who are too devout are suspected of being a fox in disguise.

30. Conversation, April 5, 1996.

31. The Okusha (literally "back shrine")—changed from its former name "Okunoin" to one less Buddhist-sounding about thirty years ago—is also part of the shrine proper and its office is run by Fushimi priests. Believers practice more popular forms of worship here (such as folk divination and the offering of candles, votive plaques, and small prayer flags) than at the main shrine.

32. March 25, 1991. Toyokawa Inari celebrates Hatsuuma rather minimally on its date in the lunar calendar, about a month later than it occurs in the solar. The branch temple in Tokyo celebrates it in a major way on the earlier date.

33. In fact, one priest said he saw a television program in which three dishes containing meat, fish, and fried tofu were set out before a fox—and the tofu was the last choice of the fox.

34. That all foxes in Japan go as pilgrims to Fushimi Inari was a tradition at least as early as 1697 (De Visser 1908a:99).

35. Fox owning, *kitsune mochi,* was a discriminatory category applied to certain households that had acquired sudden wealth—thought to have derived from the presence of seventy-five tiny foxes living in the house. The ascription was hereditary, and other families refused to intermarry with fox owners. See Blacker (1975:51-68) and Hayashimi (1976).

36. *Kitsune ken* is portrayed in a netsuke in Joly (1908:facing p. 74) and in a woodblock print in Linhart (1995:44-45).

37. Poem 3824, *NKBT* 7:140.

38. Examples of stories in which people know that a monk is really a fox, but respect his loyalty and treat him kindly, can be found in Manabe and Vidaeus (1975:14-15).

39. This was the case at Anamori Inari, concerning a miraculous sand tradition, and at Daitsūji in Nagahama about the fox Ohana-gitsune who saved the temple from burning (Nomura and Abe 1982; Nakajima 1989).

40. See Smith (1989), particularly p. 722.

41. While working on the final revisions of this text, I deleted this sentence as somewhat gratuitous—and soon thereafter lost the entire chapter and the backups as well.

42. *Nihon ryōiki* (2.4) version in Nakamura (1973:163-164; *NKBT* 70:183-185); *Konjaku monogatari* (23.17) version in *NKBT* 25:254-255.

43. One tale replaces the fox with Inari—who gives a magic hood, enabling the wearer to understand animal speech, to a fervent devotee (Mayer 1986:124-125).

44. This story, from the *Konjaku monogatari,* is presented more fully in the next chapter.

45. This man was the older brother of a shamaness. He told me this story at the party after the spring ritual for Inari held at this woman's tiny home for her believers.

46. The longer form of the name is *"kitsune no kan segyō"* ("meritorious feeding of foxes at the Great Cold"). In some areas of Japan, *"segyō"* is pronounced *"sengyō."*

47. The term *"kitsune-gari"* is ambiguous here: it literally means fox hunting, but the *"kari"* suffix is also used to mean sighting or collecting, as in *momiji-gari,* maple viewing, and *kinoko-gari,* mushroom gathering. The ac-

tivity is also ambiguous regarding the fox, for the good ones are in a sense collected while the bad ones are hunted.

48. Rice cooked with red beans is also a common popular offering at Inari shrines, perhaps because of the red color.

Chapter 4 Symbolizing Inari: The Jewel

1. See Plutchow (1990) for a wide-ranging discussion of this aspect of *tama;* see Ebersole (1989) for an extremely insightful description of *tama* based on the evidence of ancient Japanese funeral laments.

2. There are many variants on this tale within the *Nihon shoki* (Aston 1972, I:92-108). The *Kojiki* version is a single narrative (Philippi 1968:148-155).

3. Now, adjusted to the solar calendar, the rite occurs about one month before the winter solstice.

4. See Ebersole (1989:160) on this ritual for Amaterasu.

5. See Newall (1971) for wide-ranging examples of egg imagery and fertility, alchemy, creation myths, resurrection, renewal, and rebirth throughout the world.

6. See *Nihon shoki* variant in Aston (1972,I:166-70), where the jewel is a white stone, and a related Korean myth described in Philippi (1968:423).

7. See Blacker (1975:45f) for a discussion of ideas and scholarship concerning the relation of the dead soul as *tama* to the *kami.*

8. Definitions combined from Ross (1965:39-40), Katō (1937:32-33), and Herbert (1967:61-64).

9. Conversations with head priest Suzuki Kazuo on February 17, 1991.

10. This reliquary was originally at Kongōji, the temple *(bettō)* connected with Ise Shrine. Purchased by the twenty-eighth head priest of this temple in early Meiji, when shrines were forced to remove all Buddhist objects, it is said to have been given to Ise by Gyōki Bosatsu when he went to Ise to get permission from the sun goddess to build Tōdaiji (conversation with priest, May 15, 1991, and information on back of donation receipt for December 9, 1990). Gyōki and the relic are mentioned in Kitagawa (1966:43).

11. There is, however, a reproduction of it in Yasui (1986:111), a book for sale at many local shops in Toyokawa.

12. The picture talisman may be left over from more esoteric Buddhist traditions that seem to have once been a part of worship here but were expurgated during the forced sanitization of the Meiji period. A pamphlet from some decades later hints at this move by its repeated emphasis on the rational historical traditions and lack of any superstitious elements at this temple (Takahashi 1931).

13. The origin of the *maṇi* jewel, in addition to coming from the head of a dragon or mythical fish, is said to be a metamorphosis of the Buddha's bones (Furuta 1988:894).

14. This is the reworked version of the 1750 story of a fox named Heihachi-gitsune mentioned in Chapter 1. The pot still exists (pictured in Yasui 1986:119) and is enshrined in a special cupboard behind the main altar. When a young priest showed me the magic pot, he remarked that it would be a far better relic if it did not read "Heihachirō's Pot" in raised characters.

15. Summarized from Nozaki (1961:166-168) and Koizuka (1982:170-172).

16. See Goff (1991:12-14) for a history of this story in its theatrical forms.

17. Other versions say the reign of Emperor Toba (1107-1123). Some versions say that she was a woman who was reborn in these three countries, finally turning into a white fox and causing even more mischief.

18. The diviner was Abe no Yasuchika or Yasunari, descendant of Abe no Seimei, the child of a fox mother and human father in the story "Kuzuno no Ha" (Nozaki 1961:111 and 113).

19. This Life-Killing Rock, Sesshōseki, is located in Nasuno, northeast of Tokyo, in a hot springs district. Powerful sulfuric fumes that emerge from the ground near this rock actually do kill small animals and may even prove fatal to humans who ignore the signs and enter the barren area (Kusano 1953:102-105).

20. Chamberlain (1911:115-116). For various versions of the Tamamono-mae story see De Visser (1908a:51-55), Buchanan (1935:40-41), Kusano (1953:95-108), and Nozaki (1961:112-113). The earliest written version seems to be the *Kagakushu* (1444); it appears soon after in the *Nikkenroku* (1453). The incident involving Gennō is supposed to have taken place around the middle of the thirteenth century. See Bodiford (1993:173-174) for the historical background of Gennō; see Goff (1997) for a description and photograph of the play.

21. I am indebted to Anna Seidel for these references.

22. In the *Konjaku monogatari* (14.5) (*NKBT* 25:283-285); also found in the *Dainihonkoku hokekyōkenki* (Dykstra 1983:142-143) and *Kokoncho-monju* (no.681); *NKBT* 84:513-515; Tyler (1987:115-116).

23. Translation by Chambers (1994:7). Kuzunoha is the fox-woman's name as well as the word for "arrowroot leaf." See Goff (1991:15) for a history of the evolution of this story in Japanese theater.

24. Some of these rice-related rituals are late additions to the yearly round of observances. According to the priests, the rice planting festival (Taue Sai), for example, is not mentioned in the book of rituals conducted by the Hata line of priests in the Edo period, so it has been added since then. But the rituals for welcoming the *kami* from the mountain to the rice fields, and the corresponding thanks ritual in the fall, are among the oldest at the shrine.

25. I am not sure why there are twelve fox holes here. The number does resonate with the folk belief that the mountain deity, *yama no kami,* is a female who gives birth to the twelve months of the year and is therefore

known as Mrs. Twelve *(jūni sama)*. She was invoked by women in difficult labor: the husband would lead a horse toward the mountain to meet her and carry her to his home (Hori 1968:167).

26. The names mean "fifteen" and "sixteen," respectively. The significance is unclear.

27. See Greey (1882:107-108) for a similar testimonial from an earlier period.

28. It may seem that I am taking this 1935 study too seriously, but it has been the only English source on Inari for many decades. It is valuable as a starting point and for its depiction of customs at Fushimi Inari Shrine, which have changed over the last fifty years. But it must be used critically—as a document reflecting much about the scholarly concerns of the day.

29. Conversation on April 4, 1990, with Suzuki Hidetoshi, head priest of Yasaka Shrine in Kyoto, who worked at Fushimi Inari in the 1930s as a young man.

30. Another reason for this might have been the Shingon Buddhist influence at Fushimi Inari Shrine. The temple Aizenji housed the figure Aizen Myōō (Skt. Rāga Vidyārāja), who symbolized the Mahāyāna Buddhist notion that "evil passions are themselves enlightenment" *(bonnō soku bodai)* (Inagaki 1985:3 and 16). More popular interpretations turned this figure into a deity of romantic ties *(enmusubi)* (Furuta 1988:4). The *honji butsu* of the three main deities of Inari Mountain—the deities Dakiniten, Benten, and Kangiten—all have some sexual associations, at least at the popular level.

31. A geisha (literally "artist") was not necessarily a prostitute, although she could be. See Dalby (1985:54-64).

32. The characters used are literally "heavenly dog" *(tengu)*, but they are glossed with the reading "heavenly fox" (De Visser 1908b:35). In India, falling stars were seen as Garuda—a mythical half-bird, half-human creature that emitted fire from its mouth (Sasama 1988a:154; Inagaki 1985:169). There are many similarities between the fox and *tengu*. Both can possess people, have a magic pearl, can appear in the shape of a buddha, set houses on fire, and have knowledge of everything within a thousand miles (De Visser 1908b:36). The two figures come together in the syncretic deities Akiba Gongen and Izuna Gongen, depicted as *tengu* standing upon white flying foxes. *Tengu* and foxes have complex similarities and associations with dragons and snakes. See Blacker (1975) and De Visser (1908b; 1913).

33. The term "foxes' wedding" has four main meanings throughout Japan, according to studies by folklorists. The most common is the phenomenon of rain falling from a sunny sky. Strange lights at night, also called *kitsune-bi*, are called a fox wedding in some locations. In Kumamoto, when a rainbow appears they say that a fox is getting married; in Aichi, they say this when hail falls from a clear blue sky. There are countless local variations (Suzuki 1982:198-199).

34. Illustrated in Yoshino (1980: frontispiece).

35. It is interesting to note, in connection with the discussion of the jackal and Dakiniten in Chapter 3, that in the *Rāmāyaṇa* (iii.29), the jackal vomits fire and is thus a friend to the hero by being a bad omen for the monster Kharas (Gubernatis 1872:125).

36. Henry (1986:71-72) describes the anatomical structure of a fox eye that produces this effect: the tapetum lucidum is an extra layer of tissue behind the retina that acts like a mirror and causes light to pass twice over the retina, multiplying the amount of light that enters the eye.

37. Conversation with Im Dong-Kwon, Seoul, April 24, 1990.

38. See De Visser (1908a:81-82) for the 1799 version of this tradition.

39. I learned of this tradition from an undated newspaper clipping reporting traditions of over half a century ago. Although I heard no mention of such an object at the temple today, it may be there, forgotten, in a storeroom.

40. See illustrations of the Chinese and Japanese dragons and their jewels in Ball (1927:1-16).

41. Picture in author's collection.

42. A Buddhist text describes the forty-nine *kami* holes (fox holes?) on Inari Mountain and the wish-fulfilling jewels within them.

43. *Mitsu no tomoshibi; "tomoshibi"* means lights or lamps. This poem appears on Divine Oracle 2 now distributed by the shrine.

44. There is an Inari shrine in Inuyama, Aichi prefecture, with this name. The characters used to write the shrine's name are "three lights," but a small subshrine within the precincts is dedicated to "three foxes." (The names have the same pronunciation.)

45. See Blacker (1975) for a description of the human and spirit worlds in Japan, the bridge that joins them, and the circumstances under which a human can cross the bridge.

46. This seems to be the case for China as well. It would be interesting to know more about the situation in Korea, where the fox seems to have mostly a negative image.

47. Foxes lived in graves in China (De Visser 1908a:7; Watters 1874:47; Williams 1989:201) and Japan (Miyata 1988:118), and even in present-day England a fox made its home in a graveyard beneath a headstone. Although Macdonald insisted that the scattered bones were avian, not human, the church warden thought "the site of the fox's residence was in questionable taste" (Macdonald 1987:176).

48. See Monick (1987) for a fascinating exploration of this psychological quality. My descriptions do not exactly tally with his but nonetheless owe much to his study.

49. Kangiten is one-third of the composite figure called Madarajin—identified by Kūkai as the assistant of Inari and worshiped as one of the original Buddhist forms of Inari by the Shingon priests in the Inari shrine.

50. See the illustrations in Sanford (1991a:332, fig. 6) and Nishioka (1956:172-173).

Chapter 5 A God of One's Own: Individualizing Inari

1. This chapter, in a slightly different form, appeared as "'My Own Inari': Personalization of the Deity in Inari Worship," *Japanese Journal of Religious Studies* 23(1-2) (1996):101-131. It is used here with the publisher's permission.

2. In an earlier published version of this chapter (Smyers 1996) I used the term "personalization" rather than "individualization," but readers have convinced me that the latter term is generally clearer. By individualization, I mean the way a new Inari is created or customized with new functions; by personalization, I mean the process by which the deity is made one's own, made "internally persuasive" (Bakhtin 1981). I am not speaking of individualism or the constellation of a self in Japan (see Rosenberger 1992) but, rather, how some devotees make Inari personally meaningful.

3. Not all Inari shrines enshrine three or five *kami,* although that is the dominant pattern. Some enshrine a generic "Inari Ōkami," many enshrine one of the chief food *kami,* and still others include Inari and other deities that were added according to contingencies in the local history. Taikodani Inari, for example, although it has direct connections to Fushimi, enshrines only two *kami:* Ukanomitama no Ōkami and Izanami no Mikoto.

4. The son of Emperor Keikō, he subdued the Kumaso in the west in 97 C.E. and the Yemishi in the east in 110. When he died on the second campaign at age thirty, from his tomb flew a white bird, leaving behind only empty clothing in the coffin (Aston 1972, I:189 and 200-211).

5. People also act familiarly with the *kami* Ebisu, praying at the back gate or back side of his shrines, where they ring the bell loud and long. The reason commonly given for this is not intimacy, but because he is hard of hearing.

6. Jizō is the bodhisattva whose six manifestations inhabit the six realms of existence.

7. *Kanjō* was originally a Buddhist term meaning to request a sermon of the Buddha with sincere heart and, later, to urge a buddha or bodhisattva to remain in this world to spread the teachings and save sentient beings. *Kanjō* later came to mean the calling for buddhas or bodhisattvas to descend to the altar in a Buddhist service (or the actual words of supplication themselves). In Japan, the term gradually took on the broad meaning of the enshrinement of a buddha or *kami* in a building for the first time (Furuta 1988:161).

8. The *Chronology* has this as "Toyokatsu" (Fushimi 1962a:250), while the history pamphlet has it as "Toyoura" (Fushimi 1977:50). In either case, a particular name was given to this Inari: "Abundant Success" or "Abundant Bay."

9. This was a form of Shinto that included yin-yang magic and native Shinto ideas; it was also known as Abe, Anke, or Tenjin Shinto.

10. By the Edo period there were fourteen priestly lineages *(shake)* that had separate establishments at the foot of Inari Mountain, including a Shingon Buddhist establishment Aizenji, the temple within the shrine precincts.

11. Conversation with priest on January 27, 1991. I have never seen this incident described in print, although it can be gleaned from the *Chronology (Nenpyō)* (Fushimi 1962a) around the year 1875.

12. Prices calculated at the exchange rate in 1990. The prices were three to five times higher than on the price list I received in 1983. This system existed in the Edo period also, when the *wakemitama* were divided into seven ranks that varied in price accordingly.

13. In contrast to the Shinto characters, which literally mean "(honorable) deity-body," here the characters are "(honorable) true body." (See the glossary.)

14. In this way, Inari functions somewhat like the Virgin Mary in the Catholic Church. Whereas other saints share a division of labor in their specialties, Mary may be turned to for any kind of need. See Turner and Turner (1978:162).

15. Such as Sanko Inari in Inuyama, Aichi prefecture.

16. The other three are household safety, business prosperity, and dispelling evil and beckoning luck.

17. No one is quite sure how this version of Inari came to be. Priests suggested four possibilities: that Oseki Ōkami was merely another of the names for Inari, such as Suehiro; that Oseki was the name of a shamaness whose spirit was worshiped at this altar; that the name refers to the old barrier gate *(sekisho)* between Kyoto and Yamashina in that area; that it actually refers to the coughing deity. If the origin was in fact one of the first three possibilities, this new function of Inari developed through a play on words, for *"seki"* also means cough in Japanese. But on this same area of the sacred mountain are other healing and medicinal versions of Inari, so perhaps curing coughs was its original function. It does seem that there was a folk belief in Old Cough Woman, Seki no Obaasan, as well as various rocks that could cure coughs throughout Japan in the Edo period (see Joya 1963:463). And finally, I cannot resist mentioning that the onomatopoeia for a cough is *"konkon,"* also the sound of a fox barking.

18. The seven spaces where Inari was originally worshiped were simply small earthen mounds surrounded by a sacred fence, except for the one at the Chōja Sha, which has an *iwasaka* rock altar (Toriiminami 1988:147). Folk religion abhors a vacuum and tends to express with concrete symbols what purists prefer to leave abstract.

19. *Otsuka* with the word "fox" as part of the deity's name are surprisingly few. Many altars do hold a fair of fox statues, however.

20. This is the form of Inari worshiped at the Nichiren temple Saijō Inari. Forms of this and other Buddhist versions of Inari are also represented in the *otsuka* names.

21. Although this is the official policy, it did seem that exceptions were made for loyal and longtime devotees. It is not clear exactly why the shrine will not permit new altars to be built, but priests seem to feel the current balance between wooded areas and altar areas is proper. If they set up too many new altars, one priest explained, the mountain will become rock-cluttered *(ishidarake)*.

22. These forms of Inari may choose believers through divine dreams as well. See the story of Kanriki Inari later in the chapter.

23. This practice was almost certainly modeled on the Fushimi *otsuka* tradition, with terminology modified to impart a Buddhist flavor.

24. This was formerly called *oido mairi* (*oedo mairi* in Kyoto dialect). *Oido* is a women's term for buttocks.

25. I have used a pseudonym for the name of Inari as well as for the believers here for reasons of privacy.

26. The dragon is similar to the fox in being a very complex symbol embodying balance and change. It possesses great wisdom, embodies the male and female principles, has "unlimited powers of adaptation" (Volker 1950:56), and is usually associated with the wish-fulfilling jewel.

27. Women are generally thought to be in a state displeasing to the *kami* during menstruation and for a time after childbirth. While the taboo is taken much more lightly now than in past years—when a menstruating woman would not even enter the grounds of a shrine—it is still observed to some degree by some women. See Smyers (1983) for a brief review of attitudes toward "the red pollution" in Japanese religious history.

28. I have not changed the name of the deity here, as the gourd-shaped altar located at the Santoku Inari altar cluster is well known and many people pray to it. See the photo in Smyers (1996:101).

29. It is not clear whether this was the original meaning in creating the rock altar in these forms, or if this is a new interpretation.

30. The snake—and its related form the dragon—was a prevalent symbol in the narratives of my informant's spiritual experiences. It occurred in narratives almost as often as the spirit fox but was depicted only rarely in the iconography. A Jungian analyst's comments about empowered women and the snake are interesting in this context, for I generally heard this type of narrative from women, who tend to be excluded from many priestly sources of power. Bolen notes: "Whenever women begin to claim their own authority, or make decisions, or become aware of having a new sense of their own political or psychic or persoal power, snake dreams are common. The snake seems to represent this new strength" (1985:284). See Obeyesekere (1981) for a Freudian interpretation of the snake and female ascetics in Sri Lanka.

31. An exception to this is Matsuo Inari in Kobe: one of its special features is the regular use of incense. The wood of the various small shrine buildings is black from years of incense smoke.

32. See Smyers (1991) for detailed descriptions of syncretic forms in Inari worship.

33. This is a Buddhist concept; Shinto *kami* are rarely represented anthropomorphically and are enshrined behind doors. It was thus not clear in their minds that Fushimi Inari is now a Shinto rather than a Buddhist institution (or the differences between the two).

34. It is not clear whether she learned this practice in Korea; I never saw anything remotely like it in Japan. This woman also read a good deal, and her own practices changed as she got new ideas from books.

35. In the Edo period, the mountain was the property of the government, and the shrine had to request permission to use the wood from fallen trees. When the shrine was nationalized in the Meiji period, the mountai was still owned by the government but was now under direct control by the shrine. (The land that constitutes the main part of the shrine at the foot of the mountain has always been the direct property of the shrine.) In 1961 the shrine was able to reacquire the parts of the mountain containing the seven sacred sites *(nana shinseki)* by buying a parcel of land equivalent in value in Okayama and trading it to the government to get their own land back.

36. *"Kyōkai"* is the term used to translate "church," but it has a broader, non-Christian meaning as well. *Kyōkai* are often like fledgling new religions: they combine and reinterpret traditional religious ideas in novel ways, often with instructions from the deity received in dream or shamanic trance.

37. The name "Yaoki" immediately brings to mind the proverb, "To fall over seven times and spring back up eight" *(nanakorobi yaoki),* associated with the Daruma doll folk toy. The egg-shaped figure of Bodhidharma (in the popular understanding, his legs withered away because he meditated so long) is weighted at the bottom so that it always rights itself after it is pushed over. The term is used as a kind of encouragement. See McFarland (1987) for a study of the iconography and popular meanings of the Daruma figure.

38. In Chapter 6 we shall see that the intense factionalism among Inari believers may also prevent this kind of syncretic worhsip. People tend to define their Inari against other forms that are different or even heterodox.

39. For a detailed account of pilgrimage in Inari see Smyers (1997).

40. Red is not the only color of bibs, but it is the predominant one. This custom of tying bibs is not limited to fox statues but occurs with almost any kind of religious statue as a generalized votive offering.

41. This seems to be Kurosawa's idiosyncratic interpretation of the foxes' wedding, for I found no similar examples in discussions of fox folklore. Nevertheless, I find it an insightful elaboration of Japanese cultural notions concerning the fox.

42. The plate following p. 22 in that work shows a reproduction of the fox's writing.

43. Information on this phenomenon comes from Wilson (1990).

44. This is a very long time in Japan, where people rarely take vacations of even a week and make five-day trips to America.

45. From time to time I encountered this irony with other shamanesses as well: although they themselves live lives very different from that of the typical woman in Japan, they spend a fair amount of time mainstreaming other women who come to them for help.

Chapter 6 Shared Semantics and Private Persuasions

1. The creation of schisms and new sects is the tendency in Japanese religions, where there are twenty subsects within the Tendai school of Buddhism, forty-six in Shingon, twenty-three in Pure Land schools, twenty-two in Zen, and thirty-eight in Nichiren (Bunkachō 1996:106-114). The new religious movements exhibit the tendency toward schism, as well, especially following the death of a charismatic founder (Agency for Cultural Affairs 1972:98).

2. Described objectively in Befu (1984) and van Bremen (1986) and more polemically in Dale (1986), Miller (1977), and Mouer and Sugimoto (1980;1986).

3. See Kelly's (1991) review article of recent anthropological studies on Japan for a rich catalog of current ideas and emphases.

4. Henry theorizes that 40 million years ago, when canids and felids were branching off from common ancestors called miacids, a group of the canids, including foxes, retained some of the ancestral characteristics: "While the rest of the Canidae family evolved differently, the foxes went on to evolve catlike hunting equipment in their morphologies and feline hunting strategies in their behavioral repertoires." This convergent evolution occurred because both foxes and cats hunt for the same kind of small prey (Henry 1986:73).

5. See story in *Konjaku monogatari* (27.32); *NKBT* 25:521-523; translated in Tyler (1987:294-295).

6. In a sense the fox is a Trickster figure in Japan, but I avoid the term because it is only partly applicable. Stories of the Japanese fox sometimes define social boundaries by showing the fox crossing or breaking them, but he is not a part of creation myths and does not embody the kind of presocial development found in "classical" Trickster myth cycles (Radin 1956). I am grateful to Tanya Luhrman for calling this issue to my attention.

7. This information comes from a lecture given by Jonah Salz, "Breaking the Code: Performer and Audience Training in Noh and Kyōgen," at the Japan Foundation, Kyoto, October 27, 1989. See also Goff (1991:13-14).

8. The mayor of Nagasaki, Motoshima Hitoshi, was shot on January 18,

1990, by a right-wing activist who was enraged by Motoshima's comment that not only did the Shōwa emperor have some responsibility for Japan's involvement in the war, but he probably could have ended the war sooner, possibly sparing the second atomic bombing of a Japanese city *(Mainichi Shimbun,* January 19, 1990). See Field (1991) for an extended description of this event and reactions to it.

9. Not that the priests necessarily censored the richer narrative—she may not have told it to them, sensing their dislike for such narratives involving the fox. Her self-censorship can be seen as a kind of refraining, the category discussed next.

10. Interview recorded September 4, 1990.

11. At Toyokawa Inari I was never screened; in fact, the priests seemed glad to have me appear in their office and around the temple, perhaps as a symbol of "internationalization."

12. Many such renamings permeate popular lore to various ends. Even though Buddhism prohibited eating meat, wild boar was called "mountain whale" *(yama kujira)* and thus was acceptable as a kind of fish; rabbits are counted with the numerical suffix used for birds *(wa)* and were therefore regarded as birds and not meat (Saint-Gilles 1990). A whole vocabulary of substitutions exists (with regional variations) for taboo words *(imi no kotoba)* that would elicit powerful retribution if uttered directly. The substitutions permit meaning to be conveyed but screen the speaker from the powerful negative effects of the taboo term. See Umegaki (1977) for examples.

13. The account in Chamberlain quoted from an article in the newspaper *Nichi Nichi Shimbun* dated August 14, 1891. If I am correct that the fox sometimes signifies nongroup behavior in Japan, it is interesting to note that the families accused of owning foxes were those that had suddenly amassed a great deal of wealth, thereby separating themselves from the rest of the group (Hayashimi 1976; Blacker 1975). The punishment for looking too closely at this matter was fox possession, in which the victim behaved in various strange ways not consistent with group norms. The polite shunning of the family was a way to protect group norms by closing ranks against an anomaly while ensuring the smooth surface functioning of village life.

14. Jean Briggs found similar strategies among the Eskimo in her aptly titled *Never in Anger* (1970). Emotional self-control was highly valued in the small group of people with whom she lived; indeed, her directly expressed emotions caused her finally to be ostracized. She describes one struggle in which a male tried to change an established form of worship, the resistance of the women, and the preservation of the status quo—"and all without one word, to my knowledge, being spoken" (p. 56).

15. Lebra observes that although belongingness is stressed in Japan, the solitary hero is an important cultural figure (1976:27–28). (See the extended study of the solitary hero throughout Japanese history in Morris 1975.) And

in contrast to often articulated ideals of racial purity, a large proportion of movie stars and celebrities are *ainoko,* or children of mixed parentage (Lebra 1976:25).

16. See Bachnik (1983; 1986), Kelly (1991), Kondo (1990), Lebra (1976), and Plath (1980) for discussions of inside and outside in Japanese society.

17. This concept has been explored through the metaphor of wrapping in Ben-Ari et al. (1990) and Hendry (1993).

18. See Embree's description of the refusal of cooperation and ridicule, both forms of isolating the offender, as forms of social control (1939:171-172).

19. Probably the most interference from the government was the separation of Shinto and Buddhism in early Meiji, which reduced the overt syncretism within Inari worship (although it found its way back in) and was particularly hard on Buddhist Inari centers.

Chapter 7 From Rice to Riches—The Inclusiveness of Inari

1. One of the dominant cultural representations of Japan is its cultural continuity—and the quintessential expression of this continuity is the unbroken lineage of the imperial institution. In general, elite constructions tend to focus on continuity and resist change. One reason why the priests at some of Inari's centers may consider the fox an inappropriate symbol is that its strongest cultural assocation seems to be its ability to change—whereas they prefer to emphasize the unchangingness of their traditions.

Glossary

Aizenji 愛染寺

Ajisukitakahikone no Kami 味耜
高彦根神

Ake 朱

Akiba Gongen 秋葉権現

Akomachi 阿古町

Amanomihiko 天御孫命

Anamori Inari 穴守稲荷

Aoki Inari 青木稲荷

Arakuma Daimyōjin 荒熊大明神

aramitama 荒魂

Azumamaro Jinja 東丸神社

Benten; Benzaiten 弁天、弁財天

betsuin 別院

bunrei 分霊

byakko 白狐

chi no kami 地の神

chigami 地神

chinjugami 鎮守神

chinkon 鎮魂

chinpō goō 珍宝牛王

Chōei Inari 長栄稲荷

chokuzoku kōin 直属講員

Daiitokuten 大威徳天

daimyōjin 大明神

Dakiniten 荼吉尼天、荼枳尼天、
吒枳尼天、陀祇尼天

Da-ten hō 陀天法

Dōsojin 道祖神

Fukakusa 深草

Fushimi Inari Taisha 伏見稲荷大社

gobunrei 御分霊

Godai Myōō 五大明王

gokitō 御祈禱

Gokujo 御供所

goō hōin 牛王宝印

goshintai

   Shinto: "kami repository" 御神体

   Toyokawa: "true body" 御真体

Hakushinkoō Bosatsu 白辰狐王
菩薩

Hata 秦、波多、波陀

Hata no Irogu 秦伊呂具

Hatsuuma 初午

hattō 法堂

hayarigami 流行神

hibuse 火防せ

hidama 火玉

hitaki 火焚

hitaki-gushi 火焚串

hitaki no (moe)ato 火焚の
  （燃え）跡

hitodama 人玉

hōju 宝珠

hongansho 本願所

honne 本音

Hōon Daishi 報恩大師

hōtō 宝塔

Hyōtan Yama Inari 瓢箪山稲荷

Ichinomine 一ノ峯

Inari (ways of writing)

   Manyōgana (phonetic) 伊奈利

carrying rice 稲荷
rice grows 稲生
rice develops 稲成
food grows 飯生
Inari ("etymologies")
  ina-bari (granary) 稲梁
  ina-iru (rice gathering) 稲入る
  ina-kari (rice cutting) 稲刈
  form of cooked rice 飯形
  becoming cooked rice 飯成
  ina-nori (rice rises) 稲登
  i-nari (lightning sounds) 雷鳴
Inari Gokō Daimyōjin 稲生五幸
  大明神
Inari goza 稲荷五座
Inari ki 稲荷記
Inari oroshi 稲荷降ろし
Inari sage 稲荷下げ
Inari sanza 稲荷三座
ine-nari 稲成
  (in *Fudoki* text) 伊禰奈利
Izanagi no Mikoto 伊弉諾命
Izanami no Mikoto 伊弉冉命
Izuna Gongen 飯綱権現
jūgoi no ge 従五位下
Kada 荷田
Kada no Azumamaro 荷田東麻呂
kagura-me 神楽女
kahyō 華表
kaigen 開眼
kama 竈
kami 神
Kaminomusubi no Mikoto 神皇
  産霊尊
Kami no Yashiro 上の社
Kampei Taisha 官幣大社
Kangan Giin 寒巌義伊
Kangiten 歓喜天
kanjō 勧請

Kanriki Inari 間力稲荷
kenzoku 眷属
keshin 化身
Ketsu Hime 食津姫
ketsune
  dialect for *kitsune* 狐
  root [spirit] of food 食ツ根
Kiko Tennò 貴狐天王
kitō 祈禱
kitsune (phonetic) 岐都禰
  fox 狐
  come and sleep 来寝
  come always 来毎
  usual energy 気常
kitsune-bi 狐火
kitsune no kan segyō 狐の寒施行
kitsune no kedama 狐の毛玉
kitsune segyō [sengyō] 狐施行
kitsune tsukai 狐使い
kitsune tsuki 狐付き；狐憑き
Kitsune-zuka 狐塚
kō 講
Kōin Taisai 講員大祭
Kokaji 小鍛冶
kokkuri 狐狗狸
Kōmuhonchō 講務本庁
Kōsha 講社
Kōshūkai 講習会
kozō 小僧
Kuchi-ire Inari 口入稲荷
Kumadaka 熊鷹
Kuroo 黒尾
kushimitama 奇魂
Madarajin 摩多羅神
magamono-barai 曲物祓い
magatama 曲玉
makaru kaeshi no tama 死反玉
mani 摩尼
meidō 鳴動

Miketsu no Kami 御食津神
Miketsu Ōkami 御食津大神
   miketsu = three foxes 三狐
misaki 御先；御前
Mitama
   honorable spirit 神魂/神霊
   three jewels 三玉
mitamashiro 御霊代
Miyukibe 御幸
Motomiya Sai 本宮祭
Muei Inari 夢栄稲荷
Myōbu Sha 命婦社
Myōgonji 妙厳寺
Myōkyòji 妙教寺
Naka no Yashiro 中の社
nana fushigi 七不思議
nana shinseki 七神蹟
narigama 鳴竈
Nenjū gyōji hisshō 年中行事秘抄
nigatsu no hatsuuma 二月の初午
nigimitama 和魂
Ninigi no Mikoto 瓊瓊杵尊
Ninomine 二ノ峯
nin'ō 人黄
nyōi hōju 如意宝珠
Nyōi Hōshō Sonten 如意宝生尊天
Ochobo Inari (Ochiyobo Inari)
   お千代保稲荷
Ōgetsu Hime 大気都比売、大宜
   津姫
   ōgetsu = big fox 大狐
Ohitaki Sai お火焚祭
Ōichi Hime no Mikoto 大市姫命
Ōji Inari 王子稲荷
Okunoin 奥院
Okusha 奥社
Ōmiya Hime 大宮姫
Ōmiyanome no Ōkami 大宮能
   賣大神

omokaru ishi 重軽石
Ōnamuchi no Mikoto 大巳貴命
osaki 御先；御前
O-Sanba-san お産婆さん
Osusuki 小薄、小芒、尾薄
Ōta no Mikoto 太田命
otsuka お塚
oyama o suru お山をする
Ōyama Sai 大山祭
Ōyamatsume 大山祇女
Reikozuka 霊狐塚
Ruijū kokushi 類聚国史
ryūjin 龍神
Sadahiko no Ōkami 佐田彦大神
Saijō Inari 最上稲荷
Saijōi Kyōō Daibosatsu 最上位経
   王大菩薩
sakimitama 幸魂
Sanba Inari 産場稲荷
Sangyō Anzen Sai 産業安全祭
Sangyō Sai 産業祭
Sannomine 三ノ峯
Sanshūden 参集殿
Santen 三天
Sarutahiko no Ōkami 猿田彦大神
segyō 施行
Seimeitaki 清明滝
Senbon-dorii 千本鳥居
Senbon Nobori 千本幟
shake 社家
Shamusho 社務所
Shi no Ōkami 四の大神
shibu 支部
Shichijū Shichi Massha 七十七末社
Shichijūshi Michi no Naka no Ō
   七十四道の中の王
Shimo no Yashiro 下の社
Shinatōbe no Mikoto 級長戸辺命

Shinko-ō 辰狐王
shinpu 神符
shintai 神体
shintoku 神徳
Shiragiku Inari 白菊稲荷
Shirayabu Inari 白薮稲荷
shirushi no sugi 験の杉
shisha 使者
Shitateru Hime 下照姫
shō o ireru 生を入れる
shōgitaisan 障凝退散
shōichii 正一位
Shōten 聖天
Suehiro Inari 末広稲荷
sugi 杉
Susanoo no Mikoto 素戔鳴尊
ta no kami 田の神
Taikodani Inari 太鼓谷稲荷
Takakōmusubi no Mikoto 高皇
  産霊尊
Takamatsu Inari (Saijō) 高松稲荷
Takayama Inari 高山稲荷
Takekoma Inari 竹駒稲荷
tama 玉
tama shizume 鎮魂
tamafuri 招魂
tamagaki 玉垣
tamagushi 玉串
tamashii 魂
Tamatsukuri Inari 玉造稲荷
tamaya 玉屋
Tanaka no Ōkami 田中大神
tanuki 狸
tatari 祟
tatemae 建前

ten 天
tennō 天皇
Tōji 東寺
Tōkai Gieki 東海義易
tōme 専女
Toshitokujin 歳徳神
Tōume Sha 登宇女社
Toyokawa Inari 豊川稲荷
Toyokawa Kaku Myōgonji 豊川
  閣妙厳寺
Toyotsu Inari 豊津稲荷
Toyouke Hime no Kami 豊受姫
  神
Toyouke no Kami 豊受神
tsuka 塚
Ugajin 宇賀神
Uganomitama no Mikoto;
Ukanomitama no Mikoto 倉稲魂
  命、宇迦之御魂命
ujigami 氏神
Ukemochi no Kami 保食神
uma
  horse 馬
  "horse" part of cycle 午
Waka-ukanomitama no Mikoto
  若倉稲魂命
wakemitama 分霊
Wakumusubi no Kami 稚産霊神
yakan 野干；射干
yako 野狐
yama no kami 山の神
Yamashiro fudoki 山城風土記
yashikigami 屋敷神
Yūtoku Inari 祐徳稲荷
Yūzū Inari 融通稲荷

Bibliography

Agency for Cultural Affairs. 1972. *Japanese Religion: A Survey*. Tokyo: Kodansha International.

Amino Yūshun 1959. *Denpōin chingodoshi*. Tokyo: Chingo daishi kō hombu.

Anzu Motohiko and Umeda Yoshihiko. 1968. *Shinto jiten*. Osaka: Hori Shoten.

Asō Isoji. 1976. *Inari no senryū*. In Nakamura (1976:22–28).

Aston, W. G. 1905. *Shinto (The Way of the Gods)*. New York: Longmans, Green.

———. 1972. *Nihongi: Chronicles of Japan from the Earliest Times to A.D. 697*. Rutland, Vt.: Tuttle.

Atkinson, Jane Monnig. 1992. "Shamanisms Today." *Annual Review of Anthropology* 21:307–330.

Azuma Ryūshin. 1984. "Sōtō shū to jingi." *Daihōrin* 51(10):136–139.

Babcock, Barbara. 1978. *The Reversible World: Symbolic Inversion in Art and Society*. Ithaca: Cornell University Press.

Bachnik, Jane. 1983. "Recruitment Strategies for Household Succession: Rethinking Japanese Household Organization." *Man* 18:160–182.

———. 1986. "Time, Space and Person in Japanese Relationships." In Hendry and Webber (1986:49–75).

Bakhtin, Mikhail. 1981. *The Dialogic Imagination: Four Essays*. Austin: University of Texas Press.

———. 1984a. *Problems of Dostoevsky's Poetics*. Minneapolis: University of Minnesota Press.

———. 1984b. *Rabelais and His World*. Bloomington: Indiana University Press.

———. 1986. *Speech Genres and Other Late Essays*. Austin: University of Texas Press.

Ball, Katherine M. 1927. *Decorative Motives of Oriental Art*. New York: Dodd, Mead.

Batchelor, John. 1901. *The Ainu and Their Folk-Lore*. London: Religious Tract Society.

————. 1971. *Ainu Life and Lore: Echoes of a Departing Race*. Tokyo: Kyobunkwan.

Beasley, W. G., ed. 1975. *Modern Japan: Aspects of History, Literature and Society*. Berkeley: University of California Press.

Befu, Harumi. 1980a. "A Critique of the Group Model of Japanese Society." In Mouer and Sugimoto (1980:29–43).

————. 1980b. "Alternative Models: The Next Step." In Mouer and Sugimoto (1980:188–193).

————. 1984. "Civilization and Culture: Japan in Search of Identity." In Umesao et al. (1984:59–75).

Ben-Ari, Eyal, Brian Moeran, and James Valentine. 1990. *Unwrapping Japan: Society and Culture in Anthropological Perspective*. Honolulu: University of Hawai'i Press.

Benedict, Ruth. 1946. *The Chrysanthemum and the Sword: Patterns of Japanese Culture*. Rutland, Vt.: Tuttle.

Blacker, Carmen. 1973. "Animal Witchcraft in Japan." In Newall (1973: 1–19).

————. 1975. *The Catalpa Bow: A Study of Shamanistic Practices in Japan*. London: Allen & Unwin.

Bodiford, William M. 1993. *Sōtō Zen in Medieval Japan*. Kuroda Institute Studies in East Asian Buddhism 8. Honolulu: University of Hawai'i Press.

Boger, H. Batterson. 1964. *The Traditional Arts of Japan: A Complete Illustrated Guide*. London: W. H. Allen.

Bolen, Jean Shinoda. 1985. *Goddesses in Everywoman: A New Psychology of Women*. New York: Harper.

Boscaro, Adriana, Franco Gatti, and Massimo Raveri. 1990. *Rethinking Japan*. 2 vols. New York: St. Martin's Press.

Bouchy, Ann Marie. 1985. "Inari shinkō to fugeki." In Gorai (1985:171–305).

Bourguignon, Erika. 1976. *Possession*. Prospect Heights, Ill: Waveland Press.

Briggs, Jean L. 1970. *Never in Anger: Portrait of an Eskimo Family*. Cambridge, Mass.: Harvard University Press.

Brower, Robert Hopkins. 1952. "The *Konzyaku Monogatarisyū*: An Historical and Critical Introduction, with Annotated Translations of Seventy-Eight Tales." Ph.D. dissertation, University of Michigan.

Brown, Karen McCarthy. 1991. *Mama Lola: A Vodou Priestess in Brooklyn*. Berkeley: University of California Press.

Brown, Norman O. 1947. *Hermes the Thief: The Evolution of a Myth*. Madison: University of Wisconsin Press.

Brown, Robert, L., ed. 1991. *Ganesh: Studies of an Asian God*. Albany: State University of New York Press.

Buchanan, D. C. 1935. "Inari: Its Origin, Development, and Nature." *Transactions of the Asiatic Society of Japan*, 2nd ser., 12:i–191.

Bunkachō (Agency for Cultural Affairs). 1996. *Shūkyō nenkan, Heisei nana nen ban.* Tokyo: Gyōsei.

Burrows, Roger. 1968. *Wild Fox.* New York: Tapinger.

Casal, U. A. 1949. "Inari-sama: The Japanese Rice-Deity and Other Crop-Divinities." *Ethnos* (Ethnographical Museum of Sweden and Swedish Oriental Society) 14(1):1–64.

———. 1959. "The Goblin Fox and Badger and Other Witch Animals of Japan." *Folklore Studies* 18:1–93.

———. 1970. "Jewels and Stones in Oriental Lore." *Bulletin of the Japan Society of London* 4(8):15–18.

Chamberlain, Basil Hall. 1911. *Japanese Poetry.* London: John Murray.

———. 1971. *Japanese Things: Being Notes on Various Subjects Connected with Japan.* Rutland, Vt.: Tuttle.

Chambers, Anthony Hood. 1994. *The Secret Window: Ideal Worlds in Tanizaki's Fiction.* Harvard East Asian Monographs. Cambridge, Mass.: Harvard University Press.

Chang, Duk-soon. 1970. *The Folk Treasury of Korea: Sources in Myth, Legend and Folktale.* Seoul: Society of Korean Oral Literature.

Clark, Katerina, and Michael Holquist. 1984. *Mikhail Bakhtin.* Cambridge, Mass.: Harvard University Press.

Cleaver, Charles Grinnell. 1976. *Japanese and Americans: Cultural Parallels and Paradoxes.* Rutland, Vt.: Tuttle.

Cohen, Abner. 1974. *Two Dimensional Man: An Essay on the Anthropology of Power and Symbolism in Complex Society.* London: Routledge & Kegan Paul.

Coppinger, Raymond and Mark Feinstein. 1991. "'Hark! Hark! The Dogs Do Bark . . .' and Bark and Bark." *Smithsonian* 21(10):119–129.

Czaja, Michael. 1974. *Gods of Myth and Stone: Phallicism in Japanese Folk Religion.* New York: Weatherhill.

Daigo Hachirō. 1977. *Ishigami shinkō.* Tokyo: Kiji Shakō.

———. 1984. *Yama no kami no zō to matsuri.* Tokyo: Kokusho Kankōsha.

Dalby, Liza Crihfield. 1985. *Geisha.* New York: Vintage.

Dale, Peter. 1986. *The Myth of Japanese Uniqueness.* New York: St. Martin's Press.

Davis, Winston. 1980. *Dōjō: Magic and Exorcism in Modern Japan.* Palo Alto: Stanford University Press.

de Garis, Frederic, and Sakai Atsuharu. 1964. *We Japanese: Being Descriptions of Many of the Customs, Manners, Ceremonies, Festivals, Arts & Crafts of the Japanese Besides Numerous Other Subjects.* Hakone: Fujiya Hotel.

De Visser, M. W. 1908a. "The Fox and Badger in Japanese Folklore." *Transactions of the Asiatic Society of Japan* 36(3):1-159.

———. 1908b. "The Tengu." *Transactions of the Asiatic Society of Japan* 36(2):25-99.

———. 1913. *The Dragon in China and Japan.* Amsterdam: Johannes Muller.

———. 1914. "Fire and Ignes Fatui in China and Japan." *Sonderabdruck aus den Mitteilungen des Seminars für Orientalische Sprachen zu Berlin* 17(1):1-97.

Dorson, Richard M. 1962. *Folk Legends of Japan.* Rutland, Vt.: Tuttle.

Douglas, Mary. 1957. "Animals in Lele Religious Symbolism." *Africa* 27(1):46-56.

———. 1966. *Purity and Danger: An Analysis of the Concepts of Pollution and Taboo.* London: Routledge & Kegan Paul.

Dower, John W. 1986. *War Without Mercy: Race and Power in the Pacific War.* New York: Pantheon.

Duquenne, Robert. 1972. "Sanshakubō Gongen, an Aspect of Fudō Myō-ō." *Transactions of the International Conference of Orientalists in Japan* 17:119-120.

Dykstra, Yoshiko Kurata. 1983. *Miraculous Tales of the Lotus Sutra from Ancient Japan: The* Dainihonkoku hokekyōkenki *of priest Chingen.* Hirakata: Kansai University of Foreign Studies.

Earhart, H. Byron. 1974. *Religion in the Japanese Experience: Sources and Interpretations.* Encino, Calif: Dickenson.

Eberhard, Wolfram. 1986. *A Dictionary of Chinese Symbols: Hidden Symbols in Chinese Life and Thought.* London: Routledge & Kegan Paul.

Ebersole, Gary L. 1989. *Ritual Poetry and the Politics of Death in Early Japan.* Princeton: Princeton University Press.

Eliade, Mircea. 1964. *Shamanism: Archaic Techniques of Ecstasy.* Princeton: Princeton University Press.

Ellwood, Robert S. 1973. *The Feast of Kingship.* Tokyo: Sophia.

Ellwood, Robert S., and Richard Pilgrim. 1985. *Japanese Religion: A Cultural Perspective.* Englewood Cliffs, N.J.: Prentice-Hall.

Embree, John F. 1939. *Suye Mura: A Japanese Village.* Chicago: University of Chicago Press.

———. 1941. "Acculturation Among the Japanese of Kona, Hawaii." *Memoirs of the American Anthropological Association* 59:1-162.

Fernandez, James. 1965. "Symbolic Consensus in a Fang Reformative Cult." *American Anthropologist* 67:902-929.

Field, Norma. 1991. *In the Realm of a Dying Emperor: A Portrait of Japan at Century's End.* New York: Pantheon.

Foucault, Michel. 1988. *The History of Sexuality.* vol. 1. New York: Vintage.

Frazer, James George. 1912. *Spirits of the Corn and of the Wild.* 2 vols. London: Macmillan.

Fukuda Hideo, ed. 1975. *Hiroshige. (Taiyō ukiyo shiriizu 3.)* Tokyo: Heibonsha.

Furuta Shōkin et al., eds. 1988. *Bukkyō daijiten.* Tokyo: Shogakkan.

Fushimi Inari Taisha, Kōmuhonchō, ed. 1969. *Fushimi Inari Taisha: Shinkō no kaisetsu.* Kyoto.

———. 1977. *Fushimi Inari Taisha no rekishi.* Kyoto.

———. 1985. *O-Inari No.100.* Kyoto.

Fushimi Inari Taisha, Shamusho, ed. 1951. *Inari no shinkō.* Kyoto.

———. 1953-1983. *Inari Taisha yuishoki shūsei.* Kyoto.

    1953. *Shikan choshakuhen.*

    1957. *Shinkō choshakuhen.*

    1972. *Kenkyū choshakuhen.*

    1976. *Kyōka choshakuhen.*

    1979. *Zoku shikan choshakuhen.*

    1983. *Hoi hen.*

———. 1954. *Fushimi Inari Taisha ki.* Kyoto: Nakamura Oshōdō.

———. 1958. *Inari hyakuwa.* Kyoto.

———. 1962a. *Fushimi Inari Taisha Nenpyō.* Kyoto.

———. 1962b. *Inari no shinkō,* no. 1, July 1.

———. 1965. *Oyama no otsuka.* 2 vols. Kyoto.

———. 1966. *Zoku oyama no otsuka.* 2 vols. Kyoto.

———. 1967-. *Ake* (yearly journal).

Geertz, Clifford. 1973. *The Interpretation of Cultures.* New York: Basic Books.

Giles, Herbert A. 1926. *Strange Stories from a Chinese Studio.* Shanghai: Kelly & Walsh.

Goff, Janet. 1991. "Foxes and Transformation in Classical Japanese Theater." *Japan Foundation Newsletter* 19(3) (December):12-17.

———. 1997. "Foxes in Japanese Culture: Beautiful or Beastly?" *Japan Quarterly* 44(2):66-77.

Gorai Shigeru. 1985. *Inari shinkō no kenkyū.* Okayama: Sanyō shimbun sha.

Grapard, Allan G. 1983. "Shinto." *Encyclopedia of Japan* 7:125-132.

———. 1988. "Institution, Ritual, and Ideology: The Twenty-Two Shrine-Temple Multiplexes of Heian Japan." *History of Religions* 27(3):246-269.

———. 1992. *The Protocol of the Gods: A Study of the Kasuga Cult in Japanese History.* Berkeley: University of California Press.

Greey, Edward. 1882. *The Golden Lotus and Other Legends of Japan.* Boston: Lee & Shepard.

Griffis, William Elliot. 1876. *The Mikado's Empire.* New York: Harper & Brothers.

Gubernatis, Angelo de. 1872. *Zoological Mythology, or, The Legends of Animals.* Vol. 2. New York: Macmillan.

Gubler, Greg. 1974. "Kitsune: The Remarkable Japanese Fox." *Southern Folklore Quarterly* 38(2):121-134.

Hagiwara Ryūō. 1983. "Edo no Inari." In Naoe (1983c:151-164).

Halford, Aubrey S., and Giovanna M. Halford. 1956. *The Kabuki Handbook: A Guide to Understanding and Appreciation, with Summaries of Favourite Plays, Explanatory Notes, and Illustrations.* Rutland, Vt.: Tuttle.

Hamabata, Matthews Masayuki. 1990. *Crested Kimono: Power and Love in the Japanese Business Family.* Ithaca: Cornell University Press.

Hanazono Jinja Shamusho. 1971. Untitled shrine pamphlet.

Hanna, Willard A. 1976. *Bali Profile: People, Events, Circumstances (1001-1976).* New York: American Universities Field Staff.

Harada, Violet H. 1976. "The Badger in Japanese Folklore." *Asian Folklore Studies* 35:1-6.

Hardacre, Helen. 1989. *Shinto and the State, 1868-1988.* Princeton, N.J.: Princeton University Press.

Harding, M. Esther. 1963. *Psychic Energy: Its Source and Its Transformation.* Princeton, N.J.: Princeton University Press.

Harries, Phillip Tudor, trans. 1980. *The Poetic Memoirs of Lady Daibu.* Palo Alto: Stanford University Press.

Hartshorne, Anna C. 1902. *Japan and Her People.* 2 vols. Philadelphia: Winston.

Hayashimi Yasutaka. 1976. *Izumo no meishin: "kitsune mochi" meishin no minzoku to nazo.* Tokyo: Gakuseisha.

Hearn, Lafcadio. 1974. *Glimpses of Unfamiliar Japan.* Rutland, Vt.: Tuttle.

Hendry, Joy. 1987. *Understanding Japanese Society.* London: Croom Helm.

———. 1993. *Wrapping Culture: Politeness, Presentation and Power in Japan and Other Societies.* Oxford: Clarendon Press.

Hendry, Joy, and Jonathan Webber, eds. 1986. *Interpreting Japanese Society: Anthropological Approaches.* Occasional Paper 5. Oxford: Journal of the Anthropological Society of Oxford.

Henry, J. David. 1986. *Red Fox: The Catlike Canine.* Washington, D.C.: Smithsonian.

Herbert, Jean. 1967. *Shintō: At the Fountain-head of Japan.* New York: Stein & Day.

Higo Kazuo. 1983. "Inari shinkō no hajime." In Naoe (1983c:3-16).

Hiraiwa Masatoshi. 1989. "O-Inari san to nihonjin." *O-Inari* 104 (October):2-5.

Hobsbawm, Eric, and Terence Ranger. 1983. *The Invention of Tradition.* Cambridge: Cambridge University Press.

Holtom, D. C. 1928. *The Japanese Enthronement Ceremonies—with an Account of the Imperial Regalia.* Tokyo: Kyobunkwan.

Hori Ichirō. 1968. *Folk Religion in Japan: Continuity and Change.* Chicago: University of Chicago Press.

Inagaki Hisao. 1985. *A Dictionary of Japanese Buddhist Terms.* Kyoto: Nagata Bunshodo.

Iwai Hiromi. 1983. "Inari to kitsune, Inari no ema." In Naoe (1983c:287–297).

Jameson, R. D. 1932. *Three Lectures on Chinese Folklore.* Beijing: North China Union Language School.

———. 1951. "The Chinese Art of Shifting Shape." *Journal of American Folklore* 64(253):275–280.

Japan Times. 1990. "New Public Servants Liken Themselves to Dogs and Ants." October 30.

Johnson, Chalmers. 1980. "*Omote* (Explicit) and *Ura* (Implicit): Translating Japanese Political Terms." *Journal of Japanese Studies* 6(1):89–115.

Johnson, T.W. 1974. "Far Eastern Fox Lore." *Asian Folklore Studies* 33:35–68.

Joly, Henri. 1908. *Legend in Japanese Art: A Description of Historical Episodes, Legendary Characters, Folklore, Myths, Religious Symbolism Illustrated in the Arts of Old Japan.* London: J. Lane.

Jones, S.W. 1959. *Ages Ago: Thirty-Seven Tales from the* Konjaku Monogatari *Collection.* Cambridge, Mass.: Harvard University Press.

Joya, Mock. 1963. *Things Japanese.* Tokyo: Tokyo News Service.

Kagawa Toyohiko. 1924. *Before the Dawn.* Translated by I. Fukumoto and T. Satchell. New York: Doran.

———. 1971. *Shisen o kōete.* Tokyo: Kirisuto shinbunsha.

Kameyama Keiichi. 1983. "Gyoson ni okeru Inari shinkō." In Naoe (1983c:217–223).

Kamikawa Michio. 1990. "Accession Rituals and Buddhism in Medieval Japan." *Japanese Journal of Religious Studies* 17(2–3):243–280.

Kamishima Jirō. 1990. "Society of Convergence: An Alternative for the Homogeneity Theory." *Japan Foundation Newsletter* 17(3):1–6.

Kamstra, Jacques H. 1989. "The Goddess Who Grew into a Bodhisattva Fox: Inari." In *Bruno Lewin zu Ehren: Festschrift aus Anlass seines 65. Geburtstages.* Bochum: Fakultät für Ostasienwissenschaften der Ruhr-Universität Bochum.

Katō, Genchi. 1937. *A Study of Shintō: The Religion of the Japanese Nation.* Tokyo: Meiji Japan Society.

Kawai Hayao. 1984. "Beauty in Japanese Fairy-Tales." In Rudolf Eitsema, ed., *Eranos Conference: Beauty of the World.* Frankfurt: Insel Verlag.

———. 1988. *The Japanese Psyche: Major Motifs in the Fairy Tales of Japan.* Dallas: Spring Publications.

Kelly, William W. 1991. "Directions in the Anthropology of Contemporary Japan." *Annual Review of Anthropology* 20:395–431.

Kendall, Laurel. 1985. *Shamans, Housewives, and Other Restless Spirits: Women in Korean Ritual Life.* Honolulu: University of Hawai'i Press.

Kerenyi, Karl. 1976. *Hermes, Guide of Souls: The Mythologem of the Masculine Source of Life.* Zurich: Spring.

Kida Teikichi. 1976. *Fukugami.* Tokyo: Hōbunkan.

Kimura Hiroshi. 1986. "Kasamori Inari: Izu ni okeru kasamori gami no ichi shiryō." *Ake* 30:220-223.

Kirby, R. J. 1910. "*Uke-mochi-no-kami,* the Shinto Goddess of Food." *Transactions of the Asiatic Society of Japan* 28(2):39-56.

Kitagawa, Joseph. 1966. *Religion in Japanese History.* New York: Columbia University Press.

Kodansha Encyclopedia of Japan. 1983. Tokyo: Kodansha.

Koike Nagayuki. 1976. "Gensei riyaku shinkō to Inari sha." In Nakamura (1976:59-69).

Koizuka Minoru. 1982. "*Kitsune monogatari.*" Tokyo: Sanichi Shobō.

Kokugakuin University. 1985. *Basic Terms of Shinto.* Rev. ed. Tokyo: Kokugakuin University Institute for Japanese Culture and Classics.

Komatsu Kazuhiko. 1990. "Kitsune no bakekata o megutte." *Ake* 34:44-56.

Kondo, Dorinne K. 1990. *Crafting Selves: Power, Gender, and Discourses of Identity in a Japanese Workplace.* Chicago: University of Chicago Press.

Kornicki, P. F., and I. J. McMullen. 1996. *Religion in Japan: Arrows to Heaven and Earth.* Cambridge: Cambridge University Press.

Koschmann, Victor. 1974. "The Idioms of Contemporary Japan VIII: *Tatemae to honne.*" *Japan Interpreter* 9(1):98-104.

———. 1975. "The Idioms of Contemporary Japan X: *Kō to shi.*" *Japan Interpreter* 9(3):361-367.

Krappe, Alexander H. 1944. "Far Eastern Fox Lore." *California Folklore Quarterly* 3(2):124-147.

Krauss, Ellis S., Thomas P. Rohlen, and Patricia G. Steinhoff. 1984. *Conflict in Japan.* Honolulu: University of Hawai'i Press.

Kuroda Toshio. 1981. "Shinto in the History of Japanese Religion." *Journal of Japanese Studies* 7(1):1-21.

Kuroita Katsumi, ed. 1964. *Engi shiki.* Shintei zōho kokushi taikei (2). Vols. 8-10. Tokyo: Yoshikawa Kobunkan.

Kusano Eisaburo. 1953. *Weird Tales of Old Japan.* Tokyo: Tokyo News Service.

Kyoto Shimbun sha, ed. 1984. *Fushimi Inari Taisha.* Kyoto.

LaFleur, William R., ed. 1985. *Dōgen Studies.* Kuroda Institute Studies in East Asian Buddhism 2. Honolulu: University of Hawai'i Press.

Leach, Edmund R. 1972. "Anthropological Aspects of Language: Animal Categories and Verbal Abuse." In Lessa and Vogt (1972:206-220).

Lebra, Takie Sugiyama. 1976. *Japanese Patterns of Behavior.* Honolulu: University of Hawai'i Press.

Leiter, Samuel L. 1979. *Kabuki Encyclopedia.* Westport, Conn.: Greenwood Press.

Lessa, William A., and Evon Z. Vogt, eds. 1972. *Reader in Comparative Religion: An Anthropological Approach.* 3rd ed. New York: Harper & Row.

Lewis, I. M. 1971. *Ecstatic Religion: A Study of Shamanism and Spirit Possession.* London: Routledge.

———. 1986. *Religion in Context: Cults and Charisma.* Cambridge: Cambridge University Press.

Li Wei-tsu. 1948. "On the Cult of the Four Sacred Animals." *Folklore Studies* 7:1-94.

Lim, Lucy. 1987. *Stories from China's Past: Han Dynasty Pictorial Tomb Reliefs and Archaeological Objects from Sichuan Province, People's Republic of China.* San Francisco: Chinese Culture Center.

Linhart, Sepp. 1995. "Rituality in the *Ken* Game." In van Bremen and Martinez (1995:38-66).

Lloyd, Arthur. 1909. *Every-Day Japan, Written After Twenty-Five Years' Residence and Work in the Country.* London: Cassell.

Lockhart, Russell A., et al. 1982. *Soul and Money.* Dallas: Spring Publications.

Lopez, Donald S., Jr., ed. 1995. *Curators of the Buddha: The Study of Buddhism Under Colonialism.* Chicago: University of Chicago Press.

Maaru sha, ed. 1983. *Edo no moyō—II: Saiku. (Kurashikku pataan shiriizu.)* Tokyo: Maaru sha.

McCullough, Helen Craig. 1980. *Okagami, The Great Mirror: Fujiwara Michinaga (966-1027) and His Times.* Princeton and Tokyo: Princeton University Press and University of Tokyo Press.

Macdonald, David. 1987. *Running with the Fox.* New York: Facts on File.

———. 1992. *The Velvet Claw: A Natural History of the Carnivores.* London: BBC Books.

McFarland, H. Neill. 1987. *Daruma: The Founder of Zen in Japanese Art and Popular Culture.* Tokyo and New York: Kodansha International.

Mainichi Daily News. 1986. "'Man with Foxy Eyes' Has No Driver's License." February 28.

———. 1990a. "Nagasaki Mayor Shot." January 19.

———. 1990b. "Clowns Enjoying Popularity Boom." May 24.

Manabe, Masahiro, and Kerstin Vidaeus. 1975. "The Old Fox and the Fairy Child: A Study in Japanese Folklore and Miyazawa Kenji." *Journal of Intercultural Studies* 2:5-28.

Marcus, George E., and Michael M. J. Fischer. 1986. *Anthropology as Cultural Critique: An Experimental Moment in the Human Sciences.* Chicago: University of Chicago Press.

Matsumae Takeshi, ed. 1988. *Inari myōjin: shōichii no jitsuzo.* Tokyo: Chikuma Shobō.

Matsumoto Michihiro. 1988. *The Unspoken Way: Haragei: Silence in Japanese Business and Society.* New York: Kodansha.

Matsunaga, Alicia. 1969. *The Buddhist Philosophy of Assimilation: The Historical Development of the* Honji-Suijaku *Theory*. Tokyo: Sophia.

Matsuyama Masatoshi. 1990. "Kogane no butsuzo ya sodatsu fukuju seki." *Higashi Aichi Shimbun*. August 3.

Mayer, Fanny Hagin, trans. 1984. *Ancient Tales in Modern Japan: An Anthology of Japanese Folk Tales*. Bloomington: Indiana University Press.

———. 1986. *The Yanagita Kunio Guide to the Japanese Folk Tale*. Bloomington: Indiana University Press.

Mayers, William Frederick. 1924. *The Chinese Reader's Manual: A Handbook of Biographical, Historical, Mythological, and General Literary Reference*. Shanghai: Presbyterian Mission Press.

Miller, Roy Andrew. 1977. *The Japanese Language in Contemporary Japan: Some Sociological Observations*. Washington, D.C.: American Enterprise Institute for Public Policy Research.

Mills, D. E. 1970. *A Collection of Tales from Uji: A Study and Translation of Uji Shūi Monogatari*. Cambridge: Cambridge University Press.

Mitford, A. B. 1977. *Tales of Old Japan*. Rutland, Vt.: Tuttle.

Miyamoto Kesayo. 1984. "Inari gami to bukkyō." *Daihōrin* 51(10):170–173.

Miyata Noboru. 1983. "Inari shinkō no shintō to minshū." In Naoe (1983c:137–150).

———. 1988. "Inari to minshu seikatsu." In Matsumae (1988:115–140).

Miyoshi, Masao. 1974. *Accomplices of Silence: The Modern Japanese Novel*. Berkeley: University of California Press.

———. 1991. *Off Center: Power and Culture Relations Between Japan and the United States*. Cambridge, Mass.: Harvard University Press.

Moeran, Brian. 1985. *Okubo Diary: Portrait of a Japanese Valley*. Palo Alto: Stanford University Press.

———. 1989. *Language and Popular Culture in Japan*. Manchester: Manchester University Press.

Monick, Eugene. 1987. *Phallos: Sacred Image of the Masculine*. Toronto: Inner City Books.

Mori Saburō. n.d. *O Chiyobo Inari to shamusho no munagi*. Shrine pamphlet. Ochiyobo Inari Jinja.

Morris, Ivan, trans. and ed. 1971. *As I Crossed a Bridge of Dreams: Recollections of a Woman in Eleventh-Century Japan [Sarashina Nikki]*. New York: Harper.

———. 1975. *The Nobility of Failure: Tragic Heroes in the History of Japan*. New York: Holt.

———, trans. and ed. 1991. *The Pillow Book of Sei Shōnagon*. New York: Columbia University Press.

Morsbach, Helmut. 1983. "Nonverbal Communication." *Encyclopedia of Japan* 6:36–37.

Morson, Gary Saul, and Caryl Emerson. 1990. *Mikhail Bakhtin: Creation of a Prosaics*. Palo Alto: Stanford University Press.

Mouer, Ross E., and Yoshio Sugimoto. 1980. "Japanese Society: Reappraisals and New Directions." *Social Analysis* 5/6:29-43.

————. 1986. *Images of Japanese Society: A Study in the Social Construction of Reality*. London and New York: KPI.

Murai Ichirō. 1990. "Chinsho kikōga no shinpiteki tansaku." *Kyō furuhonya yukiki* 50(October 15):6-8.

Nagata Seiji. 1986. *Hokusai manga—I*. Tokyo: Iwasaki Bijutsu sha.

Naito Masatoshi and Shimokawa Koshi. 1979. *Goriyaku—Kyoto hen* (Densetsu to reiken gaido). Tokyo: Sankei Shimbun sha.

Nakajima Chieko. 1989. *Ohana gitsune. (Shiga no mukashi banashi 5.)* Kyoto: Kyoto Shimbun sha.

Nakamura, Kyoko Motomochi, trans. 1973. *Miraculous Stories from the Japanese Buddhist Tradition: The Nihon Ryōiki of the Monk Kyōkai*. Cambridge, Mass.: Harvard University Press.

Nakamura Naokatsu, ed. 1976. *O-Inari san*. Tokyo: Asunaro sha.

Nakane Chie. 1973. *Japanese Society*. New York: Penguin.

Nannichi Gimyō. 1974. *Inari o tazunete: Inari shinkō no yurai to goshintoku*. Osaka: Bunshindō.

Naoe Hiroji. 1950. "Amakusa Goshoura no yako sōdō." *Minkan denshō* 15(7):29.

————. 1983a. "Inari shinkō fukyū no minzokuteki kiban," In Naoe (1983c:113-133).

————. 1983b. "Inari shinkō no kenkyū seika to kadai." In Naoe (1983c:301-323).

————, ed. 1983c. *Inari shinkō*. Tokyo: Yūzankaku shuppan.

Nelson, Andrew N. 1962. *The Modern Reader's Japanese-English Character Dictionary*. 2nd rev. ed. Rutland, Vt.: Tuttle.

Nelson, John K. 1993. "Enduring Identities: The Guise of Shinto in Contemporary Japan." Ph.D. dissertation, University of California, Berkeley.

————. 1996. "Freedom of Expression: The Very Modern Practice of Visiting a Shinto Shrine." *Japanese Journal of Religious Studies* 23(1-2):117-153.

Newall, Venetia. 1971. *An Egg at Easter: A Folklore Study*. London: Routledge & Kegan Paul.

————, ed. 1973. *The Witch Figure: Folklore Essays by a Group of Scholars in England Honouring the 75th Birthday of Katharine M. Briggs*. London: Routledge & Kegan Paul.

Nihon rekishi daijiten. 1970. "Inari" entries. Vol. 1, pp. 405-407. Tokyo: Kawade shobō shinsha.

Nippon Gakujutsu Shinkōkai. 1965. *The Manyōshu*. New York: Columbia University Press.

Nishida Nagao. 1983. "Inari sha no kigen." In Naoe (1983c:227-267).

Nishigaki Seiji. 1983. "Inari shinkō no shosō." In Naoe (1983c:165-173).

Nishimaki Kozaburo, ed. 1975. *Kitsune*. Special edition of *Anima* 3. Tokyo: Heibonsha.

Nishioka Hideo. 1956. *Seijin taisei: Nihon ni okeru seiki sūhai no shiteki kenkyū*. Tokyo: Myōgi shuppan.

Nishiyama Kōsen, trans. 1975. *Shōbōgenzō: The Eye and Treasury of the True Law*. Tokyo: Nakayama Shobō.

Nomura Shōji and Abe Kōyō. 1982. *Anamori no suna*. Nupun furusato ehon shiriizu 2. Tokyo: Nupun jidō tosho shuppan.

Nozaki, Kiyoshi. 1961. *Kitsune: Japan's Fox of Mystery, Romance and Humor*. Tokyo: Hokuseido Press.

Obeyesekere, Gannanath. 1981. *Medusa's Hair: An Essay on Personal Symbols and Religious Experience*. Chicago: University of Chicago Press.

O'Flaherty, Wendy Doniger. 1987. "Indian Religions: Mythic Themes." *The Encyclopedia of Religion* 7:182-190. New York: Macmillan.

Ohnuki-Tierney, Emiko. 1981. *Illness and Healing Among the Sakhalin Ainu: A Symbolic Interpretation*. Cambridge: Cambridge University Press.

———. 1987. *The Monkey as Mirror: Symbolic Transformations in Japanese History and Ritual*. Princeton: Princeton University Press.

———. 1993. *Rice as Self: Japanese Identities Through Time*. Princeton: Princeton University Press.

Okada Shōji. 1985. "Reii-jin to sūkei-kō." *Nihon shūkyō jiten*:73-80.

O'Keefe, Daniel Lawrence. 1982. *Stolen Lightning: The Social Theory of Magic*. New York: Vintage.

Okumura Hirozumi. 1983. "Inari shinkō to Fushimi ningyō." *Ake* 27:34-42.

Ōmori Keiko. 1989. "Kitsune denshō to Inari shinkō—toku ni henkakei kitsune denshō to dakiniten shinkō o chūshin ni shite." *Nihon Minzokugaku* 177:94-116.

———. 1994. *Inari shinkō to shūkyō minzoku*. Nihon shūkyō minzokugaku sōsho 1. Tokyo: Iwata shoin.

Ono Yasuhiro et al., eds. 1985. *Nihon shūkyō jiten*. Tokyo: Kobundo.

Opler, Morris E. and Robert Seido Hashima. 1946. "The Rice Goddess and the Fox in Japanese Religion and Folk Practice." *American Anthropologist* 48(1):43-53.

Ortner, Sherry. 1984. "Theory in Anthropology Since the Sixties." *Comparative Studies in Society and History* 26(1):126-166.

Osaka shiritsu bijutsukan, ed. 1986. *Osaka shiritsu bijutsukan zōhin senshū*. Osaka.

Ouwehand, C. 1964. *Namazu-e and Their Themes: An Interpretative Approach to Some Aspects of Japanese Folk Religion*. Leiden: Brill.

Ōzuka minzoku gakkai. 1978. *Nihon minzoku jiten*. Tokyo: Kōbundō.

Paris, Ginette. 1990. *Pagan Grace: Dionysos, Hermes, and Goddess Memory in Daily Life*. Dallas: Spring Publications.

Perera, Sylvia Brinton. 1986. *The Scapegoat Complex: Toward a Mythology of Shadow and Guilt*. Toronto: Inner City Books.

Philippi, Donald L. 1968. *Kojiki*. Tokyo: University of Tokyo Press.

Plath, David W. 1980. *Long Engagements: Maturity in Modern Japan*. Palo Alto: Stanford University Press.

Plutchow, Herbert. 1990. "Towards a Definition of Tama." In Boscaro et al. (1990, I:146-161).

Radin, Paul. 1956. *The Trickster: A Study in American Indian Mythology*. New York: Schocken Books.

Reader, Ian. 1985. "Transformations and Changes in the Teachings of the Sōtō Zen Buddhist Sect." *Japanese Religions* 14(1):28-48.

———. 1986. "Zazenless Zen? The Position of Zazen in Institutional Zen Buddhism." *Japanese Religions* 14(3):7-27.

———. 1991a. *Religion in Contemporary Japan*. Honolulu: University of Hawai'i Press.

———. 1991b. "Letters to the Gods: The Form and Meaning of *Ema*." *Japanese Journal of Religious Studies* 18(1):23-50.

———. 1993a. "Dead to the World: Pilgrims in Shikoku." In Reader and Walter. (1993:107-136).

———. 1993b. *Sendatsu and the Development of Contemporary Japanese Pilgrimage*. Nissan Occasional Paper 17. Oxford: Nissan Institute of Japanese Studies.

Reader, Ian, and Tony Walter, eds. 1993. *Pilgrimage in Popular Culture*. New York: Macmillan.

Reischauer, Edwin O., and Joseph K. Yamagiwa. 1972. *Translations from Early Japanese Literature*. Cambridge: Harvard University Press.

Robertson, Jennifer. 1987. "A Dialectic of Native and Newcomer: The Kodaira Citizens' Festival in Suburban Tokyo." *Anthropological Quarterly* 60(3):124-136.

Rohlen, Thomas. 1976. "The Promise of Adulthood in Japanese Spiritualism." *Daedalus* (Spring):125-143.

Rombauts, E., and A. Welkenhuysen. 1975. *Aspects of the Medieval Animal Epic*. Leuven: Leuven University Press.

Rosenberger, Nancy R., ed. 1992. *Japanese Sense of Self*. Cambridge: Cambridge University Press.

Ross, Floyd Hiatt. 1965. *Shinto: The Way of Japan*. Boston: Beacon Press.

Said, Edward. 1978. *Orientalism*. New York: Vintage.

Saijō Inari. n.d. *Saijō Inari*. Temple pamphlet. Okayama.

———. 1983. *Saijō sama no ohanashi*. Okayama: Saijō Kyoho sha.

Saijō Kyoho. 1979. Vol. 335(3). Okayama: Saijō Kyoho sha.

Saint-Gilles, Amaury. 1990. "Mingei: Matsue Hariko." *Mainichi Daily News,* March 12.

Sakamoto Katsushige. 1983. "Nichiren shū no Inari shinkō: Ikegami Honmonji Chōei Inari no baai." In Naoe (1983c:175–216).

Sakurai Tokutarō. 1974–1977. *Nihon no shamanizumu: Minkan miko no denshō to seitai.* 2 vols. Tokyo: Yoshikawa kōbunkan.

Sanford, James H. 1991a. "Literary Aspects of Japan's Dual-Ganesa Cult." In Brown (1991:287–335).

———. 1991b. "The Abominable Tachikawa Skull Ritual." *Monumenta Nipponica* 46(1):1–20.

———. 1997. "Wind, Waters, Stupas, Mandalas: Fetal Buddhahood in Shingon." *Japanese Journal of Religious Studies* 24(1–2):1–38.

Sansom, George. 1943. *Japan: A Short Cultural History.* New York: Appleton-Century.

Sasaki Genjun H. 1968. "Fox Obsession in Japan: The Indian Background." *Shakti* 5(3):27–29.

Sasama Yoshihiko. 1988a. *Sei no shūkyō: Shingon tachikawa ryū to wa nani ka.* Tokyo: Daiichi Shobō

———. 1988b. *Dakini shinkō to sono zokushin.* Tokyo: Daiichi Shobō.

Saunders, E. Dale. 1985. *Mudra: A Study of Symbolic Gestures in Japanese Buddhist Sculpture.* Princeton, N.J.: Princeton University Press.

———. 1964. *Buddhism in Japan: With an Outline of Its Origins in India.* Tokyo: Tuttle.

Seham, Lucy A. 1986. "Enchi Fumiko and 'Fox Fires.'" Thesis, Wesleyan University.

Seidensticker, Edward, trans. 1964. *The Gossamer Years: A Diary by a Noblewoman of Heian Japan.* Tokyo: Tuttle.

———. 1976. *The Tale of Genji.* Tokyo: Tuttle.

Seward, Jack. 1983. "Gestures." *Encyclopedia of Japan* 3:29–30.

Sharf, Robert H. 1995. "The Zen of Japanese Nationalism." In Lopez (1995:107–160).

Shimonaka Yasaburō. 1937. *Shinto Daijiten.* 3 vols. Kyoto: Ringawa Shoten.

Shively, Donald H., ed. 1971. *Tradition and Modernization in Japanese Culture.* Princeton: Princeton University Press.

Smith, Kazuko. 1995. *Makiko's Diary: A Merchant Wife in 1910 Kyoto.* Palo Alto: Stanford University Press.

Smith, Robert J. 1974. *Ancestor Worship in Contemporary Japan.* Palo Alto: Stanford University Press.

———. 1983. *Japanese Society: Tradition, Self, and the Social Order.* Cambridge: Cambridge University Press.

———. 1984. "Japanese Religious Attitudes from the Standpoint of the Contemporary Study of Civilizations." In Umesao et al. (1984:99–104).

———. 1989. "Presidential Address: Something Old, Something New—Tradition and Culture in the Study of Japan." *Journal of Asian Studies* 48(4):715–723.

Smith, Robert J., and Ella Lury Wiswell. 1982. *The Women of Suye Mura.* Chicago: University of Chicago Press.

Smits, Ivo. 1996. "An Early Anthropologist? Oe no Masafusa's *A Record of Fox Spirits.*" In Kornicki and McMullen (1996:78–89).

Smyers, Karen A. 1983. "Women and Shinto: The Relation Between Purity and Pollution." *Japanese Religions* 12(4):7–18.

———. 1991. "Of Foxes, Buddhas, and Shinto Kami: The Syncretic Nature of Inari Beliefs." *Japanese Religions* 16(3):60–75.

———. 1993. *"The Fox and the Jewel: A Study of Shared and Private Meanings in Japanese Inari Worship."* Ph.D. dissertation, Princeton University.

———. 1996. "'My Own Inari': Personalization of the Deity in Inari Worship." *Japanese Journal of Religious Studies* 23(1–2):85–116.

———. 1997. "Inari Pilgrimage: Following One's Path on the Mountain." *Japanese Journal of Religious Studies* 24(3–4):429–452.

———. n.d. "Bewitching Foxes: Animal Possession Narratives in Contemporary Inari Worship ." In preparation.

Snodgrass, Adrian. 1988. *The Matrix and Diamond World: Mandalas in Shingon Buddhism.* 2 vols. New Delhi: Rakesh Goel.

Sonoda Minoru. 1983. "Inari." *Kodansha Encyclopedia of Japan* 3:282–328.

Stallybrass, Peter, and Allon White. 1986. *The Politics and Poetics of Transgression.* Ithaca: Cornell University Press.

Steinhoff, Patricia G. 1984. "Student Conflict." In Krauss et.al., (1984:174–213).

Suzuki Kazuo. 1988. *Magatama.* Osaka: Tamatsukuri Inari Jinja.

Suzuki Tōzō. 1982. *Nihon zokushin jiten: dō-shokubutsu hen.* Tokyo: Kadokawa.

Taikodani Inari Jinja. n.d. *Taikodani Inari Jinja.* Undated shrine pamphlet.

Takahashi Chikumei. 1931. *Inari Sama.* Tokyo: Sankyōsha.

Takekoma Inari Jinja, Shamusho. n.d. *Takekoma Inari Jinja sanpai no shiori.* Undated shrine pamphlet.

Tamaru, Noriyoshi, and David Reid. 1996. *Religion in Japanese Culture: Where Living Traditions Meet a Changing World.* Tokyo: Kodansha.

Tambiah, Stanley Jeyaraja. 1990. *Magic, Science, Religion, and the Scope of Rationality.* Cambridge: Cambridge University Press.

Taniguchi Kō. 1985. "Inari." In *Nihon shūkyō jiten,* pp. 338–342.

Toriiminami Masatoshi. 1988. "Fushimi Inari Taisha no hitakisai, Shu no torii." In Matsumae (1988:141–164).

Toyokawa Inari Tokyo Betsuin. 1991. *Rishō.*

Toyokawa Kaku Myōgonji. n.d. *Toyokawa Inari ryaku engi.* Temple pamphlet.

———. 1961. *Reiba Toyokawa Inari.* Toyokawa City.

————. 1978. *Toyokawa Inari shinkō annai*. Edited by Fujii Toshimichi. Tokyo: Toyokawa Inari Betsuin.

Turner, Victor W. 1967. *The Ritual Process: Structure and Anti-Structure*. Chicago: Aldine.

————. 1972. "Religious Specialists." *International Encyclopedia of the Social Sciences* 13:437–444.

Turner, Victor W., and Edith Turner. 1978. *Image and Pilgrimage in Christian Culture: Anthropological Perspectives*. New York: Columbia University Press.

Tyler, Royall, ed. and trans. 1987. *Japanese Tales*. New York: Pantheon.

Ueda Masaaki. 1967. "Inari shinkō no genryū." *Ake* (2):32–35.

————. 1970. "Nanori no genryū." *Ake* (10):56–59.

————. 1977. "Inari to kodai shinkō." In Fushimi (1977:1–14).

————. 1983. "Otsuka no shinkō." In Naoe (1983c:281–285).

Ueda Masaaki and Tsubohara Kisaburō. 1984. "O-Inari san." In Kyoto Shimbun sha (1984:24–29).

Ui Mushū. 1976. "Rakugo no O-Inari san." In Nakamura (1976:40–45).

Umegaki Minoru. 1977. *Nihon no imi kotoba*. Tokyo: Iwasaki Bijutsusha.

Umesao Tadao, Harumi Befu, and Josef Kreiner. 1984. *Japanese Civilization in the Modern World*. Senri Ethnological Studies 16. Osaka: National Museum of Ethnology.

Ury, Marian. 1979. *Tales of Times Now Past: Sixty-Two Stories from a Medieval Japanese Collection*. Berkeley: University of California Press.

————. 1988. "A Heian Note on the Supernatural." *Journal of the Association of Teachers of Japanese* 22(2):189–194.

van Bremen, J. G. 1986. "The Post-1945 Anthropology of Japan." In Hendry and Webber (1986:14–28).

van Bremen, Jan, and D. P. Martinez. 1995. *Ceremony and Ritual in Japan: Religious Practices in an Industrialized Society*. London: Routledge.

Voegelin, Ermine W. 1972. "Fox." In Maria Leach, ed., *Funk & Wagnalls Standard Dictionary of Folklore*. Funk & Wagnalls.

Volker, T. 1950. *The Animal in Far Eastern Art, and Especially in the Art of the Japanese Netsuke, with References to Chinese Origins, Traditions, Legends, and Art*. Leiden: Brill.

Von Franz, Marie-Louise. 1980. *The Psychological Meaning of Redemption Motifs in Fairy Tales*. Toronto: Inner City Books.

Watanna, Onoto. 1910. *Tama*. New York: Harper.

Waterhouse, David. 1996. "Notes on the *Kuji*." In Kornicki and McMullen (1996:1–38).

Watters, T. 1874. "Chinese Fox-Myths." *Journal of the North-China Branch of the Royal Asiatic Society of Great Britain and Ireland*, n.s., 8:45–65.

Webb, Herschel. 1983. "Calendar, Dates, and Time." *Kodansha Encyclopedia of Japan* 1:229–232.

Weber, Max. 1949. *The Methodology of the Social Sciences.* New York: Free Press.
———. 1963. *The Sociology of Religion.* Boston: Beacon.
Whitmont, Edward C. 1969. *The Symbolic Quest: Basic Concepts of Analytical Psychology.* Princeton: Princeton University Press.
Wieger, Leon. 1927. *A History of the Religious Beliefs and Philosophical Opinions in China from the Beginning to the Present Time.* N.p.: Hsien-hsien Press.
Williams, C. A. S. 1989. *Chinese Symbolism and Art Motifs: An Alphabetical Compendium of Antique Legends and Beliefs, as Reflected in the Manners and Customs of the Chinese.* Rutland, Vt. Tuttle.
Willis, Janice D., ed. 1987. *Feminine Ground: Essays on Women and Tibet.* Ithaca: Snow Lion Publications.
Wilson, Jean. 1990. "The Superman Syndrome in Samurai Dramas." *Mainichi Daily News,* March 9, p. 9.
Wittgenstein, Ludwig. 1958. *Philosophical Investigations.* 3rd ed. New York: Macmillan.
Yamaori Tetsuo. 1986. "Inari-gami no daburu imeiji." *Ake* 30:2-7.
Yamasaki Taikō. 1988. *Shingon: Japanese Esoteric Buddhism.* Boston: Shambhala.
Yanagita Kunio. 1952. "Japanese Folk Tales." *Folklore Studies* 51(1):i-97.
———, ed. 1957. *"Japanese Manners and Customs in the Meiji Era.* Translated and adapted by Charles S. Terry. Centenary Cultural Council, Japanese Culture in the Meiji Era, vol. 4. Tokyo: Obunsha.
———. 1962. "Kitsune zuka no hanashi," In *Teihon Yanagita Kunio shū,* vol. 13. Tokyo: Chikuma Shobō.
———. 1975. *The Legends of Tōno.* Translated by Ronald A. Morse. Tokyo: Japan Foundation.
Yasui Shirō. 1986. *Jitsu roku "Toyokawa Inari Monogatari."* Tokyo: Keizai.
Yoshida Kenko. 1974. *The Miscellany of a Japanese Priest: Being a Translation of Tsurezure Gusa.* Translated by William N. Porter. Rutland, Vt.: Tuttle.
Yoshino Hiroko. 1980. *Kitsune: Inyō gogyō to Inari shinko.* Mono to ningen no bunka shi 39. Tokyo: Hōsei Daigaku Shuppankyoku.
Zhang Songlin and Zhou Dao, comps. 1988. *Zhengzhou Han huaxiang zhuan.* Beijing: Honan meishu chuban she.
Zong In-Sob. 1982. *Folk Tales from Korea.* Elizabeth, N.J.: Hollym International.

Index

References to photographs are in boldface type.

201; all Inaris not same, 10;
among priests, 38; hidden, 206–
207; inclusive, 213–214. *See also*
individualization of Inari; personalization of Inari
divided spirits *(wakemitama)*, 19, 44;
Motomiya Sai, 48; new names for,
158; nine ranks at Fushimi Inari,
158; Sogaku Inari example, 20–
21; Toyokawa Inari version, 159
divination: cedar, 15; crossroads, 4–5;
folk methods, 5; fox behaviors,
92; heavy-light rock *(omokaru
ishi)*, 54, 125; *kokkuri*, 89; rice
steamer *(kama)*, 61
Dōgen, 25, 37
dogs: compared to government officials, 177; hated by foxes, 89, 97,
108
domestication: of foxes, 97, 101
dragon deity *(ryūjin)*, 8, 124, 167–
168, 237n. 26. *See also* snake,
divine
dream, divine, 5, 40, 49, 140, 158,
237n. 22; in establishment of
Kanriki Inari, 174

Edo (Tokyo), 20
Engi shiki: Inari shrine listed, 17;
lucky foxes, 77; nine-tailed foxes,
129
expedient means *(hōben)*, 37, 119

factionalism: in Inari, 66–70; in Japanese society, 226n. 40
fertility, 124, 131–133, 142–143,
214. *See also* sexuality and Inari
field deity *(ta no kami)*: associated
with fox, 75–76; Inari as, 216. *See
also* mountain deity
fire and foxes, 104, 138–141; foxes'
warnings of fire, 140; revenge, 140
fireball, soul as, 117–118
fire prevention, 21
fire, ritual uses, 63. See also *hitaki;*
Hitaki Sai; Mikagura
fishing, 21, 159–160

fox: Chinese, 127–129, 143; Korean,
104, 129–130
fox, Inari's: amulets, 94–95; attendant, 41, 59–60, 75, 80, 92, 107–
108, 140–141, 215; Buddhist traditions, 79–80, 86; Chinese
influence, 83; Dakiniten's 301 assistants, 60, 124; devotees' experiences, 106–108; dogmatic meaning
absent, 108, 145; equated, 8, 60,
81, 92, 230n. 43; etymological associations to Inari, 78–79; iconography, 3, 74, 93, 144, 152, **161**;
Inari responsible for real foxes, 87–
88; live foxes at shrines, 88–89;
priestly insistence Inari not fox, 8,
33, 35, 59–60, 86, 92, 97, 108,
226 n. 35; signifier, 92–93; sorcery
association, 84–85; spirit fox encounters, 96–97, 193; statues, 60,
93–94, 132, 164, 177, 229n. 29;
vehicle, 60; worship, 92–97
fox, in Japan, 87, 100; signifier for
Hokkaido, 100
fox, jewel of. *See* jewel, fox's
fox, nine-tailed, 129
fox and individuality: diversity in statues, 177; tricking individuals, 176–
177
fox and nature, 97, 100; liminal status, 187; slaughter, 102
fox and sexuality: Chinese ideas, 127–
128; cultural projections, 127; fox
as victim, 130; fox wife, 72, 130–
131; jewel and key symbols, 134,
142, 144–149; Korean tale, 129;
nine-tailed, 227n. 5;
Tamamonomae, 129
fox bewitchment *(kitsune damashi)*,
90, 98, 106
fox couriers, 21, 221n. 19
fox dances, 136
fox destruction, 102; tales of, 98–99
foxes' wedding, 26, 138, 189, 233n.
33; in Kurosawa's *Yume*, 178
fox exorcism, New Religions, 103
fox feeding *(kitsune segyō)*, 21, 23,

41; as *kō* leaders, 53; ritual anger, 51. *See also* priests
shared meanings *(tatemae)*, 202–205; articulated verbally, 207, 209; centripetal tendencies, 207–208, 209
shinbutsu bunri. See separation of Shinto and Buddhism
Shingon Buddhism, 17–19. *See also* Kōbō Daishi; Tōji
shirushi no sugi. See cedar
Shōichii. See Inari, rank
Shōten. *See* Kangiten
Shōtoku Taishi, 23, 43
silkworms, 227n. 3
snake, divine, 237n. 30; Inari's assistant, 8, 227n. 3; oracle from, 48–49. *See also* dragon deity *(ryūjin)*
spirit (soul), 114–118; four autonomous souls, 118; *hitodama*, 117–118. See also *tama;* jewel
spirit pacification *(tama shizume, chinkon):* at Fushimi Inari, 115
spirit shaking *(tamafuri)*, 114–115, 116–117
spiritual inflation, 65–66
syphilis, 137–138

Taikodani Inari, 95, 155, 235n. 3
Takamatsu Inari. *See* Saijō Inari
Takayama Inari, 40
Takekoma Inari, 18, 89, 157; Hatsuuma Festival, 96; *kami* enshrined, 155; Three Great Inari Shrines, 154–155
tama, 113, 119. *See also* jewel; spirit
Tamamonomae, 129
Tamatsukuri Inari, 23, 74, 114, 119; divided spirits of Inari, 159; enshrined *kami*, 155
tanuki. See badger
tatemae. See shared meanings
tengu, 120, 233n. 32
theater, 21
this-worldly benefits *(genze riyaku)*, 18, 36, 38

Three (Five) Great Inari Shrines. *See* Inari shrines and temples
Tōji, 17, 19, 80, 221n. 14
Tōkai Gieki, 25
Toyokawa Inari (Inari Mountain, Fushimi), 175
Toyokawa Inari (main temple), 34–36, 205, 223n. 10; Buddhist reliquary, 121–122, 231n. 10; divided spirits of Dakiniten, 159; division of worship, 34; esoteric iconography, 27; Fall Festival, 2–4, 3; fried tofu offering, 95; jewel motif, 120–121; origin tradition, 25, 37; relation to Inari worship, 66. *See also* fox mounds; Heihachirō; jewel
Toyokawa Inari (Tokyo branch temple), 223n. 7; amulets, 94; borrowing fox statues, 93; child-granting foxes, 132; creation of Yūzū Inari, 48, 125; magazine for devotees, 123; meditation at, 35; Ōoka Echizen's household Inari, 20; relation to Inari worship, 66; Tarō Inari, 94
Twenty-Two Shrines *(nijūni sha)*, Inari's inclusion in, 18

uniqueness claims, 10, 67, 201

wakemitama. See divided spirits
waterfall austerity *(taki gyō)*, 41, 67, 224n. 19
worship, individual, 47
wrestling, 198–199

yakan, 84
Yamashiro fudoki, 15, 75
yashikigami. See household protector Inari
Yoshitsune senbon zakura, 99
Yoshiwara, 136
Yūtoku Inari, 20, 154,
Yūzū Inari, 48, 125

Zen. *See* Kenninji; Toyokawa Inari

About the Author

Karen A. Smyers holds a doctorate in anthropology from Princeton University. She is the recipient of a Japan Society for the Promotion of Science grant, Fulbright-Hays, Japan Foundation, and A. W. Mellon fellowships, and the author of articles on various aspects of Japanese religion. Currently assistant professor in the Department of Religion at Wesleyan University, *The Fox and the Jewel* is her first book.

CPSIA information can be obtained
at www.ICGtesting.com
Printed in the USA
BVHW03s0249150218
508190BV00001B/37/P